BANVARD'S
FOLLY

BANVARD'S FOLLY

THIRTEEN TALES OF

Renowned Obscurity,
Famous Anonymity,
and Rotten Luck

PAUL COLLINS

PICADOR USA
New York

www.picadorusa.com

Picador® USA is a registered trademark and is used by
St. Martin's Press under license from
Pan Books Limited.

Jacket image adapted by Dave Eggers from the "Orbium
Planetarum Terram Complectentium Scenographica" by
Andreas Cellarius, first published in *Harmonia
Macrocosmica* (1660); the original Cellarius illustration
provided courtesy of the George Glazer Gallery, New
York, http://www.georgeglazer.com.

Library of Congress Cataloging-in-Publication Data

Collins, Paul, J.
    Banvard's folly : thirteen tales of renowned obscurity,
famous anonymity, and rotten luck / Paul Collins.—1st
ed.
        p. cm.
    ISBN 0-312-26886-6
    1. Eccentrics and eccentricities—Biography.
    2. Biography.

CT9990 .C64 2001
920.02—dc21

2001021930

First Edition: May 2001

10   9   8   7   6   5   4   3   2   1

THIS BOOK IS DEDICATED TO MY PREDECESSORS:

Van Wyck Brooks
Isaac D'israeli
Stewart Holbrook
Edmund Pearson

AND TO ANY PUBLISHER WHO WILL PUT
THEIR WORKS BACK IN PRINT.

CONTENTS

PREFACE

Peruse the documents of any era—newspapers, bills of sale, wills—and you find nothing but forgotten names. A famous name brings an almost electric shock of recognition, that in these crowds of nobodies and once-were-somebodies is a person you can attach a face and a reputation to. The collector and the historian value those rare documents. But I always find myself wondering about the *other* people. And buried in these footnotes of history are brilliant, fatally flawed thinkers who rose to dizzying heights of intellect and even fame, only to come crashing down into disaster, ridicule, or just the utter silence of oblivion.

Occasionally, I find others who share my predilection for the forgotten ephemera of genius. There's the Dead Media web site, devoted to "the numerous experiments that died on the barbed wire of technological advance. The Edison kinetophone. Gaumont's Chronophone. The synchronoscope. The movietone. Phonofilm. The graphophonoscope. The vitaphone . . ." There are fellow antiquarians like Edmund Pearson and Van Wyck Brooks, whose books I can scarcely open without feeling the need to give the secret handshake for the Universal Brotherhood of Collectors of Obscurity. And there's my old college roommate, Shawn Lani, now the senior exhibit designer at the Exploratorium in San Francisco. He contracted a collector's mania for household photos—anonymous black-and-white photographs from yard sales or old wire service archives, many lacking a date or even a name, but occasionally capturing a serendipitous genius in their composition. We are all curators at heart, I suppose, of items that we fear no one else will have time for.

Why write about such things?—you may ask.

And if it's not you, surely *someone* will ask this question. Despite our being a nation of moralists, the only real sin in America is that of failure. The man or woman of promise who has nothing but excuses and regrets to offer at the end of the day—these people we do worse than despise. We avert our gaze and excuse ourselves from their presence.

And why not? We are also a nation of successes. This, at least, is what every demagogue, advertiser, and con artist tells us. We want to believe that we are good people, and that opportunity is there for those with the spirit to achieve it. Yet we laud men and women who have no better quality than the possession of money, and who achieve their success on the backs of the swindled and disdained. We want to believe that there is something more to their success than mere greed and luck. Even more than a moral loser, we cannot bear the thought of an immoral success.

There are moral successes, of course. But for each person credited with a winning innovation, there are the losers who pursued a similar path to failure. Perhaps their timing was wrong. Maybe they lacked the ruthless force of personality that propels the winners of history. In the end, they might even have been undone by weaknesses in character that had little to do with the merits of their ideas.

And so I began this book, an account of those who have fallen in their pursuits. Whole books could be unearthed on each of their lives—and I hope that happens someday. But for now, these excavations may suffice.

HAVE YOU HEARD THAT IT WAS GOOD TO GAIN THE DAY?
I ALSO SAY IT IS GOOD TO FALL, BATTLES ARE LOST
IN THE SAME SPIRIT IN WHICH THEY ARE WON. . . .

VIVAS TO THOSE WHO HAVE FAIL'D!
AND TO THOSE WHOSE WAR-VESSELS SANK IN THE SEA!
AND TO THOSE THEMSELVES WHO SANK IN THE SEA!
AND TO ALL GENERALS THAT LOST ENGAGEMENTS,
AND ALL OVERCOME HEROES!
AND THE NUMBERLESS UNKNOWN HEROES EQUAL
TO THE GREATEST HEROES KNOWN!

—Walt Whitman, "Song of Myself"

BANVARD'S
FOLLY

BANVARD'S FOLLY

*Mister Banvard has done more to elevate the taste for fine
arts, among those who little thought on these subjects,
than any single artist since the discovery of painting and
much praise is due him.*

—THE TIMES OF LONDON

The life of John Banvard is the most perfect crystallization of loss imaginable. In the 1850s, Banvard was the most famous living painter in the world, and possibly the first millionaire artist in history. Acclaimed by millions and by such contemporaries as Dickens, Longfellow, and Queen Victoria, his artistry, wealth, and stature all seemed unassailable. Thirty-five years later, he was laid to rest in a pauper's grave in a lonely frontier town in the Dakota Territory. His most famous works were destroyed, and an examination of reference books will not turn up a single mention of his name. John Banvard, the greatest artist of his time, has been utterly obliterated by history.

What happened?

IN 1830, A fifteen-year-old American schoolboy passed out this handbill to his classmates, complete with its homely omission of a 5th entertainment:

BANVARD'S
ENTERTAINMENTS
(To be seen at No. 68 Centre street,
between White and Walker.)

Consisting of
1st. Solar Microscope
2nd. Camera Obscura
3rd. Punch & Judy
4th. Sea Scene
6th. Magic Lantern
Admittance (to see the whole) six cents.
The following are the days of performance, viz:
Mondays, Thursdays, and Saturdays.
Performance to commence at half-past 3 P.M.
JOHN BANVARD, Proprietor

Although his classmates were not to know, they were only the first of more than two million to witness the showmanship of John Banvard. Visiting Banvard's home museum and diorama in Manhattan, they might have been greeted by his father, Daniel, a successful building contractor and a dabbler in art himself. His adventurous son had acquired a taste for sketching, writing, and science—the latter pursuit beginning with a bang when an experiment with hydrogen exploded in the young man's face, badly injuring his eyes.

Worse calamities lay in store. When Daniel Banvard suffered a stroke in 1831, his business partner fled with the firm's assets. Daniel's subsequent death left the family bankrupt. After watching his family's possessions auctioned off, John lit out for the territories—or at least for Kentucky. Taking up residence in Louisville as a drugstore clerk, he honed his artistic skills by drawing chalk caricatures of customers in the back of the store. His boss, not interested in patronizing adolescent art, fired him. Banvard soon found himself scrounging for signposting and portrait jobs on the docks.

It was here that he met William Chapman, the owner of the country's first showboat. Chapman offered Banvard work as a scene painter. The craft itself was primitive by the standards of later showboats, as Banvard later recalled:

The boat was not very large, and if the audience collected too much on one side, the water would intrude over the low gunwales into their exhibition room. This kept the company by turns in the un-artist-like employment of pumping, to keep the boat from sinking. Sometimes the swells from a passing steamer would cause the water to rush through the cracks of the weather-boarding, and give the audience a bathing. . . . They made no extra charge for this part of the exhibition.

The pay proved to be equally unpredictable. But if nothing else, Chapman's showboat gave Banvard ample practice in the rapid sketching and painting of vast scenery—a skill that would eventually prove to be invaluable.

Deciding that he'd rather starve on his own payroll than on someone else's, Banvard left the following season. He disembarked in New Harmony, Ohio, where he set about assembling a theater company. Banvard himself would serve as an actor, scene painter, and director; occasionally, he'd dash onstage to perform as a magician. He funded the venture by suckering a backer out of his life savings; this pattern of arts financing would haunt him later in life.

The river back then was still unspoiled—and unsafe. But the troupe did last for two seasons, performing Shakespeare and popular plays while they floated from port to port. Few towns could support their own theater, but they could afford to splurge when the floating dramatists tied up at the dock. Customers sometimes bartered their way aboard with chickens and sacks of potatoes, and this helped fill in the many gaps in the troupe's menu. But eventually food, money, and tempers ran so short that Banvard, broke and exhausted from bouts with malarial ague, was reduced to begging on the docks of Paducah, Kentucky. While Banvard was now a toughened showman with several years of experience, he was also still a bright, intelligent, and sympathetic teenager. A local impresario took pity on the be-draggled boy and hired him as a scene painter. Banvard, relieved, quit the showboat.

It was a good thing that he did quit, for farther downriver a bloody knife fight broke out between the desperate thespians. The law showed up in the form of a hapless constable, who promptly stumbled through a trapdoor in the stage and died of a broken neck. With a dead cop on their hands, the company panicked and abandoned ship; Banvard never heard from any of them again.

WHILE IN PADUCAH, Banvard made his first attempts at crafting "moving panoramas." The panorama—a circular artwork that surrounded the viewer—was a relatively new invention, a clever use of perspective that emerged in the late 1700s. By 1800, it was declared an official art form by the Institut de France. Photographic inventor L. J. Daguerre went on to pioneer the "diorama," which was a panorama of moving canvas panels viewed through atmospheric effects. When Banvard was growing up in Manhattan, he could gape at these continuous rolls of painted canvas depicting seaports and "A Trip to Niagara Falls."

Moving into his twenties with the memories of his years of desperate illness and hunger behind him, Banvard spent his spare time in Paducah painting landscapes and creating his own moving panoramas of Venice and Jerusalem. Stretched between two rollers and operated on one side by a crank, they allowed audiences to stand in front and watch exotic scenery roll by. Banvard could not stay away from the river for long, though. He began plying the Mississippi, Ohio, and Missouri rivers again, working as a dry-goods trader and an itinerant painter. He also had his eye on greater projects: a diorama of the "infernal regions" had been touring the frontier successfully, and Banvard thought he could improve upon it. During a stint in Louisville, he executed a moving panorama that he described as "INFERNAL REGIONS, nearly 100 feet in length." He completed and sold this in 1841, and it came as a crowning success atop the sale of his Venice and Jerusalem panoramas.

It is not easy to imagine the effect that panoramas had upon their viewers. It was the birth of motion pictures—the first true marriage of the reality of vision with the reality of physical movement. The public was enthralled, and so was Banvard: he had the heady rush of an artist working at the dawn of a new media. Emboldened by his early successes, the twenty-seven-year-old painter began preparations for a painting so enormous and so absurdly ambitious that it would dwarf any attempted before or since: a portrait of the Mississippi River.

WHEN WE READ of the frontier today, we are apt to envision California and Nevada. In Banvard's time, though, "the frontier" still meant the Mississippi River. A man setting off into its wilds and tributaries would only occasionally find the friendly respite of a town; in between he faced exposure, mosquitoes, and, if he ventured ashore, bears. But Banvard had been up and down the river many times now, and had taken at least one trip solo as a traveling salesman. The idylls of river life had charms and hazards, as he later recalled:

> All the toil, and its dangers, and exposure, and moving accidents of this long and perilous voyage, are hidden, however, from the inhabitants, who contemplate the boats floating by their dwellings and beautiful spring mornings, when the verdant forest, the mild and delicious temperature of the air, the delightful azure of the sky of this country, the fine bottom on one hand, and the romantic bluff on the other, the broad and the smooth stream rolling calmly down the forest, and floating the boat gently forward, present delightful images and associations to the beholders. At this time, there is no visible danger, or call for labor. The boat takes care of itself; and little do the beholders imagine, how different a scene may be presented in half an hour. Meantime, one of the hands scrapes a violin, and others dance. Greetings, or rude defiances, or trials of wit, or proffers of love to the girls on shore, or saucy messages, are scattered between them and the spectators along the banks.

Banvard knew the physical challenge that he faced and was prepared for it. But the challenge to his artistry was scarcely imaginable. In the spring of 1842, after buying a skiff, provisions, and a portmanteau full of pencils and sketch pads, he set off down the Mississippi River. His goal was to sketch the river from St. Louis all the way to New Orleans.

For the next two years, he spent his nights with his portmanteau as a pillow, and his days gliding down the river, filling his sketch pads with river views. Occasionally he'd pull into port to hawk cigars, meats, household goods, and anything else he could sell to river folk. Banvard prospered at this, at one point trading up to a larger boat so as to sell more goods. Recalling those days to audiences a few years later—exercising his flair for drama, of course, and referring to himself in the third person—he remembered the trying times in between, when he was alone on the river:

> His hands became hardened with constantly plying the oars, and his skin as tawny as an Indian's, from exposure to the sun and the vicissitudes of the weather. He would be weeks altogether without speaking to a human being, having no other company than his rifle, which furnished him with his meat from the game of the woods or the fowl of the river. . . . In the latter part of the summer he reached New Orleans. The yellow fever was raging in that city, but unmindful of that, he made his drawing of the place. The sun the while was so intensely hot, that his skin became so burnt that it peeled from off the back of his hands, and from his face. His eyes became inflamed by such constant and extraordinary efforts, from which unhappy effects he has not recovered to this day.

But in his unpublished autobiography, he recalled his travels a bit more benignly:

> [The river's current was] averaging from four to six miles per hour. So I made fair progress along down the stream and began to fill my portfolio with sketches of the river shores. At first it appeared lonesome to me drifting all day in my little boat, but I finally got used to this.

By the time he arrived back in Louisville in 1844, this adventurer had acquired the sketches, the tall tales, and the funds to realize his fantastic vision of the river he had traveled. It would be the largest painting the world had ever known.

Banvard was attempting to paint three thousand miles of the Mississippi from its Missouri and Ohio sources. But if his project was grander than any before, so were the ambitions of his era. Ralph Waldo Emerson, working the New England public lecture circuit, had already lamented, "Our fisheries, our Negroes, and Indians, our boasts . . . the northern trade, the southern planting, the Western clearing, Oregon, and Texas, are yet unsung. Yet America is a poem in our eyes, its ample geography dazzles the imagination. . . ." The idea had been voiced by novelists like Cooper before him, and later on by such poets as Walt Whitman. When Banvard built a barn on the outskirts of Louisville in 1844 to house the huge bolts of canvas that he had custom-ordered, he was sharing in this grand vision of American art.

His first step was to devise a tracked system of grommets to keep the huge panorama canvas from sagging. It was ingenious enough to be patented and featured in a *Scientific American* article a few years later. And then, for month after month, Banvard worked feverishly on his creation, painting in broad strokes: trained in background painting, he specialized in conveying the impression of vast landscapes. Looked at closely, this work held little for the connoisseur trained in conventions of detail and perspective. But motion worked magic upon the rough-hewn cabins, muddy banks, blooming cottonwoods, frontier towns, and medicine-show flatboats.

During this time he also worked in town on odd jobs, but if he told anyone of his own painting, we have no record of it. Fortunately, though, we have a letter from an unexpected visitor to Banvard's barn. Lieutenant Selin Woodworth had grown up a few houses away from Banvard and hadn't seen him in sixteen years, and he could hardly pass by in the vast frontier without saying hello. When he showed up unannounced at the barn, he was amazed by what maturity had wrought in his childhood friend:

> I called at the artist's studio, an immense wooden building. . . . The artist himself, in his working cap and blouse, pallet and pencil in hand, came to the door to admit us. . . . Within the studio, all seemed chaos and confusion, but the life-like and natural appearance of a

portion of his great picture, displayed on one of the walls in a yet
unfinished state. . . . A portion of this canvas was wound upon a upright roller, or drum, standing on one end of the building, and as
the artist completes his painting he thus disposes of it.

Any description of this gigantic undertaking . . . would convey
but a faint idea of what it will be when completed. The remarkable
truthfulness of the minutest objects upon the shores of the rivers,
independent of the masterly, and artistical execution of the work
will make it the most valuable historical painting in the world, and
unequaled for magnitude and variety of interest, by any work that
has been heard of since the art of painting was discovered.

This was the creation that Banvard was ready to unveil to the world.

Banvard approached his opening day with the highest of hopes.
Residents reading the *Louisville Morning Courier* discovered on June
29, 1846, that their local painter had rented out a hall to show off
his work: "Banvard's Grand Moving Panorama of the Mississippi will
open at the Apollo Rooms, on Monday Evening, June 29, 1846, and
continue every evening till Saturday, July 4." A review in the same
paper declared, "The great three-mile painting is destined to be one
of the most celebrated paintings of the age." Little did the writer of
this review know how true this first glimpse was to prove: for while
it was to be the most celebrated painting of the age, it did not last
for the ages.

Opening night certainly proved to be inauspicious. Banvard paced
around his exhibition hall, waiting for the crowds and the fifty-cent
admission fees to come pouring in. Darkness slowly fell, and a rain
settled in. The panorama stood upon the lighted stage, fully wound
and awaiting the first turn of the crank. And as the sun set and rain
drummed on the roof, John Banvard waited and waited.

Not a single person showed up.

IT WAS A humiliating debut, and it should have been enough to make
him pack up and leave. But the next day saw John Banvard move
from being a genius of artistry to a genius of promotion. He spent
the morning of the 30th working the Louisville docks, chatting

to steamboat crews with the assured air of one who'd navigated the river many times himself. Moving from boat to boat, he passed out free tickets to a special afternoon matinee.

Even if they had paid the full fee, the sailors would have got their money's worth that afternoon. As the painted landscape glided by behind him, Banvard described his travels upon the river—a tall tale of pirates, colorful frontier eccentrics, hairbreadth escapes, and wondrous vistas, a tad exaggerated, perhaps, but it still convinced a hallful of sailors who could have punctured his veracity with a single catcall. When he gave his evening performance, crew recommendations to passengers boosted his take to $10—not bad for an evening's work in 1846. With each performance the audience grew, and within a few days he was playing to a packed house.

Flush with money and a successful debut, Banvard returned to his studio and added more sections to the painting, and then he moved it to a larger venue. The crowds continued to pour in, and nearby towns chartered steamboats to see the show. With the added sections, the show stretched to over two hours in length; the canvas would be cranked faster or slower depending on audience response. Each performance was unique, even for a customer who sat through two in a row. The canvas wasn't rewound at the end of the show, so the performances alternated between upriver and downriver journeys.

After a successful shakedown cruise, Banvard was ready to take his "Three Mile Painting" to the big city. He held his last Louisville show on October 31 and then headed for the epicenter of American intellectual culture: Boston.

BANVARD INSTALLED HIS panorama in Boston's Armory Hall in time for the Christmas season. He had honed his delivery to a perfect blend of racy improvisation, reminiscences, and tall tales about infamous frontier brigands. The crank machinery was now hidden from the audience, and Banvard had commissioned a series of piano waltzes by Thomas Bricher to accompany his narration. With creative lighting and the unfurling American landscape behind him, Banvard had created a seemingly perfect synthesis of media.

Audiences loved it. By Banvard's account, in six months 251,702

Bostonians viewed his extraordinary show; at fifty cents a head, he'd made about $100,000 in clear profit. In just one year, he'd gone from modest frontier sign painter to famous and wealthy man—and probably the country's richest artist. When he published the biographical pamphlet *Description of Banvard's Panorama of the Mississippi River* (1847) and a transcription of his show's music, *The Mississippi Waltzes*, he made more money. But there was an even happier result to his inclusion of piano music—the young pianist he'd hired to perform it, Elizabeth Goodman, soon became his fiancée, and then his wife.

Accolades continued to pour in, culminating in a final Boston performance that saw the governor, the speaker of the house, and state representatives in the audience unanimously passing a resolution to honor Banvard. His success was also the talk of Boston's intellectual elite. John Greenleaf Whittier titled a book after it (*The Panorama and Other Poems*) in 1856, and Henry Wadsworth Longfellow wrote about the Mississippi in his epic *Evangeline* after seeing one of Banvard's first Boston performances. Longfellow had never seen the river himself—to him, the painting was real enough to suffice. In fact, Longfellow was to invoke Banvard again in his novel *Kavanaugh*, using him as the standard by which future American literature was to be judged: "We want a national epic that shall correspond to the size of the country; that shall be to all other epics what Banvard's panorama of the Mississippi is to all other paintings—the largest in the world."

There is little doubt that Banvard's "Three Mile Painting" was the longest ever produced. But it was a misleading appellation. John Hanners—the scholar who almost single-handedly has kept Banvard's memory alive in our time—points out: "Banvard always carefully pointed out that *others* called it three miles of canvas. . . . The *area* in its original form was 15,840 *square feet*, not three miles in linear measurement."

But perhaps Banvard was in no hurry to correct the public's inflated perceptions of his painting. His fame was now preceding him, and he moved his show to New York City in 1847 to even bigger crowds and greater enrichment; it was hailed there as "a monument of native talent and American genius." Each night's receipts were carted to the bank in locked strongboxes; rather than count the massive deposits, the banks simply started weighing Banvard's haul.

With acclaim and riches came the less sincere flattery of his fellow artists. The artist closest upon Banvard's heels was John Rowson Smith, who had painted a supposed "Four Mile Painting." For all Banvard's tendencies toward exaggeration, there is even less reason or evidence to believe that his opportunistic rivals produced panoramas larger than his. Still, it was a worrisome trend. Banvard had been hearing for some time of plans by unscrupulous promoters to copy his painting and to then show the pirated work in Europe as the "genuine Banvard panorama." With the United States success behind him, Banvard closed his New York show and booked a passage to Liverpool.

BANVARD SPENT THE summer of 1848 warming up for his London shows with short runs in Liverpool, Manchester, and other smaller cities. In London, the enormous Egyptian Hall was booked for his show. He began by suitably impressing the denizens of Fleet Street papers with a special showing. "It is impossible," the *Morning Advertiser* marveled, "to convey an adequate idea of this magnificent [exhibition]." The *London Observer* was equally impressed in its review of November 27, 1848: "This is truly an extraordinary work. We have never seen a work . . . so grand in its whole character." Banvard was rapidly achieving a sort of artistic beatification in the press.

The crowds and the money flowed in yet again. But to truly bring in the chattering classes, Banvard needed something that he'd never had in the United States: the imprimatur of royalty. After much finagling and plotting by Banvard, he was summoned to Windsor Castle on April 11, 1849, for a special performance before Queen Victoria and the royal family. Banvard was already a rich man, but royal approval could make the difference between being a mere artistic showman and an officially respected painter. Banvard gave the performance of his life, delivering his anecdotes in perfect combination with his wife at the piano; at the end, when he gave his final bow to the family assembled at St. George's Hall, Banvard knew that he had made it as an artist. For the rest of his life, he was to look back upon this as his finest hour.

His panorama show was now a sensation, running for a solid twenty months in London and drawing more than 600,000 spectators. An enlarged and embellished reprint of his autobiographical pamphlet, now titled *Banvard, or the Adventures of an Artist* (1849), also sold well to Londoners, and his show's waltzes could be heard in many a parlor. He penetrated every level of society; after attending one show, Charles Dickens wrote him in an admiring letter: "I was in the highest degree interested and pleased by your picture." To the other dwellers of this island nation, whose experience of sailing was often that of stormy seas, Banvard offered the spice of frontier danger blended with the honeyed idylls of riverboat life:

> Certainly, there can be no comparison between the comfort of the passage from Cincinnati to New Orleans in such a steamboat, and to a voyage at sea. The barren and boundless expanse of waters soon tires upon every eye but a seaman's. And then there are storms, and the necessity of fastening the tables, and of holding onto something, to keep in bed. There is the insupportable nausea of sea sickness, and there is danger. Here you are always near the shore, always see green earth; can always eat, write and study, undisturbed. You can always obtain cream, fowls, vegetables, fruit, fresh meat, and wild game, in their season, from the shore.

Toward the end of these London shows, Banvard found himself increasingly dogged by imitators—there were fifty competing panoramas in the 1849–50 season alone. In addition to suffering competition from longtime rival John Rowson Smith, Banvard now had scurrilous accusations of plagiarism flung at him by fellow expatriate portraitist George Caitlin, a jealous painter who had "befriended" Banvard in order to borrow money. Banvard also found his shows being set upon by the spies of his rivals, who hired art students to sit in the audience and sketch his work as it rolled by.

We know that a form of art has permeated a culture when cheap imitations appear, and even more so when parodies of these imitations emerge. There is a long-forgotten work in this vein by American humorist Artemus Ward, which was published posthumously as *Artemus Ward, His Panorama* (1869). Ward spent the last years of his life working in London, and had probably attended some of the numerous panoramic travelogues and travesties that darted about in Banvard's wake. His panorama, as shown by illustrations of the supposed stage (which, as often as not, is obscured by a faulty curtain), consists of a discourse on San Francisco and Salt Lake City, often interrupted by crapulous bits of tangential mumbling in small type:

> If you should be dissatisfied with anything here to-night—I will admit you all free in New Zealand—if you will come to me there for the orders.
>
> This story hasn't anything to do with my Entertainment, I know—but one of the principle features of my Entertainment is that it contains so many things that don't have anything to do with it.

For ads reproduced in the book, Ward munificently assures his audiences that his lecture hall has been lavishly equipped with "new doorknobs." But Banvard's most serious rivals were not such bumblers, and so he had to swing back into action. Locking himself in the studio again, he created another Mississippi panorama. Where the first panorama had been a view of the eastern bank, this new painting depicted the western bank. He then placed the London show in the hands of a new narrator and toured Britain himself with the second painting for two years, bringing in nearly 100,000 more viewers.

What might Banvard have done with these two paintings had he placed them onstage *together*? Angled in diagonally from each side to terminate just behind the podium, moving in unison, they would have provided a sort of stereoptical effect of floating down the center of the Mississippi River. It would have been the first "surround multimedia." For all of Banvard's innovation, though, there is no record of such an experiment.

NOT ALL OF Banvard's time in London was spent on his own art. In his spare hours, he haunted the Royal Museum; he was fascinated by its massive collection of Egyptian artifacts. He soon became a protégé of the resident Egyptologists, and under their tutelage he learned to decipher hieroglyphics—the only American of his time, by some accounts, to learn this skill. For decades afterward, he was able to pull sizable crowds to his lectures on the reading of hieroglyphics.

Banvard moved his show to Paris, where his success continued unabated for another two years. He was now also a family man: a daughter, Gertrude, was born in London, and a son, John Jr., was born in Paris. Having children scarcely slowed down his travels; on the contrary, he left the family to spend the next year on an artistic pilgrimage to the Holy Land. In a reprise of his American journey, he sailed down the Nile and filled up notebooks with sketches. But he no longer had to sleep with these notebooks as a pillow. He was now wealthy enough to travel in comfort, and he bought thousands of artifacts along the way—a task assisted by his unusual ability at translating hieroglyphics.

These travels were to become the basis for yet two more panoramas: one of Palestine, and the other of the trip down the Nile. Neither was to earn him as much as his Mississippi panorama; the market was now flooded with imitations, and the public was beginning to weary of the panoramic lecture. Even so, Banvard's abilities were greater than ever. One American reviewer commented in 1854 in *Ballou's Pictorial Drawing Room Companion*:

> Mr. Banvard made a name and fortune by his three mile panorama of the Mississippi. It was one of those cases in which contemporary justice is bestowed upon true merit. . . . His sole teacher in his art is Nature; there are few conventionalisms in his style. His present great work is far superior in artistic merit to his Mississippi— showing his rapid improvement; its effect is enhanced by its great height.

Just eight years after his voyage down the Mississippi, he had become both the most famous living artist in the world and the richest artist in history.

BANVARD RETURNED TO the United States with his family in the spring of 1852. He was a fantastically wealthy man, so wealthy that he could retire to a castle and casually dabble in the arts for the rest of his life. And at first that's exactly what he did.

The world's most famous artist needed an equally imposing home to live in. Accordingly, he bought a sixty-acre lot on Long Island and proceeded to build a replica of Windsor Castle. When the local roads didn't meet the needs of his castle, he simply built one of his own. He dubbed the castle Glenada in honor of his daughter, Ada; neighbors, who were alternately aghast and awed by the unheard-of construction expenses being incurred, simply dubbed it Banvard's Folly.

A reporter touring the site was kinder in his appraisal of Banvard's castle:

> It has a magnificent appearance, reminding you forcibly of some of the quaint old castles nestled among the glens of old Scotland. . . . There are nine offices on the first floor, as you enter from the esplanade, viz., the drawing-room, parlors, conservatory, anteroom, servant's room, and several chambers. The second story contains the nursery, school-room, guest chambers, bath, library, study, etc., with the servants' rooms in the towers. The basement is occupied with the offices, store-rooms, etc. Although the facade extends in front one hundred and fifteen feet, still Mr. Banvard says his castle is not completed, as he plans adding a large donjon or keep, to be occupied by his studio, painting-room, and a museum for the reception of the large collection of curiosities which he has gathered in all parts of the world. . . . it has been proposed to change the name of the place [Cold Spring Harbor] and call it BANVARD. . . .

Not surprisingly, the residents of the town failed to see the charm of this last proposal.

Still, Banvard spent the next decade in relative prosperity and modest continued artistic success. Indeed, his artistic horizons broadened each year. In 1861, he provided the Union military with his own hydrographic charts of the Mississippi River. General Frémont wrote back personally to thank him for his expert assistance. That same year, Banvard provided the illustration for the first successful chromolithograph in America. The process was unique in duplicating both the color and the canvas texture of the original illustration, which Banvard had titled "The Orison." The result was a tremendous success and helped assure his continued reputation as a technically innovative artist.

Banvard then turned his attention back to his first love: the theater. *Amasis, or, The Last of the Pharaohs* was a massively staged "biblical-historical" drama that ran in Boston in 1864. Banvard had both written the play and painted its enormous scenery, and was gratified by its warm reception among critics. It seemed to him that there was nothing that he could not succeed at.

EVEN AS BANVARD displayed his Egyptian artifacts to guests at Glenada, the role of museums was changing rapidly in America. By 1780, the "cabinet of wonder" kept by wealthy dilettantes had evolved into the first recognizable museum, operated by Charles Peale in Philadelphia. Joined later by John Scudder's American Museum in New York, these museums focused on educational lectures and displays—illustrations and examples of unusual natural objects, as well as the occasional memento.

This all changed when P. T. Barnum bought out Scudder's American Museum in 1841. Barnum brought in a carnivalesque element of equal parts spectacle and half-believable fraud—a potent and highly salable concoction of freak shows, dioramas, magic acts, natural history, and the sheer unrepentant bravado of acts like Tom Thumb and "George Washington's nursemaid." Barnum was not an infallible entrepreneur, but he was the shrewdest showman that the country had ever produced. Imitators attracted by Barnum's success soon found themselves crushed under the weight of Barnum's one-upmanship and his endless capacity for hyperbolic advertising.

By 1866, Barnum's total ticket sales were greater than the country's population of 35 million. John Banvard, with a castle full of actual artifacts, could scarcely ignore the fortune Barnum was making just a few miles away with objects of much more questionable provenance. Goaded by this, he paid a visit to his old sailing partner William Lillienthal. It had been more than fifteen years since the two had floated down the Nile, collecting the artifacts that now formed the core of Banvard's collection.

With Lillienthal's help—and a lot of investors' money—Banvard was going to take on P. T. Barnum. Their venture was precarious from the start. Aside from the daunting task of challenging America's greatest showman, Banvard was hampered by his own inexperience. Years of panoramic touring and a successful play had convinced Banvard that he could run a museum, but he had never really run a conventional business with a staff and a building to maintain. In all his years as a showman, he'd earned millions with the help of only one assistant, a secretary whom he eventually fired for stealing a few dollars.

Lillienthal and Banvard financed the "Banvard's Museum" by floating a stock offering worth $300,000. In lieu of cash, they paid contractors and artisans with shares of this stock; other shares were bought by some of the most prominent families in Manhattan. There was one problem, though: Banvard had never registered his business or its stock with the state of New York. No share certificates existed for the stock. Unbeknownst to Banvard's backers, and perhaps to Banvard himself, the shares were utterly worthless.

Flush with the money of the unwary, Banvard's Museum raced toward completion.

WHEN THE MASSIVE forty-thousand-square-foot building opened on June 17, 1867, it was simply the best museum in Manhattan. The famous Mississippi panorama was onstage in a central auditorium that seated two thousand spectators, and there were a number of smaller lecture rooms and displays of Banvard's handpicked collection of antiquities. The lecture rooms were important, as Banvard had invited in student groups for free to emphasize the family-friendly educational qualities of his museum, as opposed to Barnum's sensationalism. The museum also had one genuine crowd-pleaser built right in: ventilation. Poor auditorium ventilation was a constant complaint dogging panoramist shows, and Banvard took the initiative to install louvers and windows all the way around his auditorium.

P. T. Barnum had met a serious challenger in John Banvard. One week after Banvard's opening, Barnum ran ads in the *New York Times*, crowing that his own museum was "THOROUGHLY VENTILATED! COOL! Delightful!! Cool!!! Elegant, Spacious, and Airy Halls." This was hardly true, of course; Banvard's building was far superior, and Barnum knew it. But Barnum had a grasp of advertising that not even Banvard could match. The rest of the summer was to see America's greatest showmen—and its first entertainment millionaires—locked in an economic struggle to the death.

With each stab at innovation by Banvard, Barnum would parry with inferior copies but superior advertising. Banvard had the Mississippi panorama; Barnum had a Nile panorama, probably copied from Banvard's. Banvard had the real "Cardiff Man" skeleton; Barnum had a fake. On and on the showmen battled throughout the summer, with the stage and the newspapers as their respective weapons of choice.

The struggle ended with shocking speed. Banvard was in far over his head; creditors were dunning him for payments, and shareholders were furious over the discovery that their stock had been worthless all along. On September 1—scarcely ten weeks after opening—Banvard's Museum padlocked its doors.

BANVARD IMPROVISED FURIOUSLY. The building reopened one month later as Banvard's Grand Opera House and Museum. Productions dropped in and out over the next six months—first a leering dance production, then adaptations of *Our Mutual Friend* and *Uncle Tom's Cabin*. None was successful. Unable to make anything work, Banvard finally leased out the building to a group of promoters that included—perhaps to his chagrin—P. T. Barnum.

Banvard spent the next decade with the barest grasp on solvency, and then only by quietly appropriating lease money that should have been going to shareholders and other creditors. He and his wife lived virtually alone on their rambling sixty-acre estate; they were down to one servant for the whole property. After his shoddy treatment of the museum backers, no New Yorker would want to invest in a Banvard enterprise now; he wrote two more plays only to find that no producer would take them.

If his financial ethics were suspect, Banvard's artistic integrity was suffering even more. The innovator had been reduced to plagiarism: first in his history book, *The Court and Times of George IV, King of England* (1875), which was lifted from a book written in 1831; and then again the next year, when he finally managed to write a play that opened in his old museum, now named the New Broadway Theatre. *Corrina, A Tale of Sicily* was not only plagiarized, it was plagiarized from a living and thoroughly annoyed playwright.

Humiliated and surrounded by creditors, Banvard desperately sought a buyer for his theater. P. T. Barnum, when approached, sent a crushing reply back to his old rival: "No sir!! I would not take the Broadway Theatre as a *gift* if I had to run it." When Banvard finally did unload his decrepit building in 1879, he had to watch its new owners achieve exactly where he had failed. As Daly's Theatre, the building thrived for decades before finally being torn down in 1920.

Banvard's castle was not to be as long-lived as his museum. Banvard and his wife clung to Glenada for as long as they could, but by 1883, their deep entanglement in bankruptcy forced them to sell it. It eventually fell to the wrecking ball, and virtually all their other possessions were sold off to meet the demands of creditors. But the Mississippi panorama was spared from the auction block—now worn from nearly forty years of use, and nearly forgotten by the public, perhaps it was judged to be worthless anyway.

Banvard and his wife were now both well into their sixties and had scarcely any money to their name. They packed their few remaining belongings and quietly left New York. The only place left for them was what Banvard had left so long ago: the lonely, far-off American frontier. He was returning as he had left, a poor and forgotten painter.

———

IT WAS A deeply humbled and aged John Banvard that arrived in the frontier town of Watertown, in present-day South Dakota. He and his wife, the recent proprietors of a castle, had been reduced to living in a spare room of their son's house. Eugene Banvard was an attorney with some interest in local public works and construction projects, and occasionally the elder Banvard renewed his energies of yore by pitching in with his son on these projects.

For the most part, though, Banvard retreated into his writing. He was to write about seventeen hundred poems in his life—as many as Emily Dickinson—and like her, he only ever published a few of them. Unlike the more dubious plays and histories that he had "authored," his poems appear to be original to Banvard, and sincere if not particularly innovative efforts. Taking up the pen name "Peter Pallette," Banvard wrote hundreds of poems during his years in Watertown, becoming the state's first published poet. One of Banvard's more sustained efforts, published in Boston back in 1880 as *The Origin of the Building of Solomon's Temple*, centered on the biblical brothers Ornan and Araunah. It opens with a standard Romantic invocation:

> *I'll tell you a legend, a beautiful legend;*
> *A legend an Arab related to me.*
> *We sat by a fountain beneath a high mountain,*
> *A mountain that soar'd by the Syrian sea:*
> *When a harvest moon shewed its silvery sheen,*
> *Which called into thought the Arabian's theme.*

The book's epilogue descends into a miscellany of details about English church building, Egyptian obelisks, and loony speculations about Masonic oaths, a subject of apparently inexhaustible interest to the author.

On a more practical note, Banvard also authored a pocket-size treatise titled *Banvard's System of Short-Hand* (1886)—one of the first books published in the Dakota Territories. He claimed the system could be learned within a week, and that he had been using it for years, keeping in practice by surreptitiously transcribing conversations on buses and ferryboats: "The author acquired the knowledge of shorthand precisely in this manner when he was but a youth. . . . He has many of these little volumes now in his possession and they have become quite of value as forming a daily journal of these times."

For transcription practice, Banvard included his own poems and pithy maxims, such as "He jests at scars who never felt a wound." Banvard had felt some wounds himself of late, and more were to come before his strange journey came to an end. But that same year, now into his seventies, he locked himself in his studio one last time, ready to produce a final masterpiece.

DIORAMAS AND PANORAMAS were no longer a novelty by 1886, and Edison's miraculous work in motion pictures was just over the horizon. If the art form hadn't aged well, neither had its greatest proponent—along with the usual infirmities of age and his ruined finances, Banvard's eyesight had worsened with age. His eyes had never been terribly strong since his childhood laboratory mishap. Still, even now he could muster a certain heartiness. "In his mature years his appearance was like that of many Mississippi River pilots," said one contemporary. "A thickset figure, with heavy features, bushy dark hair, and rounded beard."

Nonetheless, Banvard's family was uneasy with his notions of taking the show on the road one last time, as his daughter later recalled: "My mother and the older members of the family were quite averse to his giving it [the performance], as they felt his health was too impaired for him to attempt it." If the older members of the family were against it, one can imagine the solace Banvard took in his grandchildren, who were only now seeing the family patriarch revive the art that had made him rich and famous long before they were even born.

For his diorama, Banvard had chosen a cataclysm still in the living memory of many Americans: "The Burning of Columbia." Most of the capital city of South Carolina was burned to the ground by General Sherman's troops in a day-long conflagration on February 17, 1865. Banvard's rendition of it was by all accounts a magnificent performance. Even more impressively—in an echo of his humble beginnings—Banvard ran the diorama and a massed array of special effects as a one-man show. One audience member recalled:

> Painted canvasses, ropes, windlasses, kerosene drums, lycopodium, screens, shutters, and revolving drums were his accessories. Marching battalions, dashing cavalry, roaring cannon, blazing buildings, the rattle of musketry, and the din of battle were the products, resulting in a final spectacle beyond belief, when one considers it was a one man show.
>
> I have read of the millions expended in the production of a single modern movie, but when I remember what John Banvard did and accomplished in a spectacular illusion in Watertown, Dakota Territory, more than fifty years ago for an outlay of ten dollars, I am rather ashamed of Hollywood.

For all the spectacle, though, Banvard's day had long passed. Dakota was simply too sparsely populated to support much of a traveling show, and the artist found himself packing away the scrims, drums, and screens for one last time, never to be used again.

A FEW YEARS later, in 1889, his wife, Elizabeth, died. They had been married for more than forty years. As is so often the case in a long companionship, the spouse followed not long afterward. A visitor to Banvard's Watertown grave will scarcely guess from the simple inscription that this was once the world's richest artist:

JOHN BANVARD

Born
Nov. 15, 1815

Died
May 16, 1891

As word of his death reached newspapers back East and in Europe, editors and columnists expressed amazement. How could this millionaire have died penniless on a lonely frontier? Had they sought to get any answers from his family, though, they would have come up empty-handed. Unable to pay their bills, the Banvards all fled town after the funeral.

In their haste to evacuate their house on 513 Northwest 2nd Street, they had left much behind, and an auction was held by creditors. Among John Banvard's remaining possessions was a yellowed scrap of paper listing his unpaid $15.51 bill for his own father's funeral service in 1831. Young John had spent his life haunted by his father's lonely death and humiliating bankruptcy. Sixty years later, still clutching the shameful funeral bill, he had met the same fate.

SO WHERE ARE his paintings?

His early panoramas of the Inferno, Venice, and Jerusalem were lost in a steamboat wreck in the 1840s. A few small panels are scattered across South Dakota; the Robinson Museum, in Pierre, has three. Two more are in Watertown: the Kampeska Heritage Museum has "River Scene with Glenada," while the Mellette Memorial Association has a hint of the "Three Mile Painting" with "Riverboats in Fog."

And what of the paintings that made his fame and fortune, the ingenious moving panoramas? One grandson, interviewed many years later, remembered playing on the massive rolls when he was little. But after Banvard's death, they lay abandoned to the auctioneer. Edith Banvard recalled in a 1948 interview: "I understood that part of it was used for scenery . . . in the Watertown opera house." From there, she conjectured, the rolls may have been cut into pieces and sold as theater backdrops. Worn from decades of touring, and torn from their original context as moving pictures, they might have seemed little more than old rags. Not surprisingly, no record is known of what theaters might have done with them.

One persistent account, however, holds that Banvard's master-pieces never left Watertown at all. They were shredded to insulate local houses—and there, imprisoned in the walls, they remain to this day.

THE CLEVER DULLARD

William Henry Ireland was a dullard. That, at least, is what everyone always told him. Born of dubious parentage in 1775 to London engraver and antiquarian Samuel Ireland, William was a muddle-headed boy who was unable to apply himself at much of anything. He was sent home from one school holding a note to his father explaining that William was simply too stupid to be taught, and that to collect any further tuition fees "was little better than robbing Mr. Ireland of his money."

William spent so little energy on the outside world because his inner world was simply more interesting. Freed from any expectations of greatness from his family or his teachers, young William Ireland would haunt the streets of London, hanging about the stage doors of theaters to observe the actors coming and going, and then going home and painstakingly building little theaters of cardboard in his bedroom.

Later he became fascinated by medieval heraldry. Old helmets and breastplates, dinged and rusty and useless in an era of gunpowder, collected dust in odd corner stalls around London, and so William happily poked around looking for odd bits from broken-up suits of armor. Once home with his newfound treasures, William scrubbed the rust off and polished them, and then sat in his bedroom trying to assemble his jumbled collection of odd pieces into a suit of armor. For the missing pieces, he cut and pasted in more bits of ornamented cardboard. Soon his bedroom became a regiment of armor pastiches, and at night he would sit up in his bed and stare at them in the moonlight, dreamily imagining himself clad in shining armor and riding up to a dark and forbidding castle.

In the meantime, William ricocheted from school to school, until finally his ill health forced his father to choose the time-honored last resort for parents of the sickly and unpromising: boarding school on the Continent. William spent four idyllic years in France, and upon his return at the age of seventeen was not only as useless as before but had also developed the impenetrable affectation of a French accent. Despairing of his son's ever making a mark, Samuel Ireland finally prevailed upon a lawyer friend in London to hire the teenager as a lowly clerk.

BY THIS TIME Samuel had built a middling reputation as an engraver and author of illustrated travelogues of the British countryside. In 1793, when William was eighteen years old, father and son journeyed up the River Avon in pursuit of material for Samuel's planned volume *Picturesque Views on the Warwickshire Avon*. The pair gravitated to Stratford-on-Avon, the birthplace of William Shakespeare. Young William knew Shakespeare by heart, since every night his father would gather his family after dinner and read them excerpts from the Immortal Bard.

To merchants in Stratford, Samuel must have looked like a moneybag endowed with limbs and a head. For while the Catholic Church invented the first tourist traps—pilgrimage stopovers that sold innumerable slivers of the True Cross and "saint's bones" butchered from unfortunate pigs—Stratford was the first secular tourist trap. No one in town had paid much attention to Shakespeare after his death, but the steady stream of devotees spurred actor David Garrick in 1769 to establish the town's first Shakespeare Festival. Local shops began offering Shakespeare relics carved from the inexhaustible supply of wood offered by the old mulberry tree that once sat in his backyard; enough Shakespeare personal effects were sold each year to furnish an entire neighborhood.

It was into this gruesome chamber of tchotchkes that Samuel and his son wandered. Samuel enthusiastically snapped up the stool upon which the Bard had once courted Anne Hathaway, as well as a goblet carved from the Great Bard's Most Wonderfully Proliferating Mulberry Tree. Sensing a fine pair of rubes, a local "historian" directed the two to a country estate outside Stratford where—so it was said—old papers of Shakespeare's might still be found. The antiquarian book collector and his son excitedly rushed out to the country estate of a Mr. Williams, where they were led into a small and gloomy parlor. Samuel could barely contain himself before he blurted out a question to Williams: had he seen any Shakespeare papers lying about the mansion?

Oh dear, said the expression on the landlord's face.

"By God!" he cried. "I wish you had arrived a little sooner! Why, it isn't a fortnight since I destroyed several baskets-full of letters and papers, in order to clear a small chamber for some young partridges which I wish to bring up alive: and as to Shakespeare, why, there were many bundles with his name wrote upon them."

Williams may have paused here, just to watch the blood drain from his guests' faces. He then pointed out the room's fireplace.

"Why, it was in this very fireplace I made a roaring bonfire of them. My dear," he called to his wife, "don't you remember bringing me down those baskets of paper from the partridge room? And that I told you there were some about Shakespeare the poet?"

—I told you, his wife replied, not to burn those papers.

Samuel rose from his chair in unutterable anguish, gasping *My God!* He demanded to be taken to the partridge pens, where he and his son spent the rest of their Stratford stay poking around the rafters and floorboards, all while Mr. Williams relaxed by the fire downstairs and, one suspects, enjoyed a snifter of brandy and a good laugh.

After they returned to London, the truth dawned on the younger Ireland: they had been had. Samuel Ireland, though, clung tenaciously to his delusions. He put Shakespeare's courting stool in a place of honor in his sitting room, and often invited visitors to rest their backsides upon that very same seat where the Immortal Derrière had once sat. Watching this, William now saw his father was gullible. Realizing the full extent of parental fallibility is a jarring moment in young adulthood, all the more so when that parent is widely thought to be smarter than you. William did not gloat in this, but it did present a way by which he might gain that which his father had always with-held: recognition of his son's intelligence and talents as a writer.

THE OFFICE OF Bingley, Esq., was not a busy one, and his employer's many trips out left William Henry plenty of opportunities to haunt old bookstalls, as well as to shut himself into the office to work un-interrupted on poetry; with a vast store of office supplies on hand, in a time when pen and ink were still rather dear for most citizens, Ireland was free to chase whatever literary whim might seize him during his supposed working hours. William Henry set about the fanciful task of writing out some of Shakespeare's plays in longhand—in Shakespeare's hand, to be precise. He did not get very far in this project, but it did give him an idea.

One afternoon in late 1794, while poking through old obscure tracts in a street stall, he came across a small volume of prayers beau-tifully bound in vellum and stamped in gold with Queen Elizabeth's arms—probably a presentation copy from the author to the Queen. But without any documentation to prove this, it was worth little. Ireland bought it cheaply from the bookseller and took it back to the office. The law records there dated back hundreds of years, giving William Henry a fair notion of what Elizabethan documents looked like. He pilfered a blank sheet of old paper from a file and settled down at his desk to titrate some water into a pot of ink; the weakened solution, applied to the old paper, produced appropriately faded writ-ing. William dipped his pen and proceeded to write a dedicatory epistle from the author to the Queen—all the proof one needed for the book to become collectible. Once the ink had dried, he tucked the epistle into the front cover and left the office.

His first stop was at Mr. Laurie's, a bookbinder down the street in New Inn Passage. Ireland was well-known to Laurie and his two journeymen, for he had often stopped by with books of his own and his father's in need of repair. William showed off his epistle and asked them what they thought.

—It certainly *looks* old, Laurie replied.

But one of the journeymen, examining it more closely, said: I can make a better old ink than that for you. William watched as the journeyman mixed three liquids together in a vial, compounds normally used for marbling the front and end papers of books. The concoction frothed and bubbled for a moment, and settled back into a brownish ink. The journeyman wrote out a few words with it.

—It's very faint, Ireland observed.

The journeyman held the document over an open fire. As the paper warmed and rustled in the updraft, the ink darkened into legibility—and into an oxidized brown tint that perfectly captured the appearance of two-hundred-year old ink.

—*One shilling*, the journeyman said.

Ireland paid it.

WILLIAM RETURNED TO Bingley's office and, quill in hand, scratched out a new letter to Queen Elizabeth. This forgery he tucked into the little prayer book and took it home with him that evening, where he basked in paternal admiration. His father, delighted by the find, encouraged his son to keep looking in the bookstalls. Perhaps he could succeed in the one pursuit where Samuel had been frustrated—the autograph of William Shakespeare. "I would gladly give half my library for such an autograph," Samuel mused.

William ransacked his absent employer's old files in the hope that a land deed might have Shakespeare's name on it, but it was no use. A search of stalls selling old papers and parchments turned nothing up. There was, however, a plentiful supply of the mysterious brown ink. One sleepy December morning in Bingley's office, Ireland cut the end off an ancient rent roll and used it to write up a lease agreement between Shakespeare and John Heminge. Unlike any attempt to mimic Shakespeare's own play manuscripts, a forged legal document was so mundane as to be utterly believable. At the bottom of the lease William traced out Shakespeare's signature from a published copy.

As a legal document, it needed a wax seal. William pulled a pile of neglected seventeenth-century deeds from the office files, sat down at a desk, and clicked open his penknife. Pressing the flat of the blade against the paper, he slid it across the back of the seal, paring away the wax in one whole piece from the parchment. Soon he had a small pile of authentic old wax seals ready to apply to documents, save for one problem: they had all dried out about two hundred years ago. He grabbed an ash shovel from the office fireplace, laid a few seals in it, and held it over the flaming hearth, hoping that the heat would melt the back of the seals enough to make them adhere again. But the desiccated beeswax crumbled, so he tried heating new wax and applying it to the back of the old seals like glue. To hide the difference in color between old and new wax, he darkened and dirtied the entire seal with some ash from the hearth.

By December 16, after two weeks of work, William was ready to unveil his newest discovery.

"I have a great curiosity to show you," he said as he entered his father's study.

—Yes? his father replied.

William drew out the lease from the breast pocket of his overcoat and handed it to Samuel.

"There, sir! What do you think of that?"

Samuel opened the parchment and read over it carefully. Then he examined the seal. William watched with mounting anxiety as his father carefully folded the document back up and handed it back to him.

"I certainly believe it to be a genuine deed of the time."

William pressed it back into his father's hand.

"If you think so, I beg your acceptance of it."

This document—the signature of Shakespeare—was what his father had so long wanted that he would have given half his library for it. Clearly moved, Samuel took a set of keys from his pocket and passed them to his son.

"These are the keys of my bookcase. Go and take from it whatsoever you please; I shall refuse you nothing."

William handed back the keys.

"I thank you, sir; but I shall accept of nothing."

His father rose from his chair, unlocked the case, and drew out a slim volume published by Will Stokes in 1652, *The Vaulting-Master, or, The Art of Vaulting*. Almost half of the book consisted of engraved plates, which William recognized as a sign of the book's rarity and value. His father knew this, too.

—Take it, he said. Please.

William had pleased his father at last.

BEING A DUTIFUL son, the junior Ireland continued forging documents for his father over the next few days. When asked how he had found them, he had a tale prepared. An older gentleman, informed of young William's interest in old books and papers, had invited him to a mansion where he had a large store of them at hand. Visible among these were a few—and perhaps, hinted William, many—bearing Shakespeare's signature. The gentleman, not wishing to attract attention to himself, was only to be known as Mr. H. The good nobleman proved to be a very generous friend indeed. On December 18, William returned home with an IOU from Shakespeare to John Heminge, of the Globe Theatre. On the 20th he unveiled Shakespeare's draft letter to his patron Lord Southampton; both documents were received with incredulous joy by his father.

William even added another authentic element to his ruse. One day, probably when he should have been at work, he sauntered over to the Parliament building to watch the proceedings from the visitors' gallery at the House of Lords. While bewigged lords droned on below, William noticed an ancient and ragged tapestry hanging on the back wall. Moving himself next to it, he stealthily tore off a swatch of fabric, which he pocketed while innocently continuing to watch the debate below. Now he had genuine old thread for tying up his rolled-up documents.

William pondered what his next discovery might be. He knew that readers were vexed by the possibility that their Bard might have been Catholic. There is, after all, that suspicious reference to Purgatory by the ghost of Hamlet's father. In an era when anti-Catholic legislation was favorably viewed by many, such papist skullduggery was improper in a national literary hero. And so, on Christmas Day of 1794, William presented his nation with a fine gift—Shakespeare's Profession of Faith, in which he disowns any Catholic sympathies.

His father was awed by the import of this, so much so that he could no longer keep the discoveries secret. All holiday frivolity was to be set aside now.

—I must bring in reputable men to examine these papers, he said.

Young William went pale at this. To fool his father was one thing, but scholars? The waters were rising, and any minute he would be in over his head.

When Drs. Parr and Wharton arrived at the Ireland household, Samuel was waiting in the study for them. Young William stayed away from the room; he had no desire to witness what was about to happen. But finally the call came, and William entered his father's study almost paralyzed with terror. After a few formal questions about the origins of the manuscripts, the doctors warmly praised the young man for his discovery, at which William bowed his head—as much from fright as from modesty. Samuel then commenced the reading of the Profession of Faith:

> I beynge nowe ofe sounde Mynde doe hope thatte thys mye wyshe wille atte mye deathe bee acceeded toe as I nowe lyve in Londonne ande as mye soule maye perchance soone quitte thys poore Bodye it is mye desire thatte inne such case I maye bee carryed toe mye native place ande thatte mye Bodye bee there quietlye interred wythe as little pompe as canne bee, ande I doe nowe inne these mye seyriouse moments make thys mye professione of fayth. . . .

William agonized through each syllable. At the end of the reading, Dr. Parr spoke first.

"Sir, we have very fine passages in our church service, and our litany abounds with beauties; but here, sir, here is a man who has distanced us all!"

Dazed, William excused himself from the room and walked blindly into the dining room. The teenager leaned heavily against the window and pressed his face against the cold glass, his mind a mass of chaos.

He had become the country's Greatest Writer.

WILLIAM NOW POSSESSED something that no one suspected in him: literary genius. Over the following weeks he wrote at a desperate white heat. Legal documents, theater receipts, letters between Queen Elizabeth and Shakespeare; and finally a love letter from Shakespeare to Anne Hathaway, complete with a lock of hair and a sonnet attached:

> *Is there inne heavenne aught more rare*
> *Thanne thou sweete Nymphe of Avon fayre*
> *Is there onne Earthe a manne more trewe*
> *Thanne Willy Shakspeare is toe you. . . .*

The precious lock was quickly split up and set into rings for fashionable Londoners. Words of the discoveries spread quickly, and so many visitors descended upon Norfolk Street that Samuel had to print up admission tickets. But he basked in the attention; once a mediocre engraver and antiquarian book collector, he was now the possessor of the greatest literary discovery of the century. The rich and the powerful knocked on his door: the Prince of Wales came to visit, as did Prime Minister William Pitt and Poet Laureate Henry Pye. When James Boswell, the biographer of Samuel Johnson, stopped in, he was so overcome with emotion at the sight of the papers that he could only recover with the aid of a tumbler of warm brandy and water—which, in truth, he might have asked for even were he not overcome with emotion. Finishing off his brandy, he pulled himself from his chair and declared, "Well, I shall now die contented, since I have lived to witness the present day." A few months later he most obligingly made good on this promise.

The praise of Britain's elite fired William's imagination; even as Samuel shone in the reflected glory of the Shakespeare papers, William watched from outside his father's study and alone knew who the real literary genius was. Soon his promises to his father became more and more ambitious, even rash.

—I've found a handwritten manuscript of *King Lear*, he said one day.

He had been hard at work on this for some time. But it was not a mere transcription of *King Lear* from the published editions. William decided he was going to improve on the original. It was a typical impulse for his time; eighteenth-century theaters were infamous for removing unseemly humor in Shakespeare tragedies, or excising tragic moments from comedies. And since Georgians dearly wished their Bard could be more refined in his tastes, William replaced Shakespeare's lines with improved versions that removed any earthy humor.

Samuel and a throng of experts were delighted, and William topped it off by discovering books from Shakespeare's library—volumes which, had anyone noticed, looked suspiciously similar to ones for sale the previous week on Charing Cross, but which now bore the great poet's comments in the margins.

In churning out a blizzard of false documents, William developed a steady forged handwriting in which he could write as assuredly as in his natural hand. But as he set about writing his next discovery, a manuscript of *Hamlet*—or "Hamblette," as he had renamed it in a bizarre attempt at archaic spelling—he was getting restless. He no longer wanted to merely invent legal documents and improve on famous plays. He wanted something more.

ONE DAY, BETWEEN visits from the famous and the merely curious, William sat alone in his father's study on Norfolk Street. In a display case he could see the rapidly growing pile of Shakespeare papers; none, though, had given him a chance to exercise his own literary talents. As he brooded and looked about the room, his eye fell upon a picture hanging over the fireplace: a painting of King Vortigern, an infamously ruthless king of fifth-century Britain. Now here, William reflected, was a subject worthy of a Shakespeare play. He pulled down his father's old copy of Raphael Holinshed's *Chronicles* (1577)—the same account Shakespeare relied on when writing his history plays.

Holinshed portrayed King Vortigern as a rather nasty piece of work. He had no claim on the throne, but served as the scheming adviser to a simple-minded heir:

> Ye have heard how Constantius was made a moonke in his fathers life time, bicause he thought to be too soft and childish in wit, to have anie publike rule committed to his hands: but for that cause speciallie did Vortigerne seeke t'advance him, to the end that the king being not able to governe of himselfe, he might have the chiefest swaie, and so rule all things as it were under him.

Hidden behind this legitimate heir, Vortigern sowed discord amongst his enemies and rivals, and sent innocent men to the gallows. When Constantius was no longer of any use to him, Vortigern simply had him murdered and seized the throne. Still married, he announced his intention of taking a second wife, who promptly attempted to poison him; he was then overthrown by Constantius's legitmate heirs and by citizens disgusted with the usurper's murderous debauchery.

After reading Holinshed, William proudly announced to his father the discovery of an entire original play by Shakespeare: *Vortigern*. His father was so delighted that he badgered William about it every day. William, writing as fast as he could in the unsafe sanctuary of his workplace—one morning the cleaning lady burst in on him in mid-forgery—had to keep stalling Samuel. Mr. H, he explained, was transcribing his own copy before allowing it to leave the mansion.

It took William two months to finish the play. When he presented it to Samuel in late March 1795, his father did something unusual— he wouldn't let anyone else see it. This play, Samuel knew, was pure gold. He quietly began inquiring at some of London's biggest theaters: might they be interested in staging Shakespeare's lost play?

Producers offered Samuel contracts for *Vortigern* sight unseen. But the most prestigious to rise to the bait was Robert Brinsley Sheridan of the Theatre Royal on Drury Lane—the most prominent producer and playwright in London, and a member of Parliament to boot. But after reading the first few pages, with Samuel looking on, Sheridan's ardor cooled a bit: "There are certainly some bold ideas here, but they are crude and undigested. It is very odd: one would be led to think that Shakespeare must have been very young when he wrote the play." Lest Samuel become alarmed, Sheridan then added, "As to the doubting whether it is his or not, who can possibly look at the papers and not believe them ancient?"

Samuel wanted £500. Sheridan, knowing that he could not back out of the deal now, sensibly haggled him down to £250. He felt it was simply a mediocre Shakespeare play; few people questioned the authenticity of the papers. Why would they? The paper was real enough, as were the seals. And everyone knew that William Ireland wasn't clever enough to write well in his own modern tongue, never mind forge a document in Elizabethan English. They would have been right on the last count, if only they could see it. William *couldn't* forge a document in Elizabethan English, as his love letter to Anne Hathaway demonstrates:

> O Anna doe I love doe I cheryshe thee inne mye hearte forre thou arte as a talle Cedarre stretchynge forthe its branches ande suc-courynge smaller Plants fromme nyppynge Winneterre orr the boysterouse Wyndes Farewelle toe Morrowe bye tymes I wille see thee tille thenne Adewe sweete Love

This was the work of an ambitious but inexperienced youth who mimicked old writing by arbitrary additions of double consonants, replacing *i* with *y*, and tacking *e* at the end of words. It wasn't Eliz-abethan dialect.

It wasn't *any* dialect.

THERE IS A truism among museum curators that the best forgeries are the ones still hanging on the walls. Any example of forgery is necessarily an example of a flawed forgery, because it is known to be a forgery. The best forgeries are beyond reproach in their authentic-ity: they have so successfully insinuated themselves into a body of work that they are eternally part of its history. Like the Velveteen Rabbit, if you love a forgery enough it *becomes real*. But most forgers are not this successful. Forgeries generally succeed for no more than a generation or so, if that, because rather than looking like the works they purport to be, they look like what we *want* these works to be. They caricature the aesthetic prejudices of an age, and when that age has passed the ruse becomes embarrassingly obvious.

But discovery loomed closer for William with each passing day. After running out of ink, he went back to Mr. Laurie's for more; surely the journeymen had their suspicions. William had picked his employer's law office clean of old paper and had to bribe a bookseller on St. Martin's Lane with five shillings so that he could to slice the blank front and back pages out of old books. Then a friend named Talbot, suspicious all along of William, crept into the law offices one day and caught him red-handed. So far, though, these potential informants kept his secret.

Even so, Samuel's incessant demands for more papers were exhausting William, as were the constant pleas to meet with Mr. H. Since Mr. H. had such sway over his father, William began to address letters from him to his father. They were replete with praise for his brilliant son's poetic gifts and deeply ironic comparisons to Shakespeare:

> ... I would not scruple giving £2000 a year to have a son with such extraordinary facilities. If at twenty he can write so what will he do hereafter. The more I see of him the more I am amazed. If your son is not a second Shakespeare I am not a man ... Your son is brother in genius to Shakespeare. He is the only man that ever walked with him hand in hand.

William would watch his father's face for any sign of agreement. But Samuel didn't want to hear about paying William more attention and a greater allowance; he wanted Shakespeare papers. Exasperated, William made another bid for attention: he discovered a second trunk full of documents at the house of Mr. H. He rashly produced a list of the contents of this second trunk: complete manuscripts of *Richard II* and *Henry V*, partial manuscripts for six other plays, a new play titled *Henry the Second*, and—most incredibly—Shakespeare's autobiography.

William hatched schemes to ensure that the document windfall would continue far into the future. Hearing that the butcher living in Shakespeare's house in Stratford-on-Avon was selling it, William attempted to buy it. Had he succeeded, it would have presented infinite opportunity for new discoveries: under every floorboard, behind every fireplace brick, and over every rafter could be found a new sonnet, a secret love letter, an undiscovered play!

Unable to secure the house, William handily produced a Letter of Deed from Shakespeare recounting the heroic deeds of one... William Henry Ireland. There had indeed been a William Ireland in London in Shakespeare's day; only now, this Ireland became the young man who rescued Willy from drowning by diving into the Thames after him. In gratitude, Shakespeare had written a rider to his will bequeathing William Ireland the rights to eight plays—including *Vortigern* and *Henry the Second*.

Perhaps, William hinted to anyone who would listen, this other Ireland was a direct ancestor of his, and this was why Mr. H had chosen him as the recipient of the Shakespeare papers. An ancient will was now being honored, and William Henry Ireland—the dullard boy who never knew for sure who his mother was—was now the fabulously lucky descendant of a friend of William Shakespeare's.

SAMUEL IRELAND WAS ready in December 1795 to present his lavish volume of transcriptions and facsimile plates, *Miscellaneous Papers Under the Hand and Seal of William Shakespeare*. William begged him not to publish it, but Samuel was not to be deterred—why, these were the papers of Shakespeare! How could he not publish them? And so William waited with growing dread, knowing that the flimsiness of his inventions would now be exposed for every scholar in Britain to pick apart, and not to simply glance at in the display case in his father's study.

He would be tested sooner than he thought. One day William strolled from Bingley's offices and back to his father's house for his midafternoon break. When he arrived, he found the house in tumult.

—What's wrong? he asked.

Albany Wallis had just visited. Though he was Samuel's friend and lawyer and a neighbor on Norfolk Street, he had long been skeptical of the papers. Wallis informed Samuel that he had discovered a genuine old deed signed by John Heminge. Wallis presented Samuel with his document, and Samuel pulled the other out from the display case—the very one that William had affixed Heminge's name and signature to for his very first Shakespeare forgery. *The two signatures looked nothing alike.* William was horror-struck: he'd picked Heminge because he thought there were no extant signatures, and now his bluff was called.

—Let us go see it, he told his father.

At Wallis's office, the lawyer once again produced the deed. William stared it, memorizing its every curve and letter. Excusing himself from the chambers, and promising an explanation from Mr. H very shortly, he calmly left Wallis's building—and then ran back to Bingley's offices. He dashed out a receipt bearing the signature of Heminge, executed as best as he could remember it from Wallis's document, and then warmed it over the fire to age the special ink. He dashed back to Wallis's office with the new receipt in hand.

It was all a silly misunderstanding, William told him. Mr. H had explained everything: there were two John Heminges, one that worked with the Globe Theatre, and one that worked over at the Curtain Theatre. Shakespeare had done business with them both, and so had signatures from both in the papers. See?—He handed him the receipt—I also have a signature from your Heminge!

Wallis examined the document and admitted that the proof was clear enough. He was sorry now that he had ever doubted the papers. William returned to Bingley's office, cranked out an improved copy of the first, and then returned to Wallis to let him look at the receipt more closely. The illusion was so perfect that Wallis didn't realize that he was looking at a different piece of paper from the one he'd stared at just minutes before.

William accomplished these forgeries in just over an hour—and that included walking back and forth between the offices. By four-thirty, the crisis was over and Wallis placated. This feat weighed much in William's favor. The papers had to be real if they could be produced on such short notice: it was inconceivable that anyone could forge that quickly and effortlessly.

SHERIDAN KEPT PUSHING the *Vortigern* premiere back, as if he was hoping to make the whole thing go away. By the time it would get staged, it would be after the publication of the Shakespeare papers, and after the inevitable attacks to follow. Samuel pleaded with Sheridan to speed up the premiere, but to no avail.

On Christmas Eve 1795, the London *Times* ran a notice that *Miscellaneous Papers Under the Hand and Seal of William Shakespeare* was now ready to be picked up at Samuel's house. London's literati stopped by Norfolk Street that day for their copy, delighted to have the Bard's personal letters to read by the Yule log. Other buyers were delighted for different reasons: they were sharpening their knives.

The first attack appeared days later in *The Tomahawk*:

Ireland, Ireland, tell to me,
"Who wrote Shakespeare's writings?"—THEE!

The following weeks did not bring much relief. The obvious target for ridicule was Ireland's bizarre spelling, and on January 14 a journalist at *The Telegraph* happily "discovered" another letter of Shakespeare's:

TOOO MISSTEERREE BEENJAAMMIINNEE JOOHNNSSONN
Deeree Sirree,
 Wille youe doee meee theee favvourree too dinnee wythee meee onnn Friddaye nextte attt twoo off theee clockee too eatee sommee muttonne choppes andd somme poottaattooeesse
 I amm deerree sirree
                              Yourre goodde friendde
                              WILLIAME SHAEKSPARE

Other newspapers followed with parodies of Shakespeare's letters, and the January issue of the *Monthly Mirror* screamed, "THE WHOLE IS A GROSS AND IMPUDENT IMPOSITION, AN INSULT TO THE CHARACTER OF OUR IMMORTAL BARD, AND A LIBEL ON THE TASTE AND

UNDERSTANDING OF THE NATION!!" Editor James Boaden flayed the papers alive, amply demonstrating to readers the "vicious and fantastic orthography" of William's mock-Tudor spelling. And there was more: by January 20, it was whispered that the pugnacious lawyer and Shakespeare scholar Edward Malone had prepared a skewering of the papers. Malone was known as a devastating cross-examiner in the courtroom, and Samuel and William waited miserably the entire winter for his onslaught.

Rumblings came back to Samuel from Drury Lane that Sheridan was not exactly doing his utmost on behalf of the play. He was recycling as many old props and costumes as he could, while lead actor John Kemble ridiculed the dialogue during rehearsals, encouraging the cast to join in with him. Many did. Then, to top it off, Sheridan wickedly chose a premiere date of April 1, 1796—April Fool's Day. Samuel protested, and Sheridan barely relented. The premiere was set for the following evening, Saturday, April 2.

VORTIGERN IS NOT a bad play. William held his inept Ye Olde Sppellingge in check enough that the play script looks convincingly Shakespearean, and it has all the grand sweep of battle and gore that one could desire from an early Shakespeare tragedy. But there are no subplots, no false leads, no irony, and not the faintest leavening of humor. Despite the Fool in the cast, *Vortigern* is humorless, whereas even in his darkest plays, Shakespeare managed to nudge the audience with a bit of bitter laughter. Still, in an aching soliloquy by Aurelius, newly arrived in Britain to reclaim the throne from Vortigern, young William's gifts were obvious:

> *O God! why shou'd I, a mere speck on earth,*
> *Tear thousands from their wives, children, and homes!*
> *O! wherefore from this transitory sleep,*
> *That now doth steal from them their inward cares,*
> *Should I send thousands to cold dreary death?*
> *'Tis true, I am a King, and what of that?*
> *Is not life dear to them, as 'tis to me?*
> *O! peasant, envy not the prince's lot;*

Thy page in life's great book is not foul charg'd,
And like to ours besmeare'd with dying breaths.
O! had I lives myself enough to answer
The ravenous and greedy jaws of death,
That will on these my friends, my soldiers,
Such havoc make, and wanton gluttony!
Father of mercy, great God, spare this blood!
And if I must alone receive the crown,
Bedeck'd with purple gore, I here resign it.

Fine words—but William's most brilliant lines could not save him now.

ON MARCH 31 the sword fell. Edward Malone had not been idle in the intervening three months—*An Inquiry into the Authenticity of Certain Miscellaneous Papers and Legal Instruments* had snowballed from a short pamphlet into a 424-page avalanche of utterly damning evidence against the papers. Malone presents his *Inquiry* as a courtroom drama, in which Malone is presenting exhibit after exhibit of evidence to the judging reader, more than backed up by two hundred voluminous footnotes. He attacks the papers for their spelling, for the use of words and phrases that didn't exist in Shakespeare's time, and for the disparity between known signatures and the ones Ireland had forged. Malone spared no cost to take each Ireland document, one by one, and tear it to pieces: he filled his book with expensive foldout plates and illustrations to compare true and false signatures side by side. He could hardly hide his scorn; when quoting from Shakespeare's love poem to Anne Hathaway, Malone interrupts himself to spit, "I shall not therefore sicken your Lordship with any more of this namby-pamby stuff."

Actually, much of Malone's evidence was wrong. Many claims that certain words were not in use during Shakespeare's time were later disproved. And yet it hardly mattered. Even if all of Malone's criticisms were wrong—and they were not—he had disillusioned London from its infatuation with the papers. With this book, Malone was also crushing the career of the most talented young writer in London. But

Malone hardly knew this. Even now, nobody imagined William as the true source of the forgeries.

A CROWD GATHERED outside the Theatre Royal hours before curtain time. It was a Saturday afternoon in the springtime, and the theatergoers were well liquored and pressing so furiously to get in that the Royal's staff had to barricade the doors. Dozens of hired boys shouted their way through the mob, dispensing a printed handbill from Samuel decrying the "*malevolent* and *impotent* attack" by Malone, and requesting that "*Vortigern* may be heard with that candour that has ever distinguished a British Audience."

The admission gate opened, and the distinguished British Audience stampeded into the Theatre Royal, pitching patrons headlong into the seating and onto the floor. Doorkeepers were pushed aside, and gate crashers poured in, ready for a bit of free play-bashing. Amid the chaos, Samuel made his way inside and took a seat in the center box. Supporters cheered him from one side of the theater, and detractors jeered from another.

Young William, not keen on sitting among thousands of half-sober partisans, quietly slipped backstage and into the green room. Nobody took much notice of his departure. Curtain call came, and actors and actresses came and went. Only one, Fanny Jordan, bothered to speak to the lad. She had always been a favorite of William's; unbeknownst to her, "Shakespeare" had actually written some of the play's dialogue and songs specifically for her. But she did know that William was miserable and nervous, and did her best to soothe him during her breaks between scenes.

—It is going well, she told him during the third act.

William believed her. But he did not believe in *Vortigern* anymore. "It will not be represented a second time," he predicted.

FANNY HAD BEEN telling the truth. Although the actor fumbling through the play's prologue had been ridiculed by the crowd to the point of nearly breaking apart in anguish—a standard hazing in Georgian theaters—the first two acts of *Vortigern* proceeded smoothly enough, with the curtain closing both times to applause from the audience. Not everyone in the audience believed it to be Shakespeare, but at least they all believed it to be a good play for their two shillings. Samuel could look about the theater from his box seat and see a motley cross-section of London, MPs and pickpockets alike, enjoying the play that he'd discovered.

And then Charles Dignum walked onstage. Dignum was not a distinguished actor. He had a high reedy voice utterly inappropriate to his role as a baron, and as he spoke the audience began to snigger, the giggling welling up and up until Dignum had to yell the line

Let them bellow on!

in his flouncing tenor. The audience burst out in laughter, wiping their eyes and applauding the ludicrous acting for minutes on end, bringing the play to a complete halt. John Kemble came onstage and pleaded with them to let the play proceed, and an increasingly drunk supporter—Charles Sturt, member of Parliament—yelled at the audience to shut up. The laughter finally died down, but only just, and Act III staggered on.

Act IV has the play's climactic battle scenes between the Saxons and the Scots. Sheridan had maliciously cast a bulbous-nosed comic actor named Phillimore in the role of the Saxon general. After falling in battle, Phillimore sprawled his body across the stage, but not where he had been told to during rehearsal. As the heavily weighted curtain descended on the scene, it landed full on Phillimore's ample gut, leaving half his body in front of and half behind the curtain.

Oooooooooohhhhhh . . . , he groaned.

This was just too much. The audience hooted with laughter that increased with each groan and yodel from Phillimore and his twitching body. Sturt, MP, became so enraged that he leaped from his box onto the stage and drunkenly grabbed Phillimore by the costume to drag him away. Audience members doubled over in comic agony. As Act V proceeded and supporters in the box seats applauded it, others in the theatre drunkenly pelted them with oranges. Sturt, a supporter but now disgusted with the hash the actors were making of the play, picked up the oranges from around his seat, peeled them with his pocketknife, and then flicked orange peel at the actors as they spoke their lines.

It got worse.

In the midst of Act V, detractors waited for a prearranged signal—a line which would set off a riot. They got it in scene 2 with the line

And when this solemn mock'ry is ended . . .

Suddenly, William recalled, "the most discordant howl echoed from the pit that ever assaulted the organs of hearing." It roared on for ten minutes until Kemble, the lead in the play, started by redelivering the exact same line, bringing down the house all over again. Sturt, who though only an MP was now as drunk as a lord, stood up in his box and bent over to moon the baying mob, for which he was rewarded with another volley of oranges.

The play staggered to its end, whereupon an unfortunate actor reappeared onstage to announce that there would be another performance of *Vortigern* the following Monday. The crowd went berserk. It took fifteen minutes for the staff to restore order so that Kemble could announce that Sheridan's *School for Scandal* would also be playing next week.

He was pelted by fruit—apples, this time.

Despite the hopeful stage announcement, William had guessed right. Sheridan sent word after the play: *Vortigern*'s first performance was its last.

THE NEXT DAY William and Samuel collected their share of the take—£102, which was very good for an opening night, but nothing like what they'd have made had the play not closed after one performance. Samuel gave William a £30 share; it was the last money William was to see for quite some time.

The Shakespeare papers still had believers, despite Malone's attacks and the fracas of *Vortigern*'s opening night. Foremost among them was Samuel himself. But his name was being tarred around town as a forger, and he complained that "the public determination is to pursue me even to ruin." He begged William to reveal the identity of Mr. H—only then, he explained, could he show the public the true and reputable source of the papers. William refused, agonized, and then refused again. Finally, after a week of Samuel's pleas, he relented.

—I will give H's identity to our lawyer, Wallis, in a sworn affidavit, he said. Mr. H will be present at the swearing. But Wallis will have to keep his identity secret from you.

It seemed a fair compromise to William, for when the forgeries were fully uncovered, Albany Wallis could vouch that Samuel had been kept in the dark the whole time, thus saving Samuel's reputation. A meeting was set for May 19 at a local inn; unknown to William, Samuel hid himself across the street so that he might see Mr. H entering the building. To his great disappointment, he saw nothing.

Wallis, though, heard everything—a complete confession.

One of the papers' believers, bursting with curiosity afterward, asked William to at least tell him this: would he recognize Mr. H if he saw him?

Oh yes, William said.

"You would recognize him at first sight."

CONFESSING TO WALLIS did little to ease William's mind. Pressed by demands for answers on all sides, he retreated into extravagant lies and make-believe about a dream life that he could scarcely distinguish any more from the real world. He talked grandly of Mr. H's generosity and distributed money and expensive gifts to friends and actors, all courtesy of Mr. H. The wealthy nobleman was to buy him a horse and a stable; soon William was seen trotting about town with his new horse and carriage. Construction on a carriage house began, too, courtesy of Mr. H, until Wallis—who knew that it was all coming out of William's rapidly shrinking pocket—stepped in and talked some sense into him.

No matter. Mr. H had promised William an estate of £300 a year! And the manager of Covent Garden, after seeing the script of *Henry the Second*, had promised a £700 advance! And—William proudly informed his delighted family—he had become engaged to a wealthy young Miss Shaw of Harley Street. Samuel began to make preparations for the wedding, calculating how many servants and linens and how much money the new couple would be needing.

But when Samuel visited Harley Street, there was no Shaw family. When he visited Covent Garden, the manager had never heard of *Henry the Second*.

And then William's thirty pounds ran out.

BY JUNE, SAMUEL was at the end of his tether. Traveling away from Norfolk Street, he wrote a wrenching letter to his son:

> I have no rest either night or day, which might be much alleviated by a more open and candid Conduct on your side. Surely if there is a person for whom you can for a moment feel, it must be for a parent who has never ceased to render you every comfort and attention, from your earliest moment of existence to the present. I think you must sometimes reflect and place yourself in your imagination at a future period of life, having a son and being in such a predicament as I stand at the moment; and then judging what must be *your state of mind*, and what must be *mine at present*.

But Samuel was too late, for William never received the letter. The day before, with his father away from home, William had quietly got married—not to a wealthy young Miss Shaw, but to an unknown "girl about town" named Alice Crudge. Two days later, while Samuel's letter was still in the mail, William left the house in the afternoon, telling the maid he'd be back in the evening to pick up his things. He never returned to Norfolk Street again.

The newlyweds had struck out on their own. Alice had a little bit of money to her name, while William had none at all. Quite to the contrary, he had left some debts for his father to be pestered by. But he did undertake one final act to relieve his father. He confessed his authorship of the papers. There was just one problem: Samuel refused to believe him. If the papers were a forgery, he snapped, then they were somebody else's forgery—William simply didn't have the capacity to produce such work.

A week after leaving home, William beseeched Samuel:

Can you think so meanly of me as to be the Tool of some person of Genius? . . . The Vortigern I wrote; if I copied anyone it was the Bard himself, in no one paper, or parchment was I furnished with language by anyone living—if there is Soul or Imagery it is *my own*.

Do not wish to meet me, my dear father, I cannot yet bear it. I will instantly retire into Wales and give myself up to that study I so ardently wish for.

If the writer of the Papers, I mean the mind that breathes through them, shows any spark of Genius and deserves Honour, *I, Sir, your son*, am that person.

It was to no avail. Samuel steadfastly refused to believe William, refused even to believe that the papers were forgeries at all. A few months later, when William published a confession titled *An Authentic Account of the Shakesperian Manuscripts*, the British public also refused to believe him. Not only did William's confession not lessen the infamy hanging over his father, it made it worse: what kind of scoundrel, newspapers cried, would put his young son up to confessing to a crime that the father had so clearly committed?

The papers still had some defenders. But most, like George Chalmers in his *Supplemental Apology for the Believers*, seemed less interested in defending the papers than in knocking the stuffing out of pompous windbags like Malone. At one point Chalmers promises to unleash the following against one doubter:

1. Proofs of your being the author of the Pursuit of Literature.
2. Proofs of your impertinence.
3. Proofs of your malignity.
4. Proofs of your jacobinism.
5. Proofs of your ignorance.
6. Proofs of your nonsense.
7. Proofs of your inability to write poetry.
8. Proofs that you cannot write at *all*.

The only true believer left, it seemed, was Samuel Ireland. Samuel died in misery a few years later in 1800, insisting on his innocence and on the papers' authenticity even on his deathbed. To his dying breath, he could not believe that his slow-witted boy had written them.

EVERYONE SEEMED TO forget something: William had written a great play. Not *Vortigern*. Ireland's great achievement, it turned out, was his sequel, *Henry the Second*. Seasoned by his experience at writing *Vortigern*, and not yet publicly unmasked, in late 1795 William had labored mightily over his second history play, pounding it out in just two months. He didn't even have time to divide it into acts and scenes. But *Henry the Second* had everything *Vortigern* lacked—snaking subplots, character development, suspense, dramatic reversals of fortune, and a hint of humor. He even created his first truly resonant character in Thomas Becket, the martyred Archbishop of Canterbury; in William's play, he becomes a tragic figure driven forward to death by the twin goads of loyalty to his church and gnawing ambition:

> *The child that hath enough, will mewl for more.*
> *We from the cradle then are still the same,*
> *Eager to climb ambition's golden tree,*
> *Looking but upward to the topmost branch;*
> *Nor thinking once, if back we wou'd return,*
> *That we the boughs have bent, and broken so,*
> *That there is but to go on and gain the point,*
> *Or headlong we must totter down again.*

But it was too late for soliloquies now. Critics and audiences across Britain were furious at the impudent boy who had made fools of them; those not angry at William simply believed him incapable of writing the forgeries, and were still convinced that it had been Samuel's fraud all along. In either case, no one was interested in seeing the new play written by William Henry Ireland. And so it went unproduced; no stage was ever graced by its lines, not to this day.

WILLIAM WAS NOT to know this, of course, and the newlywed spent his days after leaving home happily planning his next literary masterpiece. At first he and Alice drifted to the city of Bristol, where William lolled about and didn't get much writing done. One family acquaintance came across a young man walking by the roadside one day in Gloucestershire; it was William. He no longer even had a horse to his name. Yet he happily talked of his writing and of his desire to buy old books again—and then asked to borrow a few guineas.

Alice and William were living on nothing but borrowed money at this point; he borrowed from family and friends alike, telling some that it was to help finance his father's new book of engravings—an utter lie. Creditors dunned him for payment; in one letter, William pleads with his father, "The principal purport of this letter is to inform you of my wish of getting into some Situation and way of life which may keep me from *Starving*."

But the only calling for William, in the end, was that of a writer. He published his *Account* in 1797, and his two plays in 1799; that same year he also published his first novel, *The Abbess*. He spent the next three decades, until his death in 1835, churning out hack novels and satires that paid the bills but scarcely lived up to the promise of his early work. Tiring of making an honest living, he "discovered" Napoleon's will in 1821, and during 1824 miraculously discovered memoirs and letters by Henry IV of France and Joan of Arc. But these fooled nobody—by now people were wise to William's tricks.

Or so they thought.

WILLIAM NEVER DID lose his skill at quickly jotting off notes in Shakespeare's hand. Long after the frauds had been exposed, *Morning Post* editor John Taylor fell into conversation with William one night at the theatre. He asked William whether he really had been the forger, whereupon William instantly jotted off two Shakespeare signatures. When Taylor got home, he pulled down a Shakespeare book and compared the two; the likeness was uncanny. But there was a good reason for Ireland's remarkable memory: he had never really stopped forging.

The public may have stopped believing in the papers, but a fascination with the whole affair remained. Copies of William's 1797 *Account* were quickly snapped up for a shilling apiece, and in later years sometimes cost one guinea at auction. Eventually William found that he no longer had his own copy of *Account* and had to go to a bookseller to buy a used copy. He was chagrined to discover the price of his own book: "The only copy now in my possession is deficient in one leaf; and for this very mutilated impression I was compelled to pay eighteen shillings; being given to understand . . . that I was favoured in its sale at that price, because I was the author of the production."

At the Christie's estate sale for Samuel Ireland's goods in 1801, Samuel's collection of old books and papers, both real and counterfeit, attracted much interest. Among those bidding on the late and ruined antiquarian's worldly effects was a fellow with a strangely familiar face . . . Edward Malone. The very man who had destroyed Samuel and his papers now wanted to buy them.

William tried in 1805 to sate the public's interest in the forgeries by publishing a much-expanded account, *The Confession of William Henry Ireland*. By now the public had accepted the notion that William had been behind the forgeries, and for some time William had been receiving inquiries from interested collectors: did he still have any of the old Shakespeare forgeries lying around? Perhaps he would like to sell them? The manuscript of *Vortigern*, say? Might he still have that in his possession?

Oh yes, William would reply. It just so happens that I do.

It just so happened that William always had one in his possession. For ever since the forgeries had been exposed, and become a subject of morbid literary interest, he had been quietly doing something almost dazzlingly postmodern in its sheer ingenuity and conception.

He was making forgeries of the forgeries.

No fewer than seven "original" copies of the manuscript of *Vortigern* surfaced after William's death, along with a whole array of

other copies that he made of the Shakespeare papers. Each is utterly
authentic in appearance; it is impossible to tell which is the original
and which is the copy. After all, the collectors were getting them
straight from the source, and besides, who'd ever heard of a forgery
of a forgery?

Ireland couldn't resist leaving one little hint for his clients. Among
Ireland's many books is a bit of satirical verse from 1807, *Stultifera
Navis: Qua omnium mortalium narratur Stultia; The Modern Ship of
Fools*. It is an allegorical collection of a ship of fools of every variety,
illustrated with a color folding plate inside the front cover. Noticeable
among the fools is the figure of one particularly unfortunate fellow.

It is a Book Collector.

IF YOU GO today to the recently built reincarnation of the Globe
Theatre, you will find one of Ireland's forged copies of a forged letter
on display. It is his Heminge deed, the one that once nearly blew
William's cover as he stood sweating and nervous in the law office of
Albany Wallis. It is not merely a display piece—it is for sale by Bernard Quaritch Ltd., an antiquarian bookseller that has been housed
just off Piccadilly Circus for two centuries now; it went into business
not long after Ireland's death, and throughout its history it has pe-
riodically received bundles of Ireland forgeries from estate sales and
the like—the result, probably, of some familial ancestor who eagerly
laid out a few pounds to buy an entire batch of "original forgeries"
directly from William.

The forged Heminge letter on display will now set you back
£2,750.

According to Quaritch specialist Theodore Hoffman, it's getting
harder and harder each year to find Ireland forgeries. The papers
themselves are holding up fairly well—he probably used either weak
tea or lemon solution over a flame to induce browning, and neither
of those would weaken the paper fibers too greatly. But William
Henry Ireland, who worked so hard to make his papers look old and
rare, has been sentenced to poetic justice—now his papers really are
old and rare.

Finding a whole new batch of Ireland meta-forgeries might be worth quite a bit of money to someone. And since Ireland was none too careful or sophisticated in his techniques, it wouldn't be too hard . . . wait. The inevitable question is asked of Theodore—might someone be out there now, making a forgery of a forgery of a forgery?

"No, no," he says quickly. "I don't think so. . . ."

3

SYMMES HOLE

Hamilton, Ohio, is a place you could find only by accident, as you're unlikely to go there deliberately. In the 1970s the town changed its name to Hamilton!—a scheme dreamed up by some local Babbitt. When the expected vim, vigor, and pep failed to materialize, the exclamation mark faded away and the dreariness of the unadorned Hamilton returned. But Hamilton—or Hamilton!—has retained one item of interest to passersby.

Under the shade of an old oak in a weedy town park is a simple if enigmatic grave monument—a stone obelisk topped by a granite sphere. This sphere has a large hole drilled through the center. Underneath, amid a crazy quilt of patching concrete, are several bronze plaques, bolted in over original stone inscriptions that were scoured into illegibility by over a century of wind, rain, and neglect. They read, in part:

> John Cleves Symmes joined the Army of the U.S. as an ensign, in the year 1802. He afterwards performed daring feats of Bravery in the Battles of Lundy's Lane and Sortie from Fort Erie. Capt. John Cleves Symmes was a Philosopher, and the originator of the "Symmes Theory of Concentric Spheres and Polar Voids." He contended that the Earth was hollow and habitable within.

The monument, erected by Symmes's son in the 1840s, is surrounded by the sort of wrought-iron fencing typically found around old cemetery plots. Nearby, on hot and dusty summer days, locals play on a basketball court. They utterly ignore the old obelisk in their midst—a more apt reflection of the life of the man buried beneath it, perhaps, than the monument itself ever was.

SYMMES WAS INDEED a brave man, although at first this bravery took a rather obvious physical form. Born in Sussex County, New Jersey, in 1780 and the namesake of a famous uncle who had developed the Northwest Territory, Symmes received a tolerable if brief common school education. He was literate, but hardly polished; he did, however, have a love of learning that often drew him to haunt public libraries. His scant schooling was not unusual for the time—other than clergy, lawyers, and doctors, few men in the late eighteenth century had the luxury of a formal college education.

In 1802 Symmes enlisted in the army. He first saw action on an open field—in a duel, that is, with a bullying fellow officer named Lieutenant Marshall. In moments Marshall was lying on the ground with a broken leg and Symmes was bleeding from a shot to his wrist. Symmes reported shortly afterward, "I wanted to know if he desired another shot, and being informed in the negative . . . with my handkerchief wrapped around my wound, I went home and ate a hearty breakfast." He was no less fearless as a captain in the War of 1812. At the Battle of Bridgewater his company repelled three bayonet charges, and at Fort Erie he captured a British artillery position and destroyed its cannon.

Retiring as a war hero, Symmes took the well-worn career route of becoming a supplier to his old employer: he set up shop as a military provisioner and Indian trader in the upper Mississippi. He set aside some money and married a widow, and soon the two were living in St. Louis and presiding over a brood of ten children. He could have retired into the comfortable life of a respectable patriarch looking ahead to a lifetime of steady military business. But something was eating at John Cleves Symmes.

He had discovered that an entire world lay hidden beneath our feet—and only he knew how to find it.

SYMMES SPENT HIS military retirement in contemplation, observing migratory patterns and perusing books on geology and maritime exploration in his local libraries. There is no telling how long the notion of a hollow earth had occupied his mind, but he had now become obsessed by it. Writing up a brief tract in unadorned prose, he trudged down to his local printer and ordered up enough copies to send to every college, municipal government, senator, and eminent scientist in the country—and then some more copies, to go to every major foreign university as well. Titled *Circular Number 1*—for indeed many more were to follow—the publication introduced Symmes to the world on April 10, 1818:

> I declare that the earth is hollow and habitable within; containing a number of solid concentric spheres, one within the other, and that it is open at the poles twelve or sixteen degrees. I pledge my life in support of this truth, and am ready to explore the hollow, if the world will support and aid me in my undertaking.
>
> I ask one hundred brave companions, well equipped, to start from Siberia, in the fall season, with reindeers and sleighs, on the ice of the frozen sea; I engage we find a warm and rich land, stocked with thrifty vegetables and animals, if not men, on reaching one degree northward of latitude 82; we will return in the succeeding spring.

With this, Symmes thoughtfully attached a certificate of his sanity.

THE CIRCULAR WAS not well received. He was rebuffed by scholars and eminent statesmen across the country, and the French Academy of Sciences tabled his paper as unworthy of consideration. In a crowning insult, the *London Morning Chronicle* doubted the provenance of Symmes's certificate of sanity.

The theory itself was a relatively simple one, even if Symmes was at times a little unclear on specifics. Concentric spheres were, Symmes pointed out, a most efficient arrangement of natural architecture.

Bones, plant stems, trees, lava tubes, insect limbs—all showed the biodesign of hollow tubes or concentric structures.

> Enquire of the botanist, and he will tell you that the plants which spring up spontaneously agreeable to the established laws of nature, are hollow cylinders. . . . Enquire of the anatomist, and he will tell you that the large bones of all animals are hollow . . . even the minutest hairs of our heads are hollow. Go to the mineralist, and he will inform you that the stone called Aerolites, and many other mineral bodies, are composed of hollow concentric circles.

Symmes simply applied this principle of structure at a planetary level. And with the planet revolving, centrifugal force would fling material out along the axis, creating convenient holes at the poles through which intrepid souls like himself could venture into the inner world. Inside, Symmes believed, were multiple spheres, each accessible via a series of polar holes. Sunlight pouring through the holes and refracted through a dense interior atmosphere of "aerial elastic fluid" suffused these inner worlds with light and heat sufficient to sustain life.

Symmes believed this theory could account for all sorts of phenomena—magnetic fluctuations, the mysterious migrations of geese, caribou, and herring, and even the ocean's currents, for like a gigantic Charbydis, the earth's seas poured into one pole and gushed out from the other. Moreover, recent expeditions beyond the Arctic Circle had found open water where many had expected only frozen tundra. That, Symmes said, was from the outrush of warmed air from the interior world. After crossing 'the icy circle," explorers would find a liquid and perhaps even tepid sea all around the poles, thus making for easy sailing into the interior realms, or what Symmes dubbed "the midplane space."

As it turned out, Symmes was not the first person to propose a hollow earth theory, and this was seized upon by learned critics to discredit him. In his 1618 work *Epitome astrononomiae Copernicanae*, Johannes Kepler had pondered the notion of the earth and other planets being composed of concentric shells. As one reference book published by Abraham Rees in 1813, *The Cyclopedia*, put it: "If this [Kepler's theory] be the case, it is possible that the ring of Saturn may be the fragment or remaining ruin of his former exterior shell, the rest of which is broken or fallen down upon the body of the planet."

The hollow earth theory continued to attract distinguished support after Kepler's death. In 1692, Edmund Halley, the astronomer of comet fame, was confounded by distinct sets of fluctuating magnetic data. His ingenious solution was to theorize that three internal spheres within the planet, revolving at different rates, were causing these distinct sets of data to appear. Perhaps, he imagined, there existed a luminous atmosphere between these shells, giving off sufficient light and heat to sustain life. In a 1716 article he even suggested that the aurora borealis was caused by the escape of this gas.

Five years later, Cotton Mather cited Halley's theories in his book *The Christian Philosopher*, and by mid-century the Swiss mathematician Leonhard Euler, the court mathematician to Frederick the Great of Russia, also lent his support to Halley's theory. But in the intervening century little attention was paid to the notion, which in any case had never achieved any popular currency.

Symmes was unlikely to have read these obscure works, and so his was an act of discovery made all the more impressive by his humble education. Moreover, his theory included a polar opening—Symmes Hole, as it came to be widely known—and that meant that contact with the interior world could be made. In Halley's theory, the earth's outer shell was five hundred miles thick and had no hole, which gave his readers little reason to pursue the theory much further. Symmes, though, had offered them a gateway to new worlds.

SYMMES WROTE AND printed up seven more circulars over the next year, applying the hollow earth theory to such disparate subjects as the migration of caribou, the geometric principle of concentric spheres, and the formation of the Allegheny Mountains. After moving to Kentucky, he published another circular in August 1819, *Light Between the Spheres*, which was then reprinted in the *National Intelligencer* and distributed to a wide audience. Symmes was becoming known to the public, but mostly through ridicule; in Cincinnati, local mathematician Thomas Matthews derided Symmes for having written "a heap of learned rubbish." The more he wrote, the more Symmes was ridiculed. And the more he was ridiculed, the more determined and angry he got . . . and the more he wrote.

It soon became clear that neither the press nor the scientific establishment was going to bother with what they considered to be the lunatic ramblings of a half-educated veteran. His only other option was to take his case directly to the people. This was not an easy decision for Symmes. For all his bravery under fire, he was deeply uncomfortable appearing before any crowd, and he lacked magnetism or even the most basic qualities of public speaking:

> [There is] scarcely any thing in his exterior to characterize the secret operations of his mind, except . . . the glances of a bright blue eye, that often seems fixed on something beyond immediate surrounding objects. His head is round, and his face rather small and oval. His voice is somewhat nasal, and he speaks hesitatingly and with apparent labour. His manners are plain, and remarkable for native simplicity. . . . Captain Symmes's want of a classical education, and philosophic attainments, perhaps, unfits him for the office of a lecturer.

It may be a measure of Symmes's ill-suitedness for the job that this description was written by James McBride, who was one of his greatest supporters.

Still, he had dedicated himself to spending the rest of his life, if needed, to vindicate his theory. He had a polished wooden globe built, cleverly designed to reveal the polar holes and multiple shells within, and in 1820 he set about traveling from town to town on the American frontier—first in Cincinnati, and then in Kentucky and the small Ohio towns of Zanesville and Hamilton—lecturing before any crowd that would listen to him, at times even addressing rapt if rather uncritical groups of schoolchildren.

For all his fumbling inability as a speaker, when this modest man addressed a roomful of listeners, spinning his cross-sectioned globe as he spoke of worlds within worlds, a hush would fall across the room. And when he had finished and made a polite plea for his listeners to write to their civic leaders in support of his expedition, a few members of the crowd would come forth to donate a little cash or to pledge themselves as expedition volunteers should his ship ever sail. He did not make much money from lecturing—scarcely enough to travel on to the next town, really. But he did make believers. Perhaps to his consternation, his fame began to grow, and by the summer of 1820 the nature artist John Audubon even had him sit for a portrait to be displayed in the Western Museum.

It didn't take long for fiction writers to see the value of Symmes's theories. The same year that Symmes began lecturing, and just two years after his first missive, a pseudonymous "Captain Adam Seaborn" issued a science fiction novel titled *Symzonia: Voyage of Discovery* (1820). In it, Seaborn recounts how, in the thrall of the theories of the ingenious Symmes, he lured his sealing crew beyond the Antarctic rim and into the very bowels of the earth.

As they approach the icy polar circle blocking the rim of the hole to the inner earth, and the ship's compass begins to go haywire, an argument ensues on deck. *Symzonia* is so obscure and difficult to find that at this point I must give over the rudder to Captain Seaborn, if only because most readers may never have another chance to read any part of his book:

> "And a pretty condition we shall be in, Capt. Seaborn, if the ice closes the passage after we have dashed through it!" replied Mr. Slim. "We shipped with you, sir, for a sealing voyage; not for a voyage of discovery."
>
> "You will please to remember, Mr. Slim, that I am expressly authorized by articles, to cruize and seek for seals wheresoever I may judge expedient and proper, and that any opposition to my authority will involve forfeiture of your share—recollect that, Mr. Slim."
>
> "I do recollect that, sir; but at the same time I do know, Capt. Seaborn, that you have no right to hazard our lives, by running into dangers, greater than ever encountered by human beings, to

gratify your mad passion for discovery, instead of pursuing the interest of all concerned, by endeavoring to find seals in the usual manner. How will you justify yourself to the world, to our families, or to your own conscience, if we should, after effecting a passage through this 'icy hoop' you speak of, find it closed against our return, and thus be forever lost to our wives, our children, and society? We must in such a case all perish, and our blood would be upon your head."

A plague upon your lean carcass, thought I, how am I to answer so many impertinent questions. I could not tell him of my belief of open poles, affording a practicable passage to the internal world, and of my confident expectations of finding comfortable winter quarters inside; for he would take that as evidence of my being insane, and by means of it persuade the crew to dispossess me of my command, and confine me to cabin for the remainder of the voyage.

After knitting my brows a short time, I replied, "Mr. Slim, you are a sufficiently capable officer, and can get your duty well enough when you choose to do it, but you don't know every thing; your mind is too dense to admit the rays of intelligence. I would have you know, Sir, that I command this ship, and am not to be thwarted or dictated to by any man. I have noticed your rebellious spirit; now mark me, Sir, so sure as I have any more of your opposition to my will, or hear any more of your murmuring; the moment I detect you in uttering one discouraging word in the hearing of any of my officers or men,—I will confine you, and carry you home in irons, to take your trial for conspiring to make a revolt in the ship, which is death by the law; remember that, and go to your duty, Sir."

With his officers thus disciplined, Seaborn continues on to the Inner World. There he finds a strange utopian land—Symzonia, he dubs it—populated by gravely wise pale beings in plain white clothing, who know little of greed, envy, or vice. Gold and pearls are plentiful in this inner world—so much so, in fact, that they are something of a nuisance to the pragmatic inhabitants. They travel in airships and, for their defense, have developed a giant mobile flame-thrower of near-nuclear destructiveness. But, after much debate, they find the Externals (Seaborn and his crew) too corrupt in morals to be trusted, and deport them from their realm. A dejected Seaborn returns Gulliver-like to Boston, only to have his fortune swindled out of him, and is ultimately reduced to telling his fantastic tale for a publisher's pennies.

With public sentiment for a polar expedition fired by such tales and by Symmes's lectures, by 1822 members of Congress found themselves being beseeched by enough citizens and petitions that action needed to be taken. In one of the stranger moments of the Senate's history, Richard Johnson, the senator from Kentucky, took the floor with this proposal:

> Mr. R. M. JOHNSON, of Kentucky, presented a petition from John Cleves Symmes, of Cincinnati, in Ohio, stating his belief of the existence of an inhabited concave to this globe; his desire to embark on a voyage of discovery, to one or other of the polar regions . . . and suggesting to Congress the equipment of two vessels of 250 to 300 tons for the expedition, and the granting of such other aid as Government may deem requisite to promote the object. A motion was made to refer the petition to the Committee on Foreign Relations, which was refused; and after some conversation, it was decided to lay it on the table—ayes 25. (*Annals of Congress*, Senate Proceedings for Thursday, March 7, 1822)

The initial suggestion that Johnson's petition first go to the Committee of Foreign Relations was sensible, as the voyage would surely result in establishment of trade relations with inhabitants of the Interior World. But despite having a number of supporters in the Senate, the entire petition was indefinitely tabled by the end of the day's debate.

Still more petitions and letters came in. The next January it came to a vote again, this time in the House of Representatives, but was again tabled. Supporters lobbied hard, and in the following month seven more bills appeared in the House—five from Ohio, one from

Pennsylvania, and one from South Carolina. All were tabled or struck down in rapid succession.

Amid these political maneuverings, ridicule and disbelief dogged Symmes in many quarters. The August 27, 1822, issue of the Charleston, West Virginia, *Courier* was fairly typical in this regard. In an article titled "The Year 2150 Anticipated," an anonymous satirist imagines a world in which Symmes is lauded to a ludicrous extent as the greatest genius who ever lived, thanks in large part to the usefulness of the Inner World as a depository for criminals, the insane, and the criminally insane.

Symmes pushed onward. After another fruitless attempt in both houses of Congress in late 1823, he moved to a newly inherited family farm in Hamilton(!), Ohio, and took his case directly to his new home state, petitioning the Ohio general assembly to pass a bill supporting his theory. It failed. Discouraged and nearly broke, Symmes's health began to falter, and he spent much of 1824 and 1825 ill. But his earnest guilelessness had impressed some people so much that whether or not they believed his theory, they would write to him or press just enough money into his palm to sustain him. When a benefit was held for him on March 24, 1824, at the Cincinnati Theatre, Symmes was even treated to a bit of well-meaning doggerel penned for the occasion by local poet Moses Brooks:

> *Has not Columbia one aspiring son,*
> *By whom the unfading laurel may be won?*
> *Yes! history's pen may yet inscribe the name*
> *Of SYMMES to grace her future scroll of fame.*

Symmes had also attracted a disciple who was to prove both his greatest boon and bane in the remaining years of his life. Jeremiah Reynolds was an ambitious young editor of the *Wilmington Spectator*, and a great admirer of Symmes's theories, when he approached the great man himself with a plan. What good was it, he argued, if Symmes only addressed paltry crowds of frontier bumpkins? The places to go were the great urban and manufacturing centers of the

Northeast—rather than nibbling at the margins, Symmes should go straight for the financial and intellectual heart of the republic.

Symmes blanched at the thought of this. Facing crowds of simple homesteaders was nerve-racking enough for him; the idea of lecturing before audiences of cosmopolitan intellectuals was simply terrifying. But Reynolds was persistent—they would both go! This reassured Symmes somewhat, for Reynolds had the polished magnetism and youthful energy that Symmes lacked. With great hesitation, Symmes set off for the East with his twenty-six-year-old disciple in September 1825.

Their timing was fortuitous, for another Symmes admirer—one who perhaps had his best interests a little closer to heart—had during Symmes's 1824 illness set about compiling a book that would explain Symmes's theory with much greater aplomb and clarity than Symmes himself had ever managed. Released just months after the tour began, James McBride's *Symmes's Theory of Concentric Spheres* anticipated the arguments and examples of nearly every subsequent work on the subject. And while McBride does not shy from some of the more arcane aspects of Symmes theories, such as the "elastic fluid" aerating the inner earth that acts as a sort of antigravity force, it was his homely examples that struck a chord with many readers. Any reader could ascertain the truth of Symmes's theory within a matter of minutes:

> If you will take the trouble to examine a mechanic grinding cutlery on a large stone that is smooth on the sides and has a quick motion, you may observe that if a certain portion of water be poured on the perpendicular side whilst the stone is turning, it does not settle or form itself into a body round the crank or axis, but forms itself on the side of the stone into something resembling concentric circles, one within another. The surface of the earth, I apprehend, revolves with much greater velocity than any grindstone; and the substances composing the spheres are much firmer than water.

For the keen observer—or the keen believer, at least—concentric circles were everywhere in nature, whether in the ripples propagating upon a pond or in the mysterious alignments of iron filings around a lodestone.

It was just such devices that Symmes and Reynolds unveiled to audiences in their traveling show, playing to packed houses at fifty cents a head. With magnets, boxes of sand, whirling stones, and Symmes's well-worn wooden globe, audiences members were brought face to face with the laws of the universe . . . laws that inexorably led to a hollow earth. Skeptics who arrived at a Chambersburg, Pennsylvania, lecture in January 1826, one local editor observed, sat dumbstruck by the force of the pair's argument—"a breathless silence prevailed"—and erupted in applause at the end of the lecture. Even the editor, who had before written Symmes off as a loon, conceded the next day in his paper:

> Facts, the existence of which will not admit of a doubt, and the conclusions drawn from them are so natural . . . that they almost irresistibly enforce conviction on the mind. . . . The cost of an experiment [expedition] would be trifling, and discoveries of importance would most probably be made, tho' Symmes should be found erroneous.

This last sentiment proved to be Symmes's undoing. The pair moved on to Harrisburg, where they addressed the Pennsylvania legislature, which responded with an enthusiastic letter of support for the man who had managed to stand up "in awe of the world's dread laugh." Still, Symmes's fragile health was brought to the breaking point by the touring, and after the two finally reached the apex of their tour, Philadelphia, Reynolds had to take on most of the lecturing. Reynolds had noticed the audience's enthusiasm for a polar expedition, regardless of the veracity of the hollow earth theory, and started simply omitting Symmes's theory from most of his lectures. The two soon parted.

Symmes staggered on through the winter of 1826–27, lecturing with his props and his grand notions throughout New York and New England and all the way up into Canada, but the strain of stage fright exacerbating his already poor health was simply too much, and he called off the rest of his tour. For the next two years he stayed with an old friend in New Jersey, hoping merely to gain enough strength to go back home to his Ohio farm. When he finally did make the long journey back home, his son later recalled, "he was so feeble that he had to be conveyed on a bed, placed in a spring wagon, to his home near Hamilton."

From his sickbed he continued to churn out circulars on his proposed expedition, but with bitter knowledge that Reynolds, who had once promised so much, was now in Washington lobbying Congress to explore the south pole . . . for whaling and sealing.

In May 1829, Symmes died, believing right up to the end that the greatest discovery in the human history had eluded his grasp.

AND YET THE dream did not die with the dreamer. Although Reynolds succeeded in getting President Adams's approval for an expedition, successor Andrew Jackson canceled the project, and it was not revived for nearly a decade. But in the meantime, Reynolds found a sympathetic ear in a wealthy New York patron named Dr. Watson. Watson and Reynolds outfitted an expedition for the south pole and set off in the SS *Annawan* from New York Harbor in October 1829. Upon reaching sight of the shores of Antarctica, they found their way through the "icy circle" blocked by towering icebergs and crashing fields of floating ice:

> After coasting the base of several icebergs and making our way through the field-ice floating around us, we reached the neighbourhood of a long and dangerous reef. . . . The dashing of the heavy swell upon the breakers, as it poured from the south, heaved in vast quantities of field-ice. As they plunged forward upon other floes in advance, the whole body was broken into atoms, and a mist, like the smoke from the crater of a volcano. . . . Let the imagination of the reader picture the savage features of the shore, whence the overtowering cliffs of ice are not unfrequently separated from the main body by the undermining rush of the billows; let him conceive the plunge of the disparted ruin; the thundering crash of its collision with the ocean; the vortex of foam and spray

which mark where it fell; and even then, be his fancy ever so vivid,
he will fail to realize the sublime realities of the Antarctick.

Sublime as it was, it was also impassable. On their way back, the crew
mutinied and stranded Reynolds and Watson, and then turned the *Annawan* from polar expedition to a more profitable trade: piracy. Reynolds wound up wandering the rocky shores of Chile, briefly served as a
soldier in a tribal revolt, and eventually joined the passing frigate *Potomac* as a secretary, spending 1831 to 1834 circumnavigating the globe.

After returning, he quickly published a popular account of the
Potomac's voyage, and then went back to earning his pay by lecturing
on the poles and the hollow earth. At one lecture in Baltimore, it is
thought that Henry Allan sat in the audience listening intently. He
went home and related all he heard to his adopted brother—Edgar
Allan Poe—and the greatest Symmes convert ever was created.

The hollow earth became an obsession for Poe. He was broke,
alcoholic, and living on bread and molasses in cramped urban hovels
with his tubercular teenage wife, and the notion of a wide-open frontier beneath his feet had an understandable pull upon his soul. His
first published story, "MS Found in a Bottle," relates the disastrous
end of a ship approaching one of the polar holes. In the only novel
he ever wrote, *The Narrative of Arthur Gordon Pym*, the titular narrator discovers a lost Antarctic island populated by savage exiles from
Symzonia, and breaks off in the closing lines with a kaleidoscopic
plunge into the Interior World:

> And now we rushed into the embraces of the cataract, where a
> chasm threw itself open to receive us. But there arose in our path-
> way a shrouded human figure, very far larger in its proportions
> than any dweller among men. And the hue of the skin of the figure
> was of the perfect whiteness of the snow.

When Poe printed the first installment of *Pym* in the January 1837
issue of the magazine he edited, the *Southern Literary Messenger*, he
pointedly printed it alongside a factual lecture on polar exploration
by Reynolds.

By mid-century, Jules Verne had steeped himself in the work of Poe, Reynolds, and Symmes enough that he wrote not one but three hollow earth works—a continuation of Poe's *Pym* titled *An Antarctic Mystery*, his 1866 novel *The Adventures of Captain Hatteras*, and his famous *Journey to the Center of the Earth*. These were not mere works of fancy. Not only had no one ventured far enough south to entirely disprove Symmes yet, but the 1848 discovery of a frozen woolly mammoth in the Siberian tundra seemed to prove Symmes's contention that just beyond the cold polar rim was a world plentifully populated by herds of animal life.

And if the ideas of Symmes had not yet faded, it was due in no small part to the efforts of his own family. It is a mark of Symmes's good nature that even after forsaking a steady career to face a decade of poverty, illness, and ridicule, he was most fondly remembered by his family. After his son Americus Vespucci Symmes erected the monumental obelisk to his father in Hamilton, he went on to publish a booklet updating his father's writings, *The Symmes Theory of Concentric Spheres* (1878). He did this in part because hollow earth theories had now become popular enough that other writers were passing off Symmes's ideas as their own.

For his zealous lobbying for his late father in newspapers and magazines, Americus received his own share of ridicule. When he sued a company for not fixing holes in the local turnpike, during the trial their lawyer turned to the jury and archly remarked that "Mr. Symmes could see a hole where nobody else could, like his father before him: indeed, it seems to be a family failing."

Symmes's progeny could hardly help inheriting a propensity for ambitious pursuits of the impossible; another son, following in his father's quixotic footsteps, retired as a captain from the army and moved to Germany to build a "flying-machine"—which, regrettably, did not fly.

BY THE LATE nineteenth century, expeditions had begun to approach the poles; the expected holes were not there, and thus the hollow earth theory fell in a decaying cultural orbit, sinking from dreamy scientific speculation to the discredited obsession of ignorant cranks and savvy charlatans. One such fellow was a Civil War veteran and quack herbalist bearing the melodious moniker Cyrus Reed Teed. He published a divine vision in 1870, *The Illumination of Koresh: Marvelous Experience of the Great Alchemist at Utica, N.Y.* It argued that the earth was hollow and that we lived on the *inner* surface of the sphere, looking in toward a center filled with diminutive planets and stars. At the center of it all was a sun that was light on one side and dark on the other, thus producing the effect of day and night.

A handsome and charismatic thirty-one-year-old, Teed at one point attracted up to four thousand mostly female followers. And like any good prophet, he declared himself the messiah and changed his name from Cyrus to the Hebrew equivalent, Koresh. He then proceeded to move his congregation to a commune outside Fort Myers, Florida. He prepared for the arrival of eight million followers in his self-proclaimed "Capital of the World." Two hundred showed up.

Teed had made a point of sending his key works, like *Cellular Cosmogony* (1898), to libraries around the world. These and his numerous pamphlets and magazines later turned up in, of all places, Nazi Germany. Nazism's anti-intellectual bent made the Reich susceptible to pseudoscience, and so when German aviator Peter Bender started preaching Teed's doctrine, it was not too surprising that his theory found some favor in the German Admiralty. But this interest didn't do Bender much good—he died in a concentration camp.

When Teed himself died in 1908, his followers had gathered and dutifully waited for him to resurrect himself. After a few days, though, the messiah had developed a definite pong, and finally local health officials pushed their way through the crowd and unceremoniously shoveled the immortal prophet onto a waiting cart. Perhaps his ostensive employer was unamused by it all, for later Teed's body was swept out to sea in a hurricane.

STILL, FOR A long and charming spell in the history of science, it was possible for a reasonable fellow to believe that entire worlds, unexplored and teeming with life, existed right beneath our very feet. It is not strange that Edgar Allan Poe, who had spent much of his final days attempting a sort of unified field theory of the universe in his cryptic essay "Eureka," would cling until his last desperate moments to the majestic vision of Symmes and his disciples.

Poe had contracted rabies—enemies later claimed alcohol poisoning—and was found senseless in the streets of Baltimore. In the final and fatal stages of infection, delirious with a fever and maddened with the excruciating throat spasms of hydrophobia, he thrashed about in convulsions of agony on his hospital pallet. The nurses could not understand what he was raving after as he cried over and over for the unseen guide to the underworld that awaited him:

"Reynolds, Reynolds . . . *Reynolds!*"

4

THE MAN WITH N-RAY EYES

Nineteen hundred and three was a good year for radiation.

After Wilhelm Roentgen's discovery of X-rays in 1895, each year for the next decade brought news from Germany, the United States, Britain, and France of the discovery of more forms of radiation— alpha rays, beta rays, radio waves, gamma rays. Labs quickly stocked up on vacuum tubes and Ruhmkorff induction coils; piles of radioactive radium and uranium powders were left haphazardly lying about on the desks. Elusive infrared and ultraviolet radiation became laboratory playthings, and dazzling arguments arose over the dual wave and particle manifestations of radiation. Einstein capped it all off by publishing his theory of relativity and the quantum theory of radiation.

People had scarcely any idea what the long-term effect of all this radiation was, but they did know that it was new and exciting. Advertisers leaped on it, and for a while at the turn of the century, trendy consumers could buy Radium Soap, Radium Flour, and Radium Boot Polish. Radon sodas and digestives in particular were all the rage—at least, they were until members of high society started keeling over, their bodies racked and pitted with massive overdoses of radiation.

LEADING THE SCIENTIFIC charge was Professor René Blondlot, the head of the physics department at the University of Nancy, in the northeast of France. Blondlot was a brilliant scientist, famed for his discovery that electricity moved through a wire at close to the speed of light. He'd also devised ingenious experiments to examine the polarization and velocity of radio waves and X-rays.

It was the latter that was occupying his attention in the winter of 1903. No one was sure if X-rays were a stream of particles, like gamma rays, or if they were waves, like visible light and radio. To test this out, Blondlot fired X-rays into a charged electric field and placed a detector off to the side of the path of the X-rays. If the X-rays were waves, the field would polarize them—that is, shift their path and send them through the detector, causing an electric spark in it to brighten. And that's just what they did—Blondlot proved, quite correctly, that X-rays are actually waves.

Then he tried a further experiment—using the cathode tube to send X-rays through a quartz prism. It was needless, really, since it had already been shown that quartz prisms didn't deflect X-rays. But as the X-rays hit the prism, Blondlot noticed something from the corner of his eye: the detector's spark got brighter.

This wasn't supposed to happen. Blondlot tried it again, and again it got brighter—almost imperceptibly brighter, but brighter nonetheless. It couldn't be the X-rays doing it, so it had to be something else. And then it dawned on him.

He had discovered a new form of radiation.

BLONDLOT UNVEILED HIS discovery to the world in a paper titled "On a New Species of Light," in the March 23, 1903, issue of *Comptes Rendus*, the proceedings of the Académies des Sciences. News of his discovery flashed to physics and medical departments around the world.

The radiation was to be called N-rays, after Blondlot's beloved town of Nancy. Subsequent experiments in March and April 1903 by Blondlot showed that these N-rays exhibited some very curious properties. They'd pass straight through materials that would block visible light—wood, aluminum, black paper. On the other hand, some materials that visible light could pass through, like water and rock salt, proved impenetrable to N-rays. And a prism-shaped piece of aluminum, it turned out, would bend and spread N-rays just as a glass prism bent visible light.

A burgeoning array of testing apparatus filled up Blondlot's university lab. He installed phosphorescent screens of calcium sulfide; in a darkened room, they faintly lit up when struck by N-rays. He also built lightproof cardboard boxes over photographic plates; when N-rays were fired through the box, their effect on an electric spark or a gas flame inside the box was visible on the photographic plate. Soak another cardboard box with water, though, and the N-rays couldn't get in—and the wet box's photographic plate, when developed, showed just this result.

As the year passed, Blondlot and his assistants at the University of Nancy racked up one discovery after another. He found that the sun emits N-rays, although "light clouds passing over the sun considerably diminish their action." Various other kinds of electric lamps also emitted the rays, although a Bunsen burner did not. A lens-shaped chunk of aluminum or quartz could focus N-rays, much as holding a glass lens out in the sunlight will produce an intensely bright spot when held the right distance off the ground.

One didn't need fancy cathode tubes and platinum filaments to produce N-rays, either, as Blondlot told his French colleagues in a November 9, 1903, paper in the *Comptes Rendus*. Ordinary objects warming in the sunlight absorbed and then radiated N-rays:

> Pebbles picked up at about four o'clock p.m., in a yard where they had been exposed to the sun, spontaneously emitted "N" rays; bringing them near a small mass of phosphorescent sulfide was sufficient to increase its luminosity. Fragments of calcareous stone, brick, etc., picked up in the same yard, produced analogous results.

Two weeks later, Blondlot revealed that salt water also had storage properties. That meant that the entire planet—mostly covered with salt water, and in the glare of the powerful radiation of a nearby star—was in effect a giant N-ray battery, storing and then shining back the sun's N-radiation.

You didn't even need a sunny day to get N-rays. Any object with molecules under compression—like the tempered steel in a knife or chisel, a watchspring as it was wound up, or a bamboo cane as it was bent—would emit N-rays. And the radiation scarcely diminished over time. Blondlot tested a new knife, and then another knife from a local archaeological dig of Roman ruins. They had equally strong N-rays.

Spurred by Blondlot's accelerating pace of discoveries, scientists throughout France enthusiastically set up cathode tubes and calcium sulfide screens to experiment with N-rays. Physicists in London traipsed down to Charing Cross to buy Nernst lamps from the storefront of the Electrical Company, as these lamps were known to be a rich source of N-rays. These scientists were well advised to follow Blondlot's instructions scrupulously: to acclimate one's pupils to see the effect of N-rays on a dimly phosphorescent screen, one had to sit in a darkened room for at least half an hour beforehand. In any case, the effects of N-rays were not always immediately obvious, for sometimes they took several minutes to be visible to the human eye.

But most important, one had to view the screen off-axis—that is, with peripheral vision. And even then, Blondlot warned, some scientists simply wouldn't have strong enough vision to see it:

> The aptitude for catching small variations in luminous intensity is very different in different persons; some see from the outset, and without any difficulty. . . . For others, these phenomena lie almost at the limit of what they are able to discern, and it is only after a certain amount of practice that they succeed in catching them easily, and in observing them with complete certainty.

Blondlot was asking his colleagues to push at the very limits of human visual perception in their observations, and sure enough, a number of physicists—particularly elderly ones like Lord Kelvin and Robert Crooke—found themselves frustrated. But many other scientists did have sharp enough vision, and by the beginning of 1904 their experimental results were pouring into science journals.

YOU ARE GLOWING with N-radiation as you read these words. In January 1904 the French professor of medical physics Augustin Charpentier discovered that the human body emits N-rays, particularly where there is muscle under compression, or where there are certain kinds of nervous tissue. Stand behind a big enough phosphorescent screen in a dark room and flex your arms, and a faint outline of your body would appear, with slightly brighter spots around your biceps and the Broca's Area of the brain.

Charpentier's results were quickly confirmed in England by Drs. Hugh Walsham and Leslie Miller. They invited the editors of the medical journal *The Lancet* to observe the brightening of a wiggling thumb under the screen; the editors were duly impressed by the results. "There would no longer appear to be any doubt," they wrote in the February 20, 1904, issue, "that rays are given off by active muscles and nerves." Not that every *Lancet* writer was possessed of such indisputable genius; an adjacent column from an aptly named Dr. White made the curious claim that "among the North American Indians insanity is of rare occurrence . . . because they live an easygoing outdoor life free from care and worry for the future and therefore free from mental overstrain."

Still, Professor Charpentier's work had raised an interesting idea—that an entire unseen world of the human nervous system would now be visible with N-ray technology. "This effect," marveled the journal *Nature*, "may prove of the greatest importance in the case of nerves." What X-rays were just starting to do for the observation of organs and bones, N-rays could now do for brain matter and muscles. They could even help diagnose disease; in March 1904, Gilbert Ballet of the French Academy discovered that specific ailments like spastic paraplegia produced unique N-ray patterns. Meanwhile, a neurologist in Edinburgh pondered the notion of detecting brain tumors through N-ray patterns made by the brain. The miraculous diagnostic tool of brain scans, a concept that had been beyond the range of thinkable thoughts before, now opened itself to those who could develop this technology.

It made sense that medical doctors would be the most interested in the discovery of N-rays, for at the turn of the century doctors were bombarding hapless patients with every variety of radiation available; as soon as a new wavelength was discovered, doctors built lamps to generate it, and then joyfully zapped gouty joints, tubercular lungs, syphilitic brain tissue, and anything else that happened to venture into their waiting rooms. It was known that ultraviolet light helped clear up smallpox pustules, that infrared could soothe injured muscles, and that gamma radiation might shrink tumors ... so why not try N-rays?

MANY ENGLISH SCIENTISTS, though, were lagging dreadfully behind their French colleagues. The journal *Nature* received letters and articles almost every month in 1904 from scientists complaining that no matter how hard they squinted, they simply couldn't catch a glimpse of N-rays hitting their calcium sulfide screens. A few even sourly suggested that N-rays weren't put out by the body at all; rather, it was body heat that made the screen fluoresce. S. G. Brown of London noted in the January 28 issue:

> About three months ago, I independently discovered that a feebly luminous phosphorescent zinc sulfide screen when brought near the body increased in brightness. . . . [Perhaps] heat was the cause of the phenomenon. Further trials showed this to be the case; by laying the back of the screen against a fluted jar filled with warm water the zinc sulfide would brighten up.

A month later, London physicist A. A. Swinton wrote a long letter to *Nature* about his own experiments—he found that a warm coin could produce the same effect. Put your foot near the screen, and it might fluoresce with N-rays, but when you took your foot out of your boot and just left the still-warm boot behind, the screen still fluoresced. What the French were seeing on their screens, Swinton warned, was just heat. The fact that N-rays only gradually appeared on the screen was especially damning to Swinton—after all, he said, most thermal effects also take a while to appear.

Even so, these writers were careful not to dismiss N-rays out of hand. "One can scarcely believe that a man of science of M. Blondlot's antecedents and experiences can have deceived himself," Swinton vouched. And the argument over heat quieted down a little when Hugh Walsham and Leslie Miller, writing again in *The Lancet*, found that heat did indeed affect the screens—but that after you insulated the screens from heat, they still glowed in the presence of muscle contractions and nerve activity.

Wishing to settle the matter once and for all, the *Lancet* editors tried it out in their offices one day that February. They reported, "By simply placing a speck of recently excited calcium sulfide on a thick book—such as, for example, the Medical Directory—a distinct increase in the glow is obvious when the muscles of the hand or leg are contracted underneath."

BACK IN FRANCE, N-rays were consuming Blondlot's life, and throughout 1904 he was publishing papers in *Comptes Rendus* at a staggering rate. Every month saw a new paper, complete with diagrams and photographic plates. Nor was he alone: in the first half of 1904, *Comptes Rendus* published fifty-four papers on N-rays. During that same period, it published only three papers on X-rays. And the import of the discoveries was no longer about the basic nature of the rays themselves—that had been well established. Now scientists were pushing into the effect of the rays on human subjects, with Blondlot himself as one willing subject.

Closing the shutters of his laboratory one cold day, Blondlot sat in the darkness and waited for his eyes to acclimate. Even so, he could scarcely see his hands in front of his face, nor the clock on his lab's wall.

He exposed his eyes to a chunk of N-radioactive material.

Slowly, and to his amazement, his hands became visible in front of him. The clock on the wall became clearer: at first he saw the clock face turning whiter. But the clock was a full twelve feet away—he couldn't *possibly* see it from here. Then he saw its circular outline emerge from the darkness. And then—this in near pitch darkness—*he could see the hands of the clock.*

OTHERS RUSHED TO experiment with the effect of N-rays on the human senses, and published reports verified Blondlot's results. Not only did vision sharpen with exposure to N-rays, so did all the other senses. Professor Charpentier continued his experiments well into the spring, beaming N-rays at humans and at the spinal columns of unfortunate dogs and frogs. He found that exposing the tongue, the nasal membrane, and the inner ear to radioactive material made them more acutely sensitive. Firing N-rays at the frontal lobe of the brain also did the trick—a beam of N-rays directed at the glabella or the bregma, for example, would make a subject suddenly aware of hitherto indiscernible smells. Irradiate the seventh cervical vertebra, and you could make the pupils of the eye contract.

Another physicist, Jean Becquerel, found that the drug digitalis emitted N-rays, but only in the presence of a beating heart. Something about the heart caused the digitalis solution to radiate. Anesthetic drugs like chloroform, on the other hand, could cause organic and inorganic materials alike to stop emitting N-rays. With a bit of ether, you could "anesthetize" a chunk of metal to make it stop emitting N-rays. So the secret of the efficacy of drugs, some speculated, might have little to do with the chemical content—it lay in their tendency to accumulate in certain parts of the body, where they would then irradiate tissue with N-rays, or cause the tissues to stop radiating.

But others were simply not convinced. C. C. Schenk, a Canadian physicist at McGill University, archly commented in *Nature* about Blondlot's ability to make exacting wavelength measurements "with a radiation so feeble that no one outside of France has been able to detect it at all." Others wondered aloud whether France was in the grip of a spell of self-hypnosis. Furthermore, not all of Blondlot's supporters were entirely reputable. A variety of cranks had written Blondlot and others in 1904, claiming that they had discovered N-rays years before, and loony experiments with unfortunate live subjects abounded.

Indeed, just about the only place you wouldn't find N-rays was in a dead body. Although Blondlot found that the eye of an ox could store N-rays days after the ox had been butchered, experiments by Charpentier had shown that long-dead tissue did not store or give off N-rays. This gave one *Lancet* correspondent a way of disproving the theory that N-ray results were being caused by nothing but body heat. When not bathing live patients in N-rays at his office in Durham, Dr. J. Stetson Hooker also found a good use for N-rays on a dead patient:

> I had some months ago the opportunity of trying to pass the rays through the forearm of a deceased patient some time after all the natural warmth had passed off. . . . Increased luminosity on the screen was soon apparent to myself and two eye-witnesses. Surely any heat rays would have been stopped on any attempt to pass them through this particularly cold stratum.

A reasonable-sounding argument. But then Dr. Hooker goes on to describe some further experiments on rays given off by humans:

> I have conducted during odd moments of the last three years some 300 experiments to test this question of the human-ray spectrum and the extraordinary unanimity of the results is astounding. . . . Rays emanating from a very passionate man have a deep red hue . . . the ambitious man emits orange rays; the deep thinker, deep blue; the lover of art and refined surroundings, yellow; the anxious, depressed person, grey; the one who leads a low debased life throws off muddy-brown rays.

It is hard to know whether Hooker had actually seen rays emanating from his patients. He does appear, however, to have discovered the precepts governing the Mood Ring.

Faced with a wave of evidence coming in from respected scientists and crackpots alike, John Butler Baker, writing from the Cavendish Laboratory, simply threw up his hands. "I am at a loss to find any other explanation of M. Blondlot's results," he said shrugging, "than that he has come across a radiation to which some men are blind and others not so."

The problem, Blondlot patiently reminded his colleagues, was that their eyes had to be sensitive and acclimated to the dark, and they had to be viewing the rays from precisely the correct angle—anyone standing off-axis to the rays' plane of polarization might see nothing at all:

Only the observer placed exactly in front of [i.e., near] the sensitive screen perceives the effect of these rays. It also shows how illusory it would be to try to make an audience witness these experiments: the effects perceived by different persons, depending as they do on their position with regard to the screen, would certainly be contradictory or imperceptible.

Even if a few foreigners disagreed, any doubts in France about the importance of Blondlot's discoveries were silenced when he received a letter from the Académies des Sciences on August 26, 1904. He had been awarded the Lecomte Prize, with a purse of fifty thousand francs and fame as his country's greatest physicist. There was only one prize left to secure: the Nobel Prize in Physics. Only three years old at this point, it had always been won by discoverers of radiation—Wilhelm Roentgen, Henri Becquerel, and the Curies. Now it might be Blondlot's turn.

OVER IN ENGLAND, things were looking glum. It was a September day in Cambridge, and a knot of physicists gathered in a corner of a meeting of the British Association for the Advancement of Science. None of them had been able to find N-rays in their experiments, and the news of Blondlot's award was weighing heavily upon them. Professor Rubens, visiting from Berlin, was especially exasperated. Kaiser Wilhelm had ordered a command performance of N-rays, and after two weeks Rubens had to call the Kaiser in utter humiliation and admit that he simply couldn't do it.

Rubens's gaze fell upon another visitor to the meeting—Robert W. Wood, who was spending the summer off from his usual post heading the physics department at Johns Hopkins University. Wood was a mischievous fellow—he'd gone on a joyride on the Trans-Siberian Railway while it was still being built, had swooped about in a glider before its design was remotely safe to life and limb, and had written a loony spoof of nature manuals titled *How to Tell the Birds from the Flowers*. He also happened to be a brilliant physicist.

"Professor Wood," Rubens said pleasantly, "will you not go to

Nancy immediately and test the experiments that are going on there?"

Wood demurred. Rubens had been the most afflicted by the N-ray discoveries, after all, so maybe *he* should go. But Rubens persisted—it would look too impolite if he, who had been very graciously answered by Blondlot in his correspondence, were then to throw cold water on the fellow. An artless colonial like Wood would hardly have anything to lose.

"Besides," Rubens added helpfully, "you are an American, and you Americans can do *anything*."

WOOD ARRIVED AT Blondlot's laboratory in the evening of September 21. Blondlot was happy to see him; not too many foreigners made the trek hundreds of miles out of Paris to the University of Nancy, and the good professor was always delighted to show off his latest N-ray results.

Blondlot didn't speak English, though, so he and Wood decided to converse in the international language of physics—German. This left Blondlot free to make confidential asides to his lab assistant in French, although Wood secretly knew enough French to make out the gist of their conversation.

The evening commenced with a simple demonstration. Blondlot painted some circles in luminescent paint on a card, and then turned down the gaslights in his lab. With the circles glowing faintly in the dark, Blondlot irradiated the glowing card with a stream of N-rays.

Do you see the change in luminosity? he asked in the darkness.

Wood couldn't see it.

It proves nothing, Blondlot insisted. Your eyes are not sensitive enough yet.

They had reached an impasse of sorts, and Wood decided that even if his eyes weren't sensitive enough to prove the existence of N-rays, then surely Professor Blondlot's were. Standing in the darkness of the lab, they tried a new test:

I asked him if I could move an opaque lead screen in and out of the path of the rays while he called out the fluctuations of the screen. He was almost 100 per cent wrong and called out fluctuations when I had made no movement at all, and that proved a lot, but I held my tongue.

He then showed me a dimly lighted clock, and tried to convince me that he could see the hands when he held a large metal file just above his eyes. I asked if I could hold the file, for I had noticed a flat wooden ruler on his desk, and remembered that wood was one of the few substances that never emitted N-rays. . . . I felt around for the ruler and held it front of his face. Oh, yes, he could see the hands perfectly.

This also proved something.

The lab's red darkroom lights came back up, and the trio made their way over to the room where Blondlot kept his spectroscope. All the while, Blondlot's skulking assistant—"a sort of high-class laboratory janitor," Wood sniffed—was giving the American dirty looks. The assistant knew *something* was afoot, but he wasn't sure what. Blondlot, though, was blissfully unaware, and led Wood over to the spectroscope to show off his N-ray-refracting aluminum prisms.

The key to an N-ray spectroscope—any sort of spectroscope, in fact—is its prism. You need it to break the constituent parts of visible light into the bands of red, orange, yellow, and so forth. The aluminum prism in Blondlot's spectroscope did the same thing, except that it split N-rays into distinct wavelengths visible through a viewpiece to a graduated luminescent scale. Using this instrument, Blondlot took a series of precise N-ray wavelengths as Wood looked on.

It all sounded impressive, and had seemed like conclusive proof to other visiting scientists. But without looking through the viewer and being able to see the wavelength lines himself, Wood had no empirical way of verifying his colleague's figures.

So he played a very, very dirty trick.

It was with no great relish that Wood later recalled how, with a single wave of hand, he destroyed France's greatest scientist:

I asked him to repeat his measurements, and reached over in the dark and lifted the aluminum prism from the spectroscope. He turned the wheel again, reading off the same numbers as before. I put the prism back before the lights were turned up.

Without a prism in the spectroscope, Blondlot had been staring at *nothing*. And yet he was still "seeing" the N-rays and reading off their measurements.

With the lights back up, Blondlot decided to call it a night; his eyes were getting tired. But his assistant, still narrowing his eyes at the American, insisted on one more experiment. Wood was ready for him.

> As soon as the light was lowered, I moved over towards the prism, with audible footsteps, *but I did not touch the prism*. The assistant commenced to turn the wheel, and suddenly said hurriedly to Blondlot in French, "I see nothing; there is no spectrum. I think the American has made some dérangement." Where upon he immediately turned up the gas and went over and examined the prism carefully.

The assistant glared at Wood, but the American simply stared back placidly. Here was a fine pair before him: a man who didn't see a spectrum when he had a prism, and another who saw a spectrum when he didn't have one.

Wood took the long night train back to Paris, staring out the darkened windows in a deep depression. The next morning he bore an envelope to the postal service. It was addressed to the offices of the journal *Nature*.

WOOD WAS NOT a cruel man. His letter to *Nature*, which was rushed into print for the September 29 issue, does not make a single mention of Blondlot's name. It only describes "a visit to one of the laboratories in which the apparently peculiar conditions necessary for the manifestation of this most elusive form of radiation appear to exist." Wood did not even say what country he had been in.

But he didn't need to.

Everybody knew who Wood was talking about. The evidence in

his letter was absolutely crushing, and could leave few readers in doubt of his conclusion that "experimenters who have obtained positive results have been in some way deluded." Wood's revelations unleashed a tide of admissions from relieved doctors and physicists that they too had failed to see the rays. They had kept quiet in the past year because, with so many colleagues getting positive results, it was too embarrassing to admit publicly that they just weren't seeing anything.

Almost overnight, papers on N-rays mysteriously vanished from the scientific press. *Comptes Rendus*, which had been ground zero for the N-ray blast, published just two more papers on the subject—and, Wood mused later, probably only because they were already going to press.

The French scientific establishment didn't back down quite as quickly. Blondlot, after all, was one of its most esteemed and influential members. But when the award ceremonies for the Lecomte Prize were held at the Académies des Sciences that December, sharp-eyed observers noticed something curious about the award citation that accompanied the medal. It was now being inscribed in the name of "his life work, taken as a whole."

There was no mention of N-rays.

AS QUICKLY AS they had appeared on calcium sulfide screens around the world, the ghostly luminescence of N-rays faded away—gone, perhaps, to a better place in the heavens. But there remained one man utterly convinced of their existence here on earth, and that was their discoverer. Blondlot *knew* what he had seen, and could not be made to back down on any point of evidence. Even as N-rays vanished off the screens of his colleagues, Blondlot pressed ahead with the London publication of an English translation of his papers on the subject, simply titled *N-Rays*. Along with his papers, Blondlot appended a chapter on how to build and use phosphorescent screens, in effect asking readers to try it out themselves. But when *N-Rays* came out in the spring of 1905, it evoked little response, except for a pitying notice in *Nature*:

Prof. Blondlot's experiments are well-contrived, and they give every appearance of being arrangements by which accurate data should be obtained; but in every case the ultimate test is the subjective one made in the mind of the observer as to whether a spot of slightly phosphorescent surface becomes more luminous or not. . . .

Even photographs of sparks and flames being heightened by N-ray exposure, the one seemingly incontrovertible proof that Blondlot had, and which he had made a point of reproducing in plates in his book, looked useless now. Critics noted that it was almost impossible to get a perfectly uniform size in a spark or flame from one moment to the next, so the minute difference shown by the photos proved nothing. They were just the typical variations you'd see in any spark or flame if you photographed it a few times. In any case, a lab worker might unconsciously expose the N-ray photo plate a little longer, so as to get a more impressive effect.

Still, one last hope was offered for legitimacy. In the journal *Revue Scientifique*, a team of French scientists publicly offered their old colleague a chance to prove N-rays existed. They proposed a test with two identical wooden boxes, which would naturally be neutral and transparent to N-rays. They would place a tempered steel tool in one box, and an inert piece of lead in the other. Blondlot would not know which box was which. He would then take N-ray measurements and determine which box held the ray-emitting chunk of tempered steel.

There was a long silence from Blondlot. And then, in 1906, he sent a letter back to the *Revue Scientifique*:

Please permit me to decline totally your proposition to cooperate in this simplistic experiment; the phenomena are much too delicate for that. Let each one form his personal opinion about N-rays, either from his own experiments or from those of others in whom he has confidence.

With Blondlot's withdrawal from the tests, N-rays vanished from the realm of science. Physicists could only assume that Blondlot was afraid of the true results, the final humiliating admission that N-rays simply did not exist.

And yet. . . . *he could see still them.*

BLONDLOT RETIRED JUST three years later, in 1909. That year he ended his career with an unremarkable volume on thermodynamics; there was no mention in it of N-rays, of course. Yet he remained a changed and broken man from his two years of N-ray exposure. As he sank into the long obscurity that preceded his death in 1930, there were whispers among physicists that their old colleague was losing his mind.

Almost all memory of N-rays died with Blondlot. When he was remembered at all, it was among a few physicists who saw him as a cautionary tale of the dangers of self-delusion. Irving Langmuir, who had won the Nobel Prize in Physics—precisely the award that had slipped from Blondot's grasp—was fond of citing Blondlot's downfall as an example of "pathological science." Blondlot had claimed extremely accurate measurements of minute phenomena that many others simply couldn't see, a common pattern for scientific delusions throughout history. Moreover, Langmuir mused in a 1953 speech, N-rays weren't cumulative, and always remained just at the threshold of perception:

> You'd think he'd make such experiments as this—to see if with ten bricks he got a stronger effect than he did with one. No, not at all. He didn't get any stronger effect . . . because this is a threshold phenomenon. And a threshold phenomenon means that you don't know, *you really don't know*, whether you are seeing it or not.

Langmuir's remarks weren't published until October 1989, when *Physics Today* transcribed an old wire recording of the speech. The date of their reprint is not accidental: it was the precise moment at which cold fusion was imploding. Wood never identified Blondlot in his article for *Nature*, and *Physics Today* didn't mention Pons and Fleishmann in theirs. Readers knew.

BENEATH THIS TALE of self-delusion, though, there is another and more troubling story. That Blondlot suffered a sort of madness toward the end is obvious: how else could he be seeing spectral wavelength lines after Wood had removed the aluminum prism? But before the heady rush of publicity and fame, before N-rays even had a name, back on that otherwise ordinary day in the winter of 1903 . . . what had made him see that first fatal flicker in his spark detector apparatus? He hadn't even been looking for a new form of radiation, after all—he was simply experimenting with X-rays.

What led such a good scientist astray?

The answer, perhaps, can only be glanced at out of the corner of the eye. The first clue to Blondlot's downfall is contained the last page of his own book on the subject, *N-Rays*:

> It is indispensable in these experiments to avoid all strain on the eye, all effort, whether visual or for eye accommodation, and in no way to try to fix the eye upon the luminous screen whose variations in glow one wishes to ascertain. On the contrary, one must, so to say, see the source without looking at it, and even direct one's glance vaguely in a neighboring direction.

In other words, to see N-rays, you had to look slightly away from the light source. And this was how Blondlot, a careful empiricist working with reliable instruments, had first seen the effect of N-rays on his test apparatus.

There was just one problem: the human eye is not a reliable instrument. It had been long known to astronomers that peripheral vision has some very strange effects on perception. In his 1832 book *Letters on Natural Magic*, the scientist David Brewster wrote:

> It is a curious circumstance, that when we wish to obtain a sight of a very faint star, such as one of the satellites of Saturn, we can see it most distinctly by looking away from it, and when the eye is turned full upon it, it immediately disappears.

This anatomical curiosity was probably not widely known to physicists like Blondlot or Charpentier—after all, that wasn't their field of study.

But lost amid the ebullient shouting out of N-ray discoveries in hundreds of science journal articles in 1904 was a *Nature* piece on optics and N-rays, a translation of a speech by German physicist Otto Lummer, that excited little commentary among physicists. They would have done well to read their magazines more carefully. In *Nature's* February 18 issue, long before anyone else, Lummer had deduced that the key to understanding N-rays was the fact that they could only be viewed obliquely:

> A whole set of Blondlot's experiments may be almost exactly imitated in their effects without employing any source of illumination whatsoever, and . . . the changes . . . may be referred to the *contest between the rods and cones of the retina in seeing in the dark.*
>
> In the human eye, rods perceive in black and white, while cones perceive color. The rods have a much lower threshold for stimulation; that's why at nighttime, when light is limited, cones become inactive and the world seems to lose color.

The center of the eye is dominated by cones, while rest of the retina has a combination of rods and cones. This makes good evolutionary sense. You make distinctions of color by staring directly at an object, while minor gradations in light intensity—the shadows and light caused by movements of, say, a sabertooth tiger stalking up behind you at night—are more quickly perceived by the sensitive rods in your peripheral vision. This clever structuring of the eye also results in the odd quirk observed by Brewster and other astronomers so many years before, says Lummer:

> Being accustomed to gaze at what sends us light, we turn our eyes in the direction from which the rays come. As, however, the cones have not yet been stimulated . . . we cannot see the spot gazed at. Thereby we are confronted by the remarkable fact that we see

something which we are not gazing at, whilst it becomes invisible when we wish to fix our eyes upon it.

Likewise, a faintly visible light like a dim spark or phosphorescent screen can appear to become slightly brighter when viewed indirectly. The actual light source hasn't become any stronger; it's just that viewing something from periphery makes it cross a threshold of perception within the eye, by stimulating more rods than it would when stared at directly.

The great tragedy of René Blondlot is that on that fateful day in his lab in 1903, he had seen sparks and phosphorescent screens brighten out of the corners of his eyes. But he wasn't seeing a change that reflected an external reality; the excess light only existed in a ghostly electrical impulse along his own optic nerve. And so, in a sense, his critics were right all along.

It really was all in his head.

5

IF ONLY GENIUSES KNEW HOW TO SCHEME

Imagine for a moment a universal language: translatable to color, melody, writing, touch, hand signals, and endless strings of numbers. Imagine now that this language was taught from birth to be second nature to every speaker, no matter what their primary language. The world would become saturated with hidden meanings. Music would be transformed, with all the instruments in the orchestra at an opera engaged in simultaneous dialogue: cellos darkly muttering melancholy comments about the protagonist while the French horns wonder aloud about the unlikely plot, and oboes informing the audience of a sponsor's *prix fixe* menu. People could, through hand signals, hold conversations across the balcony seats, allowing them to silently critique the contralto.

The rise and fall of voice in a conversation could carry a subtext, with the internal melody of speech expressing an entirely opposite or hidden sentiment. Skilled speakers could employ a sort of musical counterpoint to their words, with meanings running in parallel, or in contrast, and commenting parenthetically upon their own words even as they uttered them.

Textiles would be elaborate documents, actual texts again. The variegated strands of color in curtains, rugs, and dresses would reveal, upon inspection, entire hidden passages of literature. Numbers would become a language in and of themselves, whether through telegraphic taps or through details as mundane as the pattern of nails across floorboards, rivets in beams, or the arrangement of phone numbers—all would hold a thought frozen within them.

MANY ATTEMPTS TO radically change language are inside jobs. After all, when we reach for our *Webster's Dictionary*, we may not realize that we are grabbing a piece of linguistic propaganda. *Webster's* is little more than a reference work today, but it was not always such. Noah Webster wrote with an explicit theological intention in mind, for he traced back the proliferation of human languages to Babel. The point of the dictionary maker was not to record language as it was used, but to direct language to how it should be—to simplify it, to return toward the Edenic universal tongue in which man, beast, and God could converse freely.

Yet even our greatest lexicographer's effort met with only modest success. True, he changed "theatre" to the more sensible "theater," but he never persuaded the American public to spell "bread" as "bred," or "give" as "giv." It was not for lack of trying—at one point Webster even published his own translation of the Bible, rendered in his own phonetic spellings. It went over about as well as a Bible in Ebonics might today. People were not prepared to dispense with their maddeningly illogical native tongues. Anything more than incremental change could come only from the creation of an entirely new universal language—a massive project that no human could undertake in one lifetime.

But an ocean away, even as Webster wrote his tomes, Jean François Sudre did just that. Born in the village of Albi in 1787, Sudre attended the Paris Conservatory and became a music instructor in Sorèze. In his early years he developed a "simultaneous method of teaching music," no trace of which remains today, although one 1819 newspaper article marveled at its brilliance. Around this time, Sudre was walking down a street when he chanced across a five-year-old boy standing by a water wagon, scraping away at a fiddle with remarkable intonation.

"Give me your violin," Sudre demanded.

The child handed it over. The teacher proceeded, rather cruelly, to turn the pegs until the violin was hopelessly out of tune, and then handed it back. The little child then methodically turned one peg after another—without so much as a tuning fork—until the instrument was back in perfect tune. Sudre asked how he'd learned to tune the instrument.

"By myself."

Sudre looked to the boy's mother, who was sitting nearby: "Madame, if this child were mine, in five or six years he'd be my fortune!"

It was to be that long before the prodigy, Ernest Deldevez, and the music professor would meet again.

SUDRE MOVED TO Paris in 1822. But at least five years before, he had turned his attentions from music lessons to the ambitious notion of developing a universal language comprised of music. The first breakthrough came in Paris, where one day he rapidly sketched out a system of transposing letters to different musical notes; it was not so much an independent musical language as a code for transmitting existing languages.

Unsure of whether his system would work, he sequestered one of his music students. After fifteen lessons, the two were holding conversations across Sudre's apartment on Rue Dauphine—Sudre asking questions while strolling about his bedroom with a violin, and his student responding from a piano in the living room. Neighbors were mystified by the atonal call-and-response that went on for hours behind Sudre's doors.

Sudre showed off his system to friends visiting his chambers, some of whom were journalists, and by late 1823, Parisians began to hear of this strange man and his even stranger invention, the Langue Musicale. The next year Sudre tracked down the man he thought best for the job of disseminating his invention—someone not yet a man at all, actually, but a boy he had heard in the streets of Sorèze years before.

Sudre spent 1824 with his two young prodigies, Ernest Deldevez and Charles Lasonneur, drilling them in playing and listening to his musical alphabet. The trio toured France the following year, with the two children fighting each other onstage to answer queries from Sudre's violin.

To bolster this tour, Sudre privately published a six-franc tract,

*Langue Musicale au moyen de laquelle on peut converser sur tous les in-
struments.* In it, he envisions a future in which his new language will
become the new standard of shorthand stenography and a boon to
long-distance communication as well, since the signal could travel "up
to 700 or 800 feet with a horn, oboe, flute, or clarinet." It also contained the first of many improvements by Sudre: hand signals for each
of the notes, so that the deaf could communicate. What had started
out as a language of sound had now also become a soundless language—and Sudre had begun his long trek toward the dream of a
truly universal system of signs.

The first real hurdle for his new invention did not come until
1827, when Sudre was invited to demonstrate it to the Institut de
France. With skills honed by several years of touring and practice,
Sudre and Deldevez amazed the scholars with quick musical communication of sentences in French, Latin, and Greek. Within a year
a commission appointed by the institute released a report lauding the
Musical Language. But the greatest potential use of the Musical Language, in the commission's view, was not so much for communicating
with our brothers as for slaughtering them—"Especially in the art of
war, the use of this language could be very useful to serve as a night
telegraph." Sudre forwarded a copy of the commission's findings to
the Minister of War, and was rewarded with an invitation to demonstrate his language before an audience of generals.

But a problem emerged: a military clarion can produce only four
pitches, not the twelve that his language relied on. Sudre spent the
next two years ratcheting his language down to just four notes. He
also had a new name for it: the Téléphonie.

Trials of the Téléphonie were held on two hilltops in December
1829, with clarions accurately relaying such cheerful messages as *You
will destroy the bridge at 6 a.m.* The officers were impressed by the
inventor's tenacity, but in their subsequent report conceded that the
Téléphonie would be "only very rarely useful." Still, Sudre continued
refining and reinventing his musical alphabet. Over the next several
years he peddled variations of it to the Institut de France as a language for the blind, the deaf, and the mute. Another commission was
convened, and Sudre received polite encouragement—but no money.

And, once again, the panel concluded that the best use for Sudre's miraculous gift of language to the disabled would be on the battlefield.

Sudre kept trying. He even demonstrated that he could teach the basics of the language in just forty-five minutes. But the problem, as repeated reports stressed, was that no instrument could project a sufficient distance in all weather conditions for the listener to clearly perceive each note. Scrambling for a solution, Sudre demonstrated the Téléphonie to the French navy with an instrument hooked into air compressors for maximum volume. He was warmly complimented, and a commission recommended that he receive a 50,000 franc reward.

But the money never materialized.

BY NOW SUDRE had spent twenty years and a whopping 32,000 francs of his own money on the Téléphonie. In desperation, he demonstrated to the French army a system of tuned cannons to communicate messages at an earthshaking magnitude. But still he had no takers, and he began to wonder whether the military was really the best venue for his work.

"While I was still working on the application of my method, either for the use of the army or for the navy, a philanthropic idea dominated my thoughts," Sudre later recalled. "It was an idea of generalizing this method of communication and using it for all the people of Europe."

Sudre also began to reconsider the basis of musical language. He had shifted his Téléphonie from a twelve-note chromatic scale (i.e., both the black and the white keys on the piano) to the limited four notes of clarion. But a middle course lay open, one so obvious and simple that it was a marvel that no one had used it before—the diatonic scale. These are the seven "natural" notes, the white keys on a piano, immediately familiar to anyone: *do re mi fa sol la si.* Today we use *ti* instead of *si*, which was the name given to the seventh note in Sudre's time in many non-English-speaking countries.

Using these seven notes as the alphabet for his language, begin-

ning around 1829 Sudre developed the La Langue Musicale Universelle. Unlike the Téléphonie, which was merely a musical code for
existing languages, this new system was an entire language in its own
right, with its own grammar, vocabulary, and syntax. Each note of
the scale acted as a basic unit of language. Combine three of these
units together—*sol*, *re*, and *sol*—and you get a word like *solresol*. In
Sudre's language, this word happens to mean "language" . . . and
eventually, it was the name applied to his ambitious invention.

Sudre limited his words to a five-syllable maximum, thinking that
anything longer would be unwieldy. This yields 11,732 possible
words, a far smaller lexicon than most languages possess, but still
sufficient for most needs. For maximum efficiency, Sudre banned syn-
onyms from his language—each word had to express a distinctly different thought. His vocabulary is also structured so that reversing the
order of syllables reverses the meaning of the word, such as in *misol*
("good") and *solmi* ("evil").

Sudre created five classes of words for his Solresol vocabulary,
composed respectively of one to five syllables. Sensibly enough, the
one-syllable words—of which there can only be seven—are for the
most common uses:

do—no, not
re—and
mi—or
fa—at, to
so—if
la—the
si—yes

The forty-nine possible permutations of two-syllable words
mostly cover pronouns like "I" (*dore*) and particles like "this" (*fami*).
They also include some of the more common phrases of speech, like
"good night" (*misi*). (Since Solresol is reversible, you'd be right in
guessing that the word for "good day" is *simi*.) The 336 permutations
of three-syllable words are wholly given over to common conversa-

tional terms, like "rain" (*sisido*), "husband" (*misifa*), and "want" (*fas-ifa*).

A traveler mastering the first 392 words of Solresol could probably express his needs at least as well as a small child does in a native tongue—and with an equally amusing melodiousness. But as any good numbers runner or state lottery knows, once you get to four or five variables, the number of permutations rises dramatically. The four-syllable vocabulary (with 2,268 words) and the five-syllable vocabulary (with 9,072 words) dwarf the rest—in fact, although his Solresol labors lasted forty years, Sudre never did make it to the five-syllable words.

Given the enormous number of four-syllable words, some system of organization was needed. Keeping the language's musical basis in mind, Sudre established a system of keys for these longer words, where the first syllable indicates its subject matter. Thus *doredofa* ("head") is much closer in meaning to *doredosi* ("hair") than to a word starting in a different key, like *fasiredo* ("railroad"). But with hundreds or thousands of words present in even just one key, the keys are necessarily broad:

do—Physical and Moral Aspects of Humanity
re—Family, Household, and Dress
mi—Human Actions
fa—Agriculture, War, and Travel
sol—Arts and Science
la—Industry and Commerce
si—Government, Law, and Society

A musician might protest that these words are actually in different modes, not keys. But Sudre was not writing for musicians. He always stressed that Solresol didn't require any musical training at all—and so the misnomer "key" stuck.

Sudre tried to apply logical design to grammar. This differentiates Solresol from such exasperating languages as English, which has a bastard grammar of Middle German, Latin, and French. Word order in Solresol is simple: subject-verb-object, and noun-adjective. Plurals are indicated by lengthening the first consonant of the final syllable: saying "Doremmmi" for *doreme* would indicate that you mean "days" and not the singular "day." And finally, parts of speech are indicated by which syllable is stressed:

redomido—to slander (no accent)
REdomido—slander
reDOmido—slanderer
redoMIdo—slanderous
redomiDO—slanderously

You'll notice there's just one verb—the infinitive "to slander." That's because there are no verb tenses to memorize. Instead, you use a word before the verb (usually a double syllable like *sisi* or *rere*) to indicate past, present, and future, and so forth: an innovation that would delight any student who's ever had to slog through index cards crammed with verb conjugations.

SUDRE'S SYSTEM WAS clever—but could he actually create an entire lexicon from scratch? Pondering the size of the task before him, Sudre often quoted one colleague's comment on it: "I am not sure that God allowed it, but it is not forbidden for the human brain to try it."

Aside from the initial act of conjuring thousands of words, Sudre also needed to create bilingual dictionaries in every major language in order for Solresol to gain usage. He planned to single-handedly write Solresol dictionaries in twelve languages: French, English, German, Portuguese, Italian, Spanish, Dutch, Russian, Turkish, Arabic, Persian, and Chinese.

On July 23, 1833, he invited the press to the Royal Academy of Fine Arts to witness public demonstrations of French-Solresol translation. In his usual fashion, he had students listen to Solresol phrases from his violin, whereupon they translated them into French with astonishing speed. The following June the Paris newspaper *La Quotidienne* asked Sudre for a private demonstration. Sudre showed up in the newspaper offices with two young students, clicked open the latches of his violin case, and asked to take dictation from the newspaper staff. The paper's editor picked up his pen and scratched out a single word onto a slip of paper: *"Victoire!"* Sudre played a few notes on his violin. His students, in another room, dutifully translated this into perfect French.

To the staff's bewilderment, Sudre then asked them to give him words in English, German, Spanish, Italian, Arabic, or Chinese—because he had already completed six dictionaries. It was, one editor later wrote, "the only fifteen minutes of my life that I seriously regretted not knowing Arabic or Chinese."

Sudre's reputation, and that of his new language, grew with each performance. When he arrived in Brussels just three months later, articles lauding the "Prophet of Sound" and his new language preceded his appearances; afterward, they marveled at the fact that Sudre was now easily rendering multiple languages into Solresol onstage. Sudre was a confident performer: to start his shows, he'd read aloud from government reports on his inventions, and as an encore he would sometimes sing his own original compositions to the audience.

By the time Sudre returned to Paris, he had become a household name, the subject of newspaper articles and satirical spoofs alike. Composers like Hector Berlioz were attending his shows and pleading with the government to hire Sudre before some foreigner did. The optimism among musicians that Sudre and his decades of effort might have raised their vocation to a new height was perhaps best expressed in a February 5, 1835, article in the music journal *Le Pianiste*: "When it comes to posterity, that which M. Sudre already belongs to, we are assured that he will be most appreciated, and that, if we have elevated a statue of Gutenberg, the inventor of printing, we will find it just later to erect one to the inventor of the musical language."

JUST WEEKS AFTER Sudre was championed in print as the next Gutenberg, he demonstrated an innovation that other constructed language creators had never even attempted: communication with the deaf and blind. At a performance on the night of February 22, Sudre dramatically wrapped a handkerchief over his eyes and asked that one of his students be silently given a phrase to translate. His pupil then walked over to the blindfolded teacher and delicately pressed his fingers into Sudre's palm. Sudre opened his mouth—and to the crowd's disbelief, out came the precise words that had been written down.

What Sudre had done was transpose the seven notes of the scale to positions on his hand:

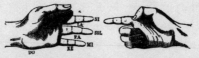

Elle est PARLÉE, lorsqu'on prononce les notes :

do, ré, mi, fa, sol, la, si.

Elle est ÉCRITE, lorsque ces mêmes notes sont tracées sur le papier, comme ci-après :

Elle est MUETTE, lorsque les notes sont indiquées sur les doigts, comme il suit :

Enfin elle est OCCULTE, lorsque le *sourd-muet*, par une légère pression, les fait reconnaître à *l'aveugle* avec lequel il veut se mettre en rapport.

Par cette courte explication, on voit évidemment que tous les hommes de la terre, lors même que la plupart d'entre eux seraient SOURDS, AVEUGLES ou MUETS, trouvent dans cette *nouvelle langue* un moyen de pouvoir communiquer leurs idées.

Sudre's *Langue Musicale Universelle* (U.S. Library of Congress)

By simply tapping away at the other person's palm, a blind man could now communicate with a mute. Such an invention, in an era where the handicapped were generally left to rot in institutions, was an extraordinary advance. And it was both a strange and strangely touching sight on stage—a boy and a man, hands clasped together, talking in earnest silence.

Now the Gutenberg comparisons were echoing throughout the Parisian press. Sudre arranged for one final performance at the Paris city hall—and then, ominously, he was to go off to England. "We do not believe that a discovery has ever received more impressive testimonies," one newspaper complained, "and we refuse again to believe that to gather fruits, the inventor should be obliged to leave the country." The British press was no less astonished at this fact. After his arrival in London in July 1835, *Mechanic's Magazine* marveled, "In spite of the serious and important reports we have received in his favor, he has only received feeble encouragement from his own country. We hope he will find a better fortune among us."

Sudre spent the rest of the summer shuttling back and forth between London and Paris; the size of his audience is hinted at by the fact that his London venue was the concert hall of King's Theatre. His six dictionaries were put on display in Paris, and another commission hastily convened to issue yet another glowing report of Sudre's latest invention. By the end of the summer, Sudre had sketched out two more dictionaries, and he was now including Solresol translations of Dutch and Swedish in his shows.

But he could not linger in Paris, for he had received word that his presence was required in England: the King and Queen wished to meet him.

IT WAS WELL that Sudre and his pupils had labored so long onstage before his command performance, for they were now seasoned linguistic performers. He first gave a polished demonstration in York to the archbishop, the Duchess of Kent, and a certain Princess Victoria—a young woman who would just two years later assume the throne.

He then traveled down to the royal retreat at Brighton, where George IV had once built a gaudy and carnivalesque Chinese pavilion for royal entertainment. Sudre and his students filed across the marble floors into a salon crammed with lacquered furniture, dragon chandeliers, and sumptuous red curtains and bowed to King William and Queen Adelaide. As bridge tables were brought in for the royals to write upon, Sudre introduced himself with a slight nervous tremor in his voice. The Queen quickly put him at ease: on the slip of paper that she passed to him for translation she had written "I wish you success." From there, the rest of his demonstration went without a hitch.

After this triumph, Sudre spent part of 1836 compiling favorable government reports and press notices, including his own translations from the British press, into a compendium titled *Rapports sur la Langue Musicale*. Sudre stuffed in every article he could lay his hands on, even ones that were direct plagiarisms of others. He took this book on the road across France and in tours over the next several years in Belgium and the Netherlands.

But Sudre had more up his cape. Over the following years he developed an extraordinary array of ways of expressing Solresol. You could do it through numbers (1 equals *do*, 2 equals *re*, etc.), which could also be expressed as a series of knocks or other sharp sounds. You could talk through visual hand signals and through the seven ROYGBIV colors of the spectrum. With each passing year, Sudre worked obsessively on further improvements—telegraphic versions of Solresol, stenographic symbols, written shorthand, and the like. He did not expect Solresol ever to replace national languages, but he desperately wished to see it become the second language to which every human would be born into.

It is hard to imagine anyone wanting to live in such a vertiginous world of hidden meanings. Awareness of Solresol can be disorienting and a little unnerving in a chaotic world that does not actually follow its strictures; one modern Solresolist, Greg Baker, recalls that after a while he started wondering how "the beginning of Beethoven's Fifth seems to talk about 'Wednesday.' " Needless to say, obsessive fans who hear already secret messages in music would not do their mental stability any favors by learning Solresol.

And yet the experience may be less cacaphonic than we might imagine. In practice, Solresol is a language in the key of C. Imagine sitting down at a piano and only hitting the white keys randomly. Or, better yet, raid your child's room and plonk away on a kiddie xylophone or toy piano. No matter how hard you try to foul it up, you'll still sound pretty good. This is why virtually every nursery rhyme is written in this key. An instrument tuned to C can give performances that aren't very structured or melodic, but they'll also never sound harsh or dissonant—and the same can be said for Solresol.

The French language, on the other hand, is a fine instrument for sour notes.

NOT EVERYONE WAS enchanted by Sudre. He began receiving nagging letters in 1839 from Aimé Paris, a scholar who became his bitterest critic. In 1821, Paris had tried to create a universal language himself, an attempt that ended with his throwing his notes in the fire. Later Paris attended Sudre's lectures and glowered at the unscientific nature of Sudre's crowd-pleasing proofs: it was, he spat, "a juggling act" put on by a "mountebank."

His hostility reached a peak in the winter of 1846, when he published a newspaper article denouncing Sudre as a fraud. A planned second attack was scrapped, probably by editors who feared a libel suit. But Paris, undeterred, went on to publish two tracts in 1846 and then 1847 containing both his articles and the broadsides fired back and forth through the mail between himself and Sudre.

In his first attack, he concedes that Sudre's Téléphonie system might have some limited usefulness, but then heaps scorn on the "so-called Universal Musical Language." Paris was enraged that prominent commissions were giving Sudre their approval, when—or so Paris thought—all Sudre had created was a childish set of "detestable" conversions from one alphabet to another; this, he claimed, hardly constituted a language:

> Who would believe, after so many celebrated people have given their seal of approval, that we weren't looking at one of these important discoveries that change the face of the world, and decide the fate of nations? And yet I regret to say that these Institute members have been deceived by Monsieur Sudre. . . . [they] gave him the stamp of a great man simply because he discovered the French language minus its orthography.

Paris goes on to charge Sudre with trying to rip off the government through his continued publicity stunts and begging for grants. He ridicules Sudre's claim of having spent decades developing the language, and even gets up a certain swagger in his attacks against Sudre's requests for a government pilot program: "Sudre has asked for two years to set up such a system at great expense. I could do it in six weeks for free."

Perhaps, Paris insinuated, he wouldn't even need six weeks, because musical language had all been done before anyway by Blaise de Vigenere in his 1587 cryptographic treatise *Traité des Chiffres, ou Secrètes Manières d'Écrire*, and by Gustavus Selenus in his 1624 work *Cryptomenytices et Cryptographiae*. Indeed, we can only imagine Sudre's chagrin when in 1830, just one year after he had begun his efforts on Solresol, B. E. A. Weyrich published in Leipzig a slim fifty-page tract on a musical language, *Die Instrumentalton-Sprechkunst*. To Sudre's great good luck, though, Weyrich's rather simplistic proposal quickly sank out of view. But by rehashing these ideas so incompetently, Paris charged, Sudre had poisoned the well for any genuine innovators:

> After all these frauds have created a public prejudice against them, it takes many men to get a real new idea to be accepted. . . . The Universal Musical Language's nature, usefulness, and power are all illusions. Sudre has destroyed its potential usefulness by his deceits. His work should be rejected as an illusion and a lie. . . . So many great plans languish in obscurity, while puerile, trendy inventions become all the rage. If only geniuses knew how to scheme.

Paris's many charges against Sudre don't bear much scrutiny. His disdain for Sudre's publicity methods may be justified, but that hardly takes away from Sudre's language. The claim that musical languages had been invented before is true but irrelevant—nobody had worked out a vocabulary and grammar to the extent that Sudre had. And the charge that Sudre had falsely claimed years of labor on Solresol was effectively disproved by the eventual publication of a Solresol dictionary and lexicon.

Sudre was bewildered by Paris's vehement attacks. "I don't know why Aimé Paris has ridiculed my invention," he shrugged. "He thinks

he has the last word on it. He hasn't even had the first word." It may
have been simple envy. Or it may have been the ink-flinging of an
opinionated crank—something that constructed languages are cursed
with a plentiful supply of.

And yet not all of Paris's criticisms proved unjustified: "You want
to force musical sounds to serve as signs represented already by codes
known by anyone who can read . . . and which you want to replace
with less convenient signs which only four in a thousand could in-
terpret," he sniped. "A stupid idea. All that you're doing with your
written notes, which are not music to nonmusicians . . . [is creating]
a time-consuming and unlearnable system."

In this, at least, Paris was absolutely correct. The limited vocabulary and confusing sameness of Solresol words were to haunt its
proponents later.

ASIDE FROM AIMÉ Paris, though, during the 1840s and 1850s Sudre
piled up accolades with one tour after another; his wife had joined
him as his onstage partner, and he continued to work on his dictionaries. There was only one thing keeping Sudre from being a smashing
success: a total lack of funding.

Why? In the face of so much praise, it is hard to understand why
Sudre didn't get rewarded for his efforts. But in retrospect, the explanation is a heartbreakingly simple one: there's no money in universal languages. There is no freight to be carried by them, no mills
to be run processing them, no wars to be won by them, no diseases
to be cured. Solresol is, at heart, the philanthropic effort of an ide-
alist—and the Brotherhood of Mankind does not issue quarterly div-
idend checks.

Sudre's many allies were understandably appalled by this, and in
June 1850 the novelist Victor Hugo, then at the height of his fame
and influence, issued this open letter from his home in Paris:

On behalf of M. Sudre, the celebrated inventor of the Musical
Language and the Téléphonie, who has been little compensated
for his work until now, I call upon the sympathy of men who, in

all countries, are interested in the progress of human intelligence
and of the pacific conquest of civilization.

Shamed by such outcries, in 1855 a jury went out of its way at the
Paris Exposition to create for Sudre a special prize of ten thousand
francs; they were certainly aware that even this generous sum hardly
began to repay Sudre for his thirty-five years of labor.

By the time Sudre dragged himself to the 1862 London Exhibition, his suitcase packed with eight completed Solresol dictionaries
for display, he was already an old and increasingly frail man. A jury
at this exposition was moved to award him a Medal of Honor, and
each word of its citation might as well have been a blow of the chisel
into his tombstone: "The remarkable project of Mr. Sudre . . . will it
ever receive a useful application? And its author, already quite old,
will he receive no other recompense other than the unanimous admiration of an unprofitable jury?"

Months later, he was dead.

A MONUMENT WAS duly erected to Sudre in his home village. But as
for the eight dictionaries, his life's work, that Sudre showed to such
great acclaim at the London Exposition just before his death . . . no
one has seen them ever since. Sudre's lifetime of work, it seems, was
utterly lost to history.

Except that one dictionary *did* survive. His widow, Josephine
Sudre, took up the Solresol cause after his death, and in 1866 published a French-language Solresol grammar and dictionary titled
Langue Universelle Musicale. Although it is Jean François Sudre's magnum opus, his widow continued the language's development after her
husband's death; the copy possessed by the Library of Congress has
a number of inked-in corrections made by hand in what appears to
be her writing. The book is an odd size, much like a modern check-
book—shaped, that is, to be slipped into the pocket of a traveling
coat. The Sudres foresaw the day when travelers around the world
might pull out their Solresol guides to melodiously converse with one
another.

Sudre's widow also lived to see the rise of the great medium of the future—the telegraph. In 1865 a major new telegraph exchange was being planned for Paris, and the government needed a standard means of communication. Her husband had seen the first glimmerings of this medium years before, and had gamely suggested a variation of his Téléphonie as a method of telegraphic code. Now his elderly widow, stringing telegraph wires around their Paris apartment and experimenting for five days solid, quickly developed a telegraphic version of Solresol in time to present it to the Minister of the Interior. The demonstration was a great success . . . but her scheme was not adopted.

Madame Sudre's frustration is clear in her piteous preface to the Solresol dictionary: "I have come to tell men of intelligence. . . . Assist me all you can, use your influence, so that music, which is universal, can become the bond of language tying together all nations!"

Her cries did not go unheard. The Société pour la Propagation de la Langue Universelle Solresol was founded in Paris, although the absence of material on Solresol in libraries today is not much of a testament to the society's effectiveness. Nonetheless, the use of Solresol grew steadily in the decades after Sudre's death, with thousands of speakers in France becoming familiar with its use.

Solresol reached a high-water mark in 1902, when society head Boleslas Gajewski published a brief *Grammaire du Solresol*, which represented a refinement and expansion of the grammar rules set down in Sudre's 1866 guide. Although Gajewski starts his guide with platitudes about how useful Solresol would be for international travelers, he makes a point of printing one key paragraph in bold type:

> Thus by means of Solresol, the blind will be able to exchange ideas with foreign deaf-mutes and vice versa, so everyone will be able to answer them and be understood by them.
>
> **There are in Europe more than 250,000 blind people and more than 210,000 deaf-mutes; there are thus 460,000 individuals, in Europe alone, who possess scarcely any means of communicating with everyone else, and who, thanks to Sudre's**

SOLRESOL, will be brought back to everyday life and see the inconveniences for their disability reduced.

Gajewski probably knew that the game was nearly up for persuading a mass worldwide audience to adopt Solresol; those with disabilities presented a captive audience that was more attainable and easily focused upon.

Gajewski and his society were at least able to make enough of an impact that when universal language advocates Louis Couturat and Leopold Leau published their 1903 volume *Histoire de la Langue Universelle*, they spent a chapter on Solresol fretting over how many people had taken up with an inept language: "One can hardly explain the relative success of this language, the poorest, most artificial, and most impractical of all constructed languages. . . . It is useless to attempt to express all human ideas with only seven syllables." At times they almost directly quote Aimé Paris's laments that Solresol was being learned at the expense of superior systems. As for its uses among the deaf, mute, and blind, they hardly felt this obliged the able-bodied to learn the language: "Why build the same bike for healthy people as for lame people?"

Couturat could have saved himself the expense of ink, and Gajewski the trouble of bindings and paper; new artificial languages like Volapuk and Esperanto were on the horizon, and their recognizably European basis helped them become embraced in a way that Solresol never was. Gajewski's book, meant to spark a new Solresol movement, proved to be a last gasp. Scarcely another word was written on Solresol for the next century, and soon the very existence of the language was forgotten.

YET SOLRESOL IS no longer entirely dead. There are about a dozen enthusiasts scattered across the world—most notably two Australian cryptographers (Greg Baker and Jason Hutchens), who discovered the language independently of each other; the Alaskan researcher Stephen Rice; California musicologist David Whitwell; and Oregon physician John Schilke. Each has worked to preserve the history of this bizarrely charming language, often while completely unaware that any other Solresolists were even out there. Fittingly enough, the reemergence of this Universal Language has largely occurred in that most universal of mediums: the Web.

Some have even attempted to compose in the language. Musician Bruce Koestner—who has also created a chromatic (i.e., twelve-note, including both a piano's white keys and black keys) language called Eaiea—has written part of a chamber opera in Solresol; in 1997 a Dutch radio presenter, Yolanda Mante, wrote and broadcast a brief skit in Solresol about Sudre.

And the revival looks as if it may even be gaining momentum. Greg Baker has registered the domain name of solresol.org.au as a future base of operations, and Jason Hutchens has floated the idea of computer programs that will convert Solresol writings into files that could be exchanged between musician-speakers worldwide. Rice has begun to make some refinements in the language; when completed, they will be the first step forward in Solresol's development since Gajewski's 1904 text.

But unlike proselytizers for international languages like Esperanto or Interlingua, the last practicing Solresolist probably passed away in a French nursing home decades ago. The difficulty in establishing pauses between words and the easily confused vocabulary dog Solresol as much today as when it was at its height a century ago. Modern Solresol followers largely pursue it as an exercise in comparative linguistics, and a worthy challenge in reconstructive history.

One enigmatic trace did turn up before the current revival: years ago, someone in the computer industry quietly inserted the seven letters of the Solresol alphabet in the Unicode sixteen-character set. "Here was a language that had very little written record," Greg Baker muses, "now being regarded by the computer industry as an important international language, on par with Thai, Tamil, or English."

Solresol domifare. . . .

6

22,000 SEEDLINGS

Grape jelly, of the T-shirt-destroying purple variety, is very much like wheat paste, Play-Doh, or crayons—that is, something that North Americans can immediately identify by taste, touch, or smell. It is a smell of childhood, an infusion of sugar on the palate that, were it not so utterly taken for granted, might be capable of evoking Proustian eloquence on days of *Land of the Lost* and *Electric Company* past. But even the very name of the variety—Concord Grape—is scarcely thought upon.

Concord grapes are still grown near a town called Concord—and what a comforting, almost quaint notion that is. But try to actually buy a Concord grape in a supermarket and you will be met by quizzical looks. The Concord grape is not a table grape, they will tell you. And yet, to look at the jam and jelly aisle in the market, you'd think that the Concord was the only grape in existence. In the American world of processed grape products, King Concord reigns supreme.

Many Americans would be surprised to find that the Concord grape is little known elsewhere in the world, and that the beloved American combination of fatty peanut butter and sugary jam on Wonder Bread is as much an object of fascinated revulsion to foreigners as anything that Elvis might have ordered from his house chef. But stranger still is the discovery that, once upon a time, not only was there no Concord grape over *there* . . . there was no Concord grape over *here*.

AMERICA IS A place of grapes; when Viking explorers nudged around the continent's edge a thousand years ago, they were so impressed by the profuse growth that they dubbed the new world Vineland. But close inspection would have revealed the tendriled inhabitants were both recognizable and strange. Native American vines are grapes, yes, but they are not the same as European grapes. And so later European settlers did what came naturally to them: they ignored the native varieties and imported vine cuttings from the Old World.

Settlers had good reasons for this. Humans shy from eating unfamiliar mushrooms and berries; catastrophic liver damage and kidney failure being what they are, immigrants to the Americas who mistake native varieties for ones from the homeland don't get a chance to repeat the error. Even the tomato, now one of the most heavily cultivated native American fruits, was allowed to rot on wild vines for years, because settlers were convinced it was poisonous.

But most of all, the classic European table grapes and wine grapes, such as muscat and tokay, were proven financial successes. Settlers, who were sometimes granted land on the condition that they improve it through clearing and planting, needed safe bets in order to survive and to hang on to the property that they had so painstakingly stolen from the Indians. And so, along with indentured servants and packets of letters, ships to America bore an even more valuable cargo: vine cuttings.

But America was not a good place to grow grapes.

Not European grapes, anyway. From the 1630s when the first vineyard was planted by William Bradford up through the mid-1800s, scarcely any American farmer made a living off of grapes. The plagues of the vine are legion: red spiders, mealy bugs, thrips, rose bugs, fretters, and beetles wielding mandibles like brutal tire irons. And even if the vines survived them, come harvest time you'd find dry rot in the roots—or wet rot in the fruit. Native varieties had, through natural selection, built up some resistance to these ailments. But European grapes, as the horticulturist Andrew Fuller recalled bluntly, "entirely failed in this country."

Farmers blamed the soil, overwatering, improper pruning, bad weather . . . everything, that is, except the grapes themselves. They found that the only way to raise grapes with any degree of consistency was in a glass house. With the mass production of glass in the nineteenth century, this no longer sounded entirely ludicrous to people. After all, the era's greatest public building, the Crystal Palace in London, was in effect a giant greenhouse. Newly designed heating systems meant that these houses could even provide fruit year-round. Guides proliferated on how to build a glass "grapery" in one's own backyard.

But for large-scale fruit agriculture, glass houses are a staggeringly inefficient way to raise a crop. Even as American agriculture boomed through various land grabs, grape acreage remained stubbornly small—by the mid-nineteenth century, a paltry 5,600 acres in all of America east of the Rockies. In the 1840s the viticulturist Elijah Fay ventured to send a shipment of grapes to Buffalo with an assistant named Baker. "Buffalonians stared at the fruit," says one historian, "asking Baker the kind of plums they were and how they were eaten." Americans scarcely even understood what grapes were; how was a farmer going to find any market for them?

But then, not all farming is done by farmers. Agriculture, which has become the most high-tech and lucrative of biosciences in our own time, also happens to be the most approachable of human endeavors. Save a pip and stick it in some soil, and with nothing more than benign neglect you might still wind up with something to show for it. Even children can do it: after all, the quintessential school science experiment for young children is to watch a seed germinate in a test tube.

The early nineteenth century, for all its careful lore of pruning and grafting and planting cycles, was still a time when you didn't need an ag science degree; the tools of the trade were still simple and graspable. Take, for example, this straightforward recipe by Fuller: "If the vines do not grow as rapidly as desired, then put a few shovelfuls of good fresh barnyard manure into a barrel of water, stir it well, let it settle, and then draw off the water and apply it to the plants." And so, liquid manure at the ready, grapes were raised by dedicated amateurs and backyard enthusiasts: after all, no serious working farmer would consider such a risky and expensive crop.

ONE SUCH AMATEUR garden could be found in the Washington Street backyard of Epaphous Bull, a Boston silversmith. His son Ephraim took a particular interest in the garden. Ephraim, born on Jefferson's inaugural day in 1806, had the signs of some sort of greatness; with his nose constantly in a book, he'd won an academic medal when he was just eleven years old. But Epaphous could not afford to keep the boy in school, and so at the age of fifteen he was sent to an apprenticeship in beating gold leaf. In his spare moments off the job, young Ephraim could still be found in his father's backyard, carefully examining the Catawba, Isabella, and Sweetwater vines that he'd planted.

Ephraim proved a quick study at goldbeating, and he grew to eventually run his own workshop, where he turned out gold leaf for bookbinders and gilders. But the hot and dusty workplace, not to mention the crowded environs of the city, was aggravating his lungs. By 1836, the situation had become plain to him and his doctor: he needed to move to the country. Ephraim and his wife moved twenty miles away to Concord, the quiet village where the Revolution had started so many years before. They were delighted to find that they could afford a seventeen-acre farm out on Lexington Road.

There was just one catch: the next-door neighbor was positively bizarre.

BRONSON ALCOTT, JUST a few years older than Ephraim, was if anything even more bookish. He too had had little formal schooling, though this hadn't prevented him from founding his own school in Boston. He'd formulated a progressive approach to education that promoted Platonic dialogue and self-paced, individually motivated learning over the traditional approach of rote memorization and instructor lecturing. Children were encouraged to keep journals, and classroom dialogues ventured into religious inquiry and a mild prototype of health and sex education. For these groundbreaking contributions to American education, the young man was of course pilloried in the newspapers for "indecency." But Alcott continued to practice his own enlightened and utterly modern educational theories on his most apt pupil: his own daughter, Louisa May.

1836 was an auspicious time for Bull to have settled next door. Alcott's close friend Ralph Waldo Emerson had just published a revolutionary essay titled *Nature*, and Alcott himself was busy finishing an extraordinary—and now forgotten—volume of transcribed dialogues with children about religion, *Conversations on the Gospels* (1837). When it came out he was roasted again in the press for having the temerity to suggest that young people might have anything meaningful to say about God. Hundreds of unsold copies ended up being bought as scrap paper and used to line trunks.

Alcott bore failure well. He had to, because ever since his first job, as a traveling salesman, pretty much everything he had tried his hand at had failed. He was a man of equally vast impracticality and vision, and eerily prescient in his pursuits: women's rights, the abolition of slavery, banning tobacco on health grounds, and eating what he dubbed a "Pythagorean diet"—today it would be called vegan. Emerson was so delighted by Alcott that at one point he seriously proposed that their families move in together.

One other subject particularly attracted Alcott's notice: the newly flowering science of genetics. This was a field in which he and Ephraim had much to enthuse over. Most interesting of all was the work of a Belgian physician, Jean Baptiste Van Mons, who possessed a seemingly miraculous skill at selectively breeding and cross-pollinating pears; by isolating the best aspects of each strain, he had bred forty distinct and superior types of the fruit.

Any conversations Ephraim and Bronson had on the latest work of Van Mons were eventually cut short, though, by Alcott's announcement that he—along with most of the members of the burgeoning Transcendentalist movement in Concord—was departing to found a utopian agrarian colony, Fruitlands. In his place came a new tenant for the farm next door—a hack writer named Hawthorne.

WRITING MANY YEARS later, Julian Hawthorne remembered watching his father, Nathaniel, and his neighbor, Ephraim Bull, philosophizing over long summer days on politics, human nature, morality, and . . . grape growing. On dusty fall days, Bull would work at installing a long fence along one border of the property, although he wasn't much interested in keeping the neighbors away; whenever he saw the Hawthorne children, he'd invite them to climb the fence and eat as many grapes right off the vine as they could hold. "It seems to me," Julian Hawthorne later mused, "that he could hardly have realized our capacity."

Bull made a vivid impression on the young boy:

> He was as eccentric as his name; but he was a genuine and sub-
> stantive man, and my father took a great liking to him, which was
> reciprocated. He was short and powerful, with long arms, and a
> big head covered with bushy hair and a jungle beard, from which
> looked out a pair of eyes singularly brilliant and penetrating. He
> had brains to think with, as well as strong and skillful hands ; he
> personally did three-fourths of the labor on his vineyard, and every
> grape vine had his separate care.

His frequent work alone in the vineyard may have been a necessity for Bull; as friendly as he was, he had a monumental temper, and whenever he brought hired laborers into his vineyard he'd get so exasperated at their stupidity that his roaring could be heard all the way across the farm and in the Hawthornes' yard—"like the sounds of a distant battle," Julian recalled.

But Bull was indeed engaged in a mighty struggle. With native varieties of grapes—which were scarcely worth noticing, to most viticulturists—he was going to try to breed a hardy open-air grape that would not only rival the best European grapes in flavor but have the native resistance and early growing cycles needed to survive New England insects, diseases, and autumnal cold snaps. Bull had some support in this; the scholar James Mease had argued for the development of native varieties in his *Domestic Encyclopedia* as early as 1804. But it was easier said than done.

Grape breeding requires patience. While grape growers typically propagate their vines by cutting and grafting, this doesn't work for breeding. Cutting and grafting is biologically static: you are growing a clone. That's great for farmers, as grafts grow quickly and consistently. But to breed a new variety, you need variation. And there's only one way to do that naturally—you plant seeds, and you wait.

Grape genetic material varies from seed to seed; the seeds that come from a single bunch can be as different from one another as sons and daughters of by the same parents. The seeds of any given grapevine provide a wide array of genetic permutations to work with, both useful and useless. But it is impossible to judge the quality of your breed until they bear fruit, and that takes at least two growing seasons. From there, you might have to go through many successive generations of seed selection and cross-pollination before you get the characteristics you want from a grape.

This can take years, decades. Even entire lives.

BREEDING BEGINS WITH a single plant, and Bull didn't find his in a vineyard or a commercial nursery. He found it by the kitchen drain behind his house. It was a *Vitis labrusca*, a northern fox grape, and this one bore fruit early in the growing season. Early fruition was crucial for any grape that would grow in New England, and so Bull tasted the grape flesh and examined the vine carefully. "The crop was abundant, and of very good quality for a wild grape," he later recalled. "I sowed the seed in the autumn of 1843."

His methods of planting were simple enough: "I put these grapes whole, into the ground, skin and all, at a depth of two inches, about the first of October, after they had thoroughly ripened. I nursed these seedlings for six years, and of this large number, only one proved worth saving." That one was, he decided, to be called the *Concord* grape. After three generations of fruition and culling, he was ready to show off his new creation to a visitor to the house. On September 10, 1849, he picked a bunch of grapes when they were their ripest and presented some to a neighbor. He watched as the man sampled the new fruits.

"Why," the man marveled, "this is better than the *Isabella!*"

This was excellent news for Bull; his new grape had already surpassed the most palatable of native grapes. Emboldened, he took some cuttings down to the offices of the *Boston Cultivator*, offering to trade one of his Concord cuttings for some of the *Cultivator's* vine samples. But he forbade the *Cultivator* staff from selling anything they grew from his vine; he needed a few years to propagate his grapes before he unveiled his work to the public.

THE TWO MEN from the Massachusetts Horticultural Society walked up to his cottage door one September day.

"Where are those grapes you promised to send in?"

Bull was taken aback.

"I did send them in, by a neighbor" he stammered. "I was too sick to make the trip myself, but I sent them just as I said I would."

The men said they'd check the exhibition tables at Horticultural Hall again. A lot was riding on their finding that bunch of grapes; the 1853 fall meeting in Boston of the Horticultural Society was to be the Concord's public debut. And it took some searching, but they *were* there—just as Bull said they'd be. They'd been mistakenly placed in the vegetable section instead, and hidden under a pile of squashes and turnips. The mistake was understandable, because the Concords didn't even look like grapes—not to American eyes, anyway. They were too *big*.

The judges raised their eyebrows.

"I'll bet he girdled the vines," ventured one. "We'd better make sure there's no trickery here."

And so the committee rode out to Concord and made the pilgrimage out to Grapevine Cottage. Bull, already too sick to make the Boston meeting, now found himself surrounded by men with notebooks, peppered on all sides by questions. How had he raised the vines? Were these really typical grapes for this variety? Could he prove it?

—There are others out back.

And Bull led them out to his vineyard, where the judges examined the vines. Not only had Bull sent them entirely typical specimens, but the grapes in his backyard were even bigger . . . and sweeter.

BULL WAS FAIRLY matter-of-fact in his own descriptions of what he had sown:

> The grape is large, frequently an inch in diameter, and bunches handsomely shouldered, and sometimes weigh a pound. In color it is ruddy black, covered with a dense blue bloom, the skin very thin, the juice abundant, with a sweet aromatic flavor. It has very little pulp. The wood is strong, the foliage large, thick, strongly nerved, with a woolly under surface, and does not mildew or rust. It ripens the 10th of September.

But a reporter at the exhibition was more to the point: "The committee announced to the world that, at last, a grape had been developed that would grow in New England—bigger and better than any grown before."

Bull's vine stock soon went on sale, available only through C. M. Hovey & Company of Boston. Bull and Hovey were sitting on a gold mine—as the only sellers of what promised to be the greatest American vine ever bred, they could charge $5 a vine and see a handsome profit. It was a tremendous hit: requests poured in from amateur viticulturists from around the country, and in 1854 alone Bull's cut was $3,200. Concord grapes were destined, it seemed, to appear on every backyard trellis in the country.

But then something strange happened. Sales went down—just a little at first. Then a little more. And then, inexorably, the sales dwindled to nearly nothing. The realization slowly sank into Bull: it wasn't just amateurs who had been sending in orders to Hovey.

His competitors had been buying the vines.

———

THERE WAS NO way that Bull could have anticipated what happened. Grapes were not a commercial crop in the United States. But the reporter at the exhibition had been right: the judging committee had told the world, perhaps a little too well, just how fine Bull's grapes were. And now commercial nurseries, who'd never bothered much with grapevines before, were quietly ordering the Concord vine and preparing enough to seed an entire domestic industry—all without a penny to go to Ephraim Bull.

In 1854, breeders in the United States had no protection whatsoever, no way to control their product. They could thank Thomas Jefferson for this: when drafting the country's patent laws, he had deliberately excluded life forms. Perhaps it seemed impious to claim the mantle of creation over life itself. But then again, Jefferson was a levelheaded Deist, a man who never let a religious qualm derail a rational train of thought. His real reason for excluding life forms might have been simple: to keep the courts from becoming solidified into a frozen block of litigation. It wasn't until 1930 that Congress finally allowed plant varieties to be patented.

What was more, patents didn't always protect the holders anyway. Quite the reverse: if you were patenting a mechanical process, your patent papers would have to describe the workings in great detail. Any crook willing to read through the public record could swipe your invention, secure in the knowledge that if the patent holder lived far enough away, he might never even find out—and even if he did, he might not be able to afford a legal battle. Some of the greatest and most lucrative inventions were never patented at all, and for precisely this reason.

When *Scientific American* readers were asked in 1899 to name the greatest invention of their century—they had tiresome lists and "best of" century wrap-ups back then, too—it was not Bell's telephone that they named. Nor, for that matter, was it Edison's lightbulb, Whitney's cotton gin, Fulton's steam engine, or photography, or the gas-powered automobile, or any other of a multitude of obvious choices. It was the Bessemer steel process.

Sir Henry Bessemer is a man little spoken of today, but his steel process, which he was perfecting even as Ephraim Bull was happily cashing his first big check from Hovey & Company, built the modern world as we know it. Virtually all steel—whether in cars or buildings—is manufactured on some variant of the Bessemer process. Sir Henry became fantastically wealthy off it. But this was not how made his *first* fortune.

His first fortune came from, of all things, powdered bronze. As a young man, Bessemer was helping his sister decorate a portfolio of flower illustrations. He needed some gold ink to complete the lettering, and to do this, he'd have to get some "gold powder" from Mr. Clark, the local art supply merchant:

> The material was not called "gold," but "bronze" powder, and I ordered an ounce of each shade of colour, for which I was to call on the following day. I did so, and was greatly astonished to find that I had to pay seven shillings per ounce for it.
>
> On my way home, I could not help asking myself, over and over again, "How can this simple metallic powder cost so much money?" for there cannot be gold enough in it, even at that price, to give it this beautiful rich colour. It is, probably, only a better sort of brass; and for brass in almost any conceivable form, seven shillings per ounce is a marvellous price. . . ."
>
> Here was powdered brass selling retail at £5 12s. per pound, while the raw material from which it was made cost probably no more than sixpence. "It must, surely," I thought, "be made slowly and laboriously, by some old-fashioned hand process; and if so, it offers a splendid opportunity for any mechanic who can devise a machine capable of producing it simply by power."

The powder, it turned out, was manufactured secretly in Nuremberg. Bessemer found the formula in an old tome at the British Museum, and it was every bit as laborious as he'd guessed—so much so that the only way to better it was to leapfrog it entirely, to invent bronze powder anew. After much experimentation, Bessemer devised an engine that ground out bronze powder far faster than any current

process. When he showed the results to one importer, the man offered him £500 yearly on the spot for use of the process.

That is when Bessemer knew it must be worth a great deal more
than £500.

Moreover, he knew that as soon as he filed a patent, he probably
wouldn't even see £500 off it. He'd have to keep it secret. But how?

> There were powerful machines of many tons in weight to be
> made; some of them were necessarily very complicated, and some-
> body must know for whom they were. . . . [So] when I had thus
> devised and settled every machine as a whole, I undertook to dis-
> sect it and make separate drawings of each part, accurately figured
> for dimensions, and to take these separate parts of the several
> machines and get them made: some in Manchester, some in Glas-
> gow, some in Liverpool, and some in London, so that no engineer
> could ever guess what these parts of machines were intended to
> be used for.

Quietly, he set about building a small factory in a London suburb.
It had only one entrance and no windows. And once the factory was
running, no worker was allowed to see more than a fraction of the
interior—ever. Time and again, industrial spies from Nuremberg
sailed back home empty-handed.

In the end, no one really knew how the process worked . . . except
for Henry Bessemer. He became very rich; on the cusp of the Gilded
Age, his factory provided the gilding. Had he patented his process, it
would have become public domain after just fourteen years, around
1870—squarely in the middle of the greatest demand. But, without
a patent, the only way to get cheap bronze powder was to go to
Bessemer and his mysterious, windowless brick building.

He kept his process secret for more than forty years.

EPHRAIM BULL FACED a special challenge: the actual process of creating the Concord grape was really no secret at all. After all, Dr. Van
Mons had already been doing it for decades with pears over in

Belgium. It was the result that had to be kept secret. And that was tricky indeed, because there is one absolutely crucial difference between making grapes and making bronze powder:

Grapes have *seeds*.

And, worse still, the vines have buds. You can clone with impunity. It was still a long way away from 1995, when the Delta & Pine Land Company's patent on the "Control of Gene Expression" resulted in the much-reviled "terminator seeds." In the nineteenth century the only way to keep seeds from proliferating was through food processing, not genetic engineering. Bull needed to somehow sell the sweetness and flavor of the Concord grape without actually selling the grape—to sell the golden eggs but not the goose. But in 1854 there was simply no way to do this.

Bull's life became occupied by other pursuits; in 1855, just as his profits were vanishing, he was elected to the Massachusetts house of representatives. The Concord grape had already become so famous that his colleagues sensibly appointed Bull chairman of the committee on agriculture. And as the years passed, he became a fixture of Concord life and lore: a member of the school board, a recruiter during the Civil War, and the caretaker for Hawthorne's house while the writer was off on diplomatic duty in Britain. Although Bull was a rather neglectful caretaker, the families stayed close—sometimes Ephraim's daughter Mary would wander into the neighbor's backyard, wanting another drawing lesson from Mrs. Hawthorne.

Yet Bull was a changed man. Although he continued breeding grape varieties for the rest of his life, he refused to let anyone else have them. His hoarded labors were enormous and exacting: "From over twenty-two thousand seedlings," he once remarked, "there are twenty-one which I consider valuable." The first was the Concord; the next twenty, which visitors described as perfectly good varieties of red and white grapes, never made it to market. It was not wise to ask Bull about the notion of selling them.

"There are no honest nurserymen," he'd snap. "I shall be cheated."

Meanwhile, he was to watch his Concord grape flourish and create fortunes around the country. Millions of acres were cultivated, and by the end of the century more Concords were being grown in the United States than every other grape variety combined. They were immensely popular for very good jelly and for very bad wine.

It is not impossible to make a decent wine from Concord grapes, but—like most native varieties—they have a "foxy" undertone that spoils the delicate flavor of any good wine. There are ways for a vintner to remove this foxiness, but cheap winemakers didn't bother. The vintner George Husmann complained that what winemakers were doing with the Concord was "reprehensible"—"These gallonizers have done a great deal of mischief by bringing their trash before the public, and calling it wine." But the Concord was such a hardy grape, and the profits from hooch jugs so good, that vintners hardly cared. Much later, during Prohibition, tipplers could even buy a thinly disguised fermentation kit called Vine-Go, designed to allow you to turn your virtuous Concord grape juice into really wretched wine.

Bull watched from the sidelines as his creation was perverted to enrich others. He could only think: it didn't have to be this way.

He was right.

BULL, PERHAPS, WAS born in the wrong time. There was a way to sell the grape essence without selling the seed: grape juice and jelly, manufactured and packaged with the latest in pasteurization and bottling technology. Had Bull been able to do this in 1854, his life might have turned out very differently. But the fortune fell to someone else.

Thomas Bramwell Welch had no intention of being a food tycoon. Originally a minister, Welch was a marvelously impractical fellow who could scarcely stay in any one profession or one state for very long. When he tired of ministering, he attended medical college and became a doctor. He tried his hand at his own bottled tonic for upset stomachs: Dr. Welch's Neutralizing Syrup. Then, ready for another change, he went to dental college and became a dentist. This profession he managed to hold for two decades, but still he could not stay settled. After experimenting with zinc and gold fillings, he founded a company to manufacture Dr. Welch's Dental Alloys. Then he established a dental magazine with a nationwide circulation. And, taking a cue from Webster, he even published his own phonetic Sistem for Simplified Spelling. The "sistem" did not catch on.

He had two great fascinations, really: religion and science. The Welch household always had carefully read copies of *Scientific American* around, as well as numerous missionary reports from Africa. It was at the intersection of these two worlds that Welch met his fortune. Welch was a teetotaler, and yet deeply believed in the holiness of the communal sacrament. But how could a good dry Christian drink wine? The problem was underscored for Welch when, after letting a visiting clergyman stay at the house, the fellow got smashed on the communion wine—a not uncommon outrage among some men of the cloth.

The trick, then, was to make nonalcoholic grape juice that would keep as well as wine would. And so it was that in 1869 "Dr. Welch's Unfermented Wine" was born. Welch himself picked the grapes from his backyard trellis, strained the juice out, and then boiled the bottles. It was an innovation that nearly bankrupted his family. "For two or three years following," his son later mused, "you squeezed grapes; you squeezed the family nearly out of the house; you squeezed yourself nearly out of money; you squeezed your friends."

He also squeezed his customers: at $12 a quart, the stuff was astronomically expensive. Furthermore, Americans had never had grape juice before: they didn't know what to make of it. "The demand had to be created," grandson Edgar Welch later commented. But eventually prices came down, and through intensive marketing at the 1893 World's Fair—the same fair that introduced most Americans to a bizarre item called grapefruit—the Welch brand became famous.

And where was the octogenarian Bull during the 1893 World's Fair? Why, at the Concord poorhouse.

BULL HAD LIVED long, though he'd never got the hang of aging gracefully—he wore a shiny blond wig in public. One neighbor witnessed his hidden countenance: "A transformation occurred almost as startling as those in a theatre, and he appeared as an aged man with snow white beard, nearly bald, oftenest seen in a dressing gown and little black cap, tending his plants lovingly."

At the age of eighty-five he was still tending his garden and clambering up ladders. But one fall day in 1893 he fell down from his ladder, and from then on he needed frequent care. After exhausting his friends' hospitality, Bull was finally sent to the Concord Home for the Aged, where he would live on in poverty. His lingering injuries were not just physical. In his old age, he'd hoped against hope one last time, and tried to introduce a new variety of grape commercially. But it failed badly and took all his money with it.

By 1894, an editorial writer in the agricultural magazine *Meehan's Monthly* was appalled by the fate of the father of the Concord grape:

> [Imagine] the commonwealth without this exquisite fruit. It is safe to say that we should be poorer to the extent of many scores of thousands of dollars annually. What Bull did for the country is certainly worthy of due reward as is the work of McCormick or Colt or Singer. He found a common species of grape such as any farmer would deem valueless and leave for his birds in hedge-rows; he spent years modifying it by the most pains-taking selection and finally gave us a delicious, cheap, and most helpful food, which will be supplying life and pleasure to millions of persons for ages after this generation has vanished.

Readers did not have to wait long to see Bull's generation vanish. One year later, the old man was dead.

THE GRAPES LIVED on, of course: if you visit his Grapevine Cottage, you can still see them growing all around. But one might wonder if, after years of shying away from selling his grapes, followed by one last final flop, Bull had really given up hope.

Had the sweet grape made a man bitter?

The epitaph on his headstone in Sleepy Hollow Cemetery, not far from his eternal neighbors Emerson, Thoreau, and Hawthorne, stands as an answer. It was ordered by Bull himself.

EPHRAIM WALES BULL
1806–1895

He Sowed,
Others Reaped.

7

PSALMANAZAR

In 1840, rare book collectors across Europe received what at first glance was an entirely ordinary item: the catalog for an upcoming estate auction. On the block was the library of a recently deceased gentleman in Binche, France, one Count J. N. A. de Fortsas.

Count Fortsas, it turned out, was a very peculiar fellow. In his sixty-nine years he focused obsessively upon collecting an utterly unique library. *He would only own books of which no other copy existed.* If he discovered the existence of another copy of a book in his collection, he would burn *his* book, so that he might once again experience the thrill of buying the only copy in existence. Over the years, this practice had dreadfully decimated his library, so that upon his death he owned only fifty-two books. And yet each of these books was priceless, the only copy. Collectors had long given up many of them for extinct, and still others were alluring obscurities never heard of before. Virtually every major collector in Europe found at least one item in the slim catalog that seemed to be written especially for him—and though the collector may never have heard of the title before, now he simply had to have it.

When the auction day of August 10, 1840, arrived, the streets of the little town of Binche were invaded by scores of book collectors from across the Continent, all clutching marked-up copies of the Fortsas auction catalog, and all eyeing each other in the streets with barely disguised distrust. Inquiries to the thick-headed locals were useless: none of them knew where Count Fortsas lived. Enough collectors got over their mutual distaste for each other to congregate in the local tavern, where they plied the regulars for any information on Fortsas and his precious fifty-two-volume library. As these fruitless attempts were proceeding, a man ambled in and read an official announcement: effective immediately, the proud people of Binche were to retain their great local treasure by purchasing the entire lot directly from the Count's family.

So sorry, he added, but the auction has been called off.

The tavern erupted in angry curses in French, Dutch, German, and English, all to the protestation of locals who insisted that they had never even *heard* of a Count Fortsas before. By the time the first collector had uttered the magic word—*hoax*—the man who had read the announcement was long gone.

It was decades before anyone discovered the handiwork of Renier Chalon, an antiquarian who had created the fake Fortsas catalog and gleefully salted it with nonexistent books so tantalizingly titled that he knew his greedy rivals would traverse a continent in pursuit of them. Chalon's descriptions of imaginary books were conjured up with a truly devilish personal animus, written with the precise knowledge of his rivals' obsessions so as to create the one perfect title that might drive a specific recipient in Amsterdam or London mad with acquisitiveness.

To achieve his illusion, all Chalon had to do was invent a deceased noble and some book titles. Tell people what they want to hear, Chalon had reasoned, and they will joyfully leap over their own ignorance and the most obvious improbabilities. But he was not the first to realize this. Over a century before, another had gone even further—inventing a language, a country, an entire living man.

IN 1704, A time when many strange people from strange lands were strolling the streets of England's burgeoning capital, George Psalmanazar was the strangest of all. He was a Formosan, a native of the island we today call Taiwan, and the first of his kind to reach the shores of Great Britain. No one had ever seen a Formosan before; and he, presumably, had never seen an Englishman before.

Always accompanied by the Scottish chaplain Alexander Innes, who had discovered and converted the lost and wandering heathen to Christianity, Psalmanazar was famous from the moment he set foot on shore. Bishops and clergy clamored to meet this miraculous convert, a man who could speak volubly in both the cleric's tongue of Latin and in his native Formosan. Nobles and wealthy merchants of London would invite him to dinner to listen to him speak Formosan; noblewomen watched in fascination as the wild heathen paused in his discourses to dine off a dinner plate heaped with raw meat and dirty roots.

He was, he would explain between bloody mouthfuls, a victim of a kidnapping. Jesuit priests setting up a mission on his island had singled him out for his amazing ability to learn languages and had spirited him away to a Jesuit retreat in Europe, where he was to be indoctrinated as a native missionary to Formosa—an agent of Christ who was both of their culture and yet able to perform a Latin mass. But I escaped, Psalmanazar would add. And Chaplain Innes, he recounted gratefully, had saved him when he was but a wanderer in a strange land, without a friend in the world.

His tale, of being the only man of his kind here, stranded half a world away from his home, was deeply affecting to Londoners. But there were a few problems with his tale. George Psalmanazar was not really named George Psalmanazar. He had never been kidnapped by Jesuits. He did not speak or write Formosan, or practice any Formosan religion. He had never been to Formosa; and was not, in fact, any sort of Formosan at all.

He wasn't even Asian.

WE DO NOT know where he was born. In the memoirs that he kept hidden in his desk, Psalmanazar only says that he was not born in Europe but did grow up there. He does not say which country it was that he grew up in. From hints that he left in his memoir, and from the perfect French that he was always able to speak, some acquaintances ventured to guess that he may have been raised in southern France. But then, George was a man who could speak many languages perfectly. He could have been from almost anywhere.

Born in 1685, he grew up in a nondescript village with his mother—his estranged father, the descendant of an "ancient but decayed family," had moved far away, to Germany, when the boy was but five years old. George was an only child of sorts. There had been other siblings, but they had not survived childhood. In those days, few people did.

His mother sent him to be educated by local Franciscan monks. They quickly noted the young boy's facility with new languages; when visitors came to the school, the monks would trot little George out first, and have him recite Latin to the impressed onlookers. By the age of nine, he was fluent.

His later schooling came among Jesuits, and then he was sent away to attend college under the tutelage of the Dominican order. He was by far the youngest student there, perhaps only fourteen or fifteen years old. But for all his abilities, George was fairly lazy, and his professors little better. His philosophy tutor was simply incompetent; another professor entirely neglected the usual course of classical studies, instead rambling on about his favorite subject, military fortifications. He might arrive and intone to the class

—Today we will be building berms.

And George would find himself and his classmates building clay models of fortified breastworks in the middle of the lecture hall. Meanwhile, his rhetoric and theology texts gathered dust.

George tired of his afternoon classes. It was a long walk from his lodgings into the city, and the coursework looked pointless to him. He began to cut class, opting instead to take meandering hikes through the city and out into the countryside. There he would thoughtfully write letters home to his mother complaining about being broke and how terrible college was.

She had already strained her finances to the breaking point just to send him. Worse still, George had an utter inability to spend money wisely, and his clothes grew shabbier by the day. He took up a tutoring job with a well-to-do family to make up the shortfall, but his tatty clothes and irritating earnestness—he'd utter pious platitudes to them that he didn't half believe himself, just hoping to impress them—soon lost him the job. He was broke enough that he had to go home, but too poor to pay for the journey.

George watched the pilgrims and travelers on the streets of his town, pondering glumly how he could ever see his mother again. And then it came to him: the key to being treated differently was to become *someone else.*

POOR IRISH PILGRIMS were well received in town when they begged for money. The best way to get home, then, was to become an Irishman. He forged a paper to prove his Irish nationality, and then hit upon a clever way to cover his utter inability at English or Gaelic: he wouldn't speak it. Instead, he would only speak in his beloved Latin, the universal language of all educated pilgrims.

He slowly made his way home. Begging in Latin wasn't exactly a bum's paradise; he later recalled that he was limited to "accosting only clergymen or persons of figure, by whom I could be understood." And as always, the moment a kindly priest gave him a few coins, it was spent. By the time he reached home, his clothes were in tatters; his mother's neighbors were scandalized.

His mother upbraided him for his appearance, and he half expected a scolding for his imitation of an Irishman. But he was wrong. His mother was now so impoverished herself that she took him aside one day and calmly suggested that perhaps he should go visit his father, and that maybe he should keep up his Irish act in order to get there. She outfitted her young impostor as best she could, fitting him with a staff, a cloak, and a long black buckram gown. Scraping up her last few gold coins, she sewed them into his clothing.

He retraced his route back to his college, and from there faced hundreds and hundreds of miles on the open road between there and Cologne. And that roadside was littered with bodies—puffed, bloated bodies, with blackened tongues half pecked out by birds: "Now and then at some lonely place lay the carcase of a man rotting and stinking on the ground by the way-side, with a rope about his neck, which was fastened to a post two or three yards distant." These were highwaymen, who were usually discharged soldiers and sailors desperate for money. They had been killed and left to rot by villagers as a warning to other thieves.

There were warnings for the likes of George, too—little crosses by the side of road, built of stone and wood, memorials to unwary travelers, young and alone, who had been robbed and murdered on that very spot. George would stop to ponder them, and then wonder what lay ahead for his own lonesome journey.

He was not yet sixteen years old.

EVENTUALLY GEORGE REACHED the great gates of the city of Lyon, where a guard asked if he wanted alms. Yes, I do, George replied quite innocently.

The guardsman led George through the streets of the city for well over an hour; the boy could scarcely keep up, as he was looking agog at the great squares and grand buildings and cathedrals of the big city. When they reached another gate at the opposite end of the city, the guard stopped and reached into his pocket.

—Here, he said, clapping a couple of copper coins into George's hand. You are to pass through that gate. If you ever come back into the city of Lyon, you will be whipped.

He walked away, leaving the boy speechless.

AFTER A JOURNEY of five hundred miles on foot, George found his father in Germany, still living in the town where he'd been told to look. But nothing prepared him for his father's house: it was bare, even poorer than his mother's. After a long and dangerous journey to meet a man he barely knew, he felt it had all been a waste. Sighing over "the forlorn condition I saw myself in, the mean figure I made in an obscure village," George longed now simply to go back home to his mother. His father, by contrast, was delighted to have his long-lost son back in his home again.

He hadn't seen his child in over ten years, and here he was again, now a strapping young man.

—You should look in town, see if they'll hire you as a tutor, he'd urge. Then you could stay here.

George reluctantly went into town looking for a school or rich family to hire him. But there was a university there, and the streets were already filled with poor students—so many, in fact, that they would go house to house as holy buskers, singing pious Latin verses for handouts. George knew Latin better than anyone, but when he attempted it, got only stares; Germans had their own way of pronouncing Latin, and George's accent simply baffled them.

His father was some comfort, for he talked incessantly of his happy younger days traveling in Holland, and young George began to imagine his own trip someday. Poor as he was, his father was a worldly man—he could readily speak Italian, Spanish, German, and French. George listened and learned, and spent his alone hours pacing about his father's house, wondering what to do next.

His Irish disguise hadn't worked well because there were so few people he could beg from, and discovery could come at the hands of the first priest who happened to be Irish. The way around this problem, George figured, was to become a nationality that everyone had heard of but no one knew anything about.

A CONVINCING FOREIGNER needs a language and a passport, and George set about procuring both. The passport was the easiest, though it was also the most badly botched. Like any self-respecting sixteen-year-old dropout, George had already forged an ID or two— his passport, after all, currently listed him as an Irishman. He forged traveling papers for a Japanese national as well as he could, though his handwriting was so sloppy that it took many attempts to get even a mildly believable document together. It still needed an official wax seal; for this, George simply melted the one off his old fake passport and melted it back onto the new one.

Forging a language was another matter altogether. The easternmost language that George knew anything about was Hebrew, in which sentences run from right to left on the page. Sensibly enough, he decided the Japanese alphabet would too. He'd heard that they had a different alphabet in the Far East, so he created a distinct set of Japanese alphabet characters, training himself to write and "read" them backward. Eventually he was able to do it with nearly the same ease as he had with any genuine language. As a finishing touch, he invented a Japanese calendar. Each year now had twenty months.

It was not easy accomplishing this in his father's house: "The truth is," he later admitted, "time was short and knowledge in what I went about so very small and confused, and what I did was by stealth, and fear of being detected by my father." But once he felt ready to assume his new identity, he approached his father and announced that he was departing to the Low Countries.

His father began to weep. How could George leave him now—his own grown son, whom he had not seen since he was but a child of five years? But the boy prevailed upon his father; was it not he, after all, who had been regaling George with tales of youthful adventures in the Netherlands? Reluctantly, his father agreed. He outlined a safe route to the Dutch, and tearfully bid his son farewell. As he left, George mailed off a letter to his mother, explaining that he was traveling to the Low Countries for a brief spell, but would be back home again soon. And then he walked away, leaving his father's cottage behind him, until it diminished into a speck far behind him, and then disappeared altogether.

George's parents never heard from him again.

OUT ON THE road, begging in fluent Latin and occasionally pausing to jabber excitedly in "Japanese," at first George found somewhat more success than he had as an Irishman. It mattered little that he didn't look the least bit Asian; later acquaintances ventured that George, with his pasty complexion and light blond hair, resembled a Dutchman. But in the 1690s almost nobody in Europe, least of all George himself, knew what an actual Asian looked like. The blond boy could be utterly fearless in his pose as an Asian because, for all he knew, he really did look like one.

In fact, when he reached the garrisoned town of Landau, his

Japanese act was a hit with the foot soldiers there. George was in mid-routine when several musketeers grabbed him and dragged him off. The boy was brought before the town's commanding officer, who demanded an explanation of his presence. George babbled some "Japanese" and flailed about through his alibis until the officer simply ordered him to be tossed in jail as a spy. He was released the following day, led to the city gates, and told never to come back.

His long travels and habitual inclination to shabbiness proved a poor combination. "I saw myself in a short time covered with rags and vermine," he lamented, "and infected with a virulent itch." His hands became disgustingly pustulent, and his mean appearance did not inspire much charity among fellow pilgrims.

Dragging himself into Liège, George found shelter with a group of fellow vagrants in a local hospital, where men passed the day by swapping stories, booze, tubercular coughs, and lice. Word came that the Dutch army was hiring "such vagrants as appeared fit to carry a musket." George persuaded six "fellow ragamuffins" to join him in a trip down to the recruiter. The recruiter sent off all six of George's companions to their fate in the army, but George was different; he wanted George as his personal servant.

But first, George had to be made presentable, and that meant getting him new clothes and curing his rash. His rash now covered most of his body, and had left him covered in scabs. And so ointments were rubbed in, special baths given, leeches applied. Nothing worked. His body was as repellent as ever.

His new mentor simply gave up on trying to cure the condition, and had George accompany him back to the city of Aix-la-Chapelle. There, it turned out, the recruiter owned a coffeehouse and billiards hall, and George was pressed into service as a waiter. In his off hours, he was to tutor his employer's son in Latin. But his new master clearly hoped that the presence of a Japanese freak might attract extra business to the coffeehouse. Unfortunately, the townspeople were too occupied with seeking out the newly fashionable springs where they could take mineral-water cures.

The coffeehouse had employees working in another sideline, a refreshment catering business for large balls and banquets. George was never sent out, on account of the rather offputting scabs that covered his inflamed hands, until one day when there was no one else available. Doling out punch to wealthy guests, George stared agog at the grandeur of the party before him. It was a world he'd scarcely known before.

His job eventually came to an unexpected end. George was sent by his employer's wife on a journey of many miles on foot to deliver a message to her husband, who had gone off to attend to some business. The boy was in an unfamiliar province, and the map his father had given him was no good now. He wandered back and forth to different crossroads, trying to remember where it was that he'd come from and where he was supposed to be going. But he was hopelessly lost, and mortified to think that even if he did find his master, he'd be terribly late with the message. And so, inquiring for the way to Cologne, he set off on his own once again.

AS HE TROD wearily into Cologne, George told himself that at least from here he could find his way back to his father's and then his mother's home again. But once in town, he again fell upon that last resort of the desperate traveler—the army recruitment officer. The regiment he joined was a ragged unit of deserters from the French army, university dropouts, and bewildered German farmboys. Most spent their off hours drunk or whoring, though George was little inclined to follow. But playing the unconverted heathen, he delighted in twisting the few pious soldiers into logical knots as they tried to explain and defend the bizarre precepts of Christian religion.

One such fellow, hoping to convert his Japanese comrade, talked him into visiting a monk:

> When we got to the monastery, we found the good old capuchin sitting on a bench . . . with a lusty young woman kneeling before him, barking like a dog, and making a great many other antick noises and postures; upon which I was told that she was

possessed, and that the good father was exorcising an evil spirit
out of her.

George did not convert that day.

HIS REGIMENT STAGGERED into the winter underfed, underclothed,
and with scarcely a freezing pallet to sleep on. George could barely
keep up, and finally the captain of the regiment recommended him
for discharge. But once he got his papers, he also got a nasty shock:
they wanted his uniform back.

George stripped down and shivered—at which point he discovered that the captain had sold off the civilian clothes that he was to
have held for discharge. George was turned out into the cold with
nothing but a blue linen frock to wear, the bare soles of his feet numb
against the frozen soil. Though he would have scarcely believed it as
he walked away from the garrison, half naked in the freezing air, his
discharge was lucky. Many of his comrades died of exposure and disease later that winter.

Begging for clothes and food, George made his way back to Cologne again, where another officer took pity on the forlorn boy.

—What is your name? he asked the ragged pilgrim.

George thought carefully.

—*Psalmanazar*, he finally answered.

THE OFFICER PERSONALLY recruited him into his regiment, and that
spring they were deployed in Holland. With his new name, Psalmanazar took on a whole new vitality in creating himself anew as a
Japanese. His favorite ploy was showing up at the regimental Sunday
services to distract the Christians:

> I would turn my back to them, and turning my face to the rising
> or setting sun, to make some awkward shew of worship, or praying
> to it . . . I made me a little book with figures of the sun, moon and
> stars, and other such imagery as my phrensy suggested to me, and
> filled the rest with a kind of gibberish prose and verse, and which
> I muttered or chanted as often as the humour took me.

His strange antics caught the attention of the regimental commander, Brigadier George Lauder, who invited him to dine with him one evening late in February 1703—an unheard-of honor for a foot soldier. George arrived to find several other officers and regimental officials with Lauder, including the chaplain, a Scotsman named Alexander Innes. As George dined hungrily on officers' fare, and suffered the droning speeches of the regiment's staff, he felt Innes, who was quieter and a little more friendly than the rest, observing him across the table.

After the meal, Innes walked over and kindly accosted him.

—We must speak in private. Will you visit my house?

AT INNES'S HOUSE, the two passed many hours in conversation; George could not yet speak English, but both were fluent in Latin. There were more visits; scarcely a one would pass without Innes thanking him and slipping a few coins into the youth's palm at the end. But when talk turned to George's other new friends—other ministers who wished, perhaps, to convert him—Innes would stop him.

—You needn't bother with them. They do not understand you as I do.

One day, when George was visiting, the two fell to discussing the Japanese language. Innes pulled down a volume of Cicero, opened it, and pointed out a passage of *De Natura Deorum* to the young man.

I want you, he said, to translate this into Japanese.

George froze. And then, without betraying his fear, he picked up a quill and began to write, moving his hand from right to left on the parchment. Innes watched him write, knowing—as George did not—that to achieve the conversion of an exotic Japanese like George would surely mean a promotion to a cushier post.

George finished writing, and Innes took the paper away.

—Here, he said, passing him another sheet. Do it again.

George sat miserably, staring at the lines of Cicero. He had just made up line after line of nonsensical shapes on a page—and now he had to repeat it? He wrote out the translation as best as he could remember it.

Innes took the second sheet and compared it to the first.

—Look, he showed them to George. Half the characters are different.

George grasped for an explanation, but Innes didn't need one.

—You need to be more careful from now on, he said.

George looked at his new mentor, shocked as the realization sank in.

They understood each other perfectly now.

IN MARCH 1703 the letter came from Henry Compton, the bishop of London, and Innes was overjoyed. They were to leave the regiment at the end of the year and proceed to England, where Bishop Compton would be waiting for them. But first a crucial matter had to be resolved: Psalmanazar was still an unconverted heathen. Innes took him to Brigadier Lauder's house for one last time, and in the presence of the commander the Formosan heathen was baptized a Christian. Lauder gratefully presented him with a gilt pistol and a glowing letter of commendation—everything Psalmanazar needed to travel to England in safety.

Innes gathered together a suit of cast-off clothing for George to wear for his voyage. It was much too big for George; he felt a bit ridiculous as his sleeves and pants flapped about in the wind. And yet the young savage was feeling rather pleased with himself as he and Chaplain Innes prepared to set off. The chaplain, too, was feeling quite clever. He had talked George into altering his story a little— he was now a native of Formosa, not Japan, as Formosa was a land about which Europeans knew nothing except its name. If asked about his old story, George was simply to say, yes, I am also Japanese, as Formosa is a possession of Japan.

Now that Innes had converted the famous Formosan, his promotion in the church was assured. The only question was how to rid himself of his convert when he was no longer of use.

—When we are in London, he said to George, I will recommend that you be sent to Oxford. They will be most interested in learning the language of the Formosans.

————

HERE IS THE sight that greeted George one wintry day, as he and Innes entered London: severed heads. Bristling from the first arch of London Bridge were frozen, disembodied heads staked through with spiked poles, gazing without sight as ships passed by on the River Thames and carriages entered the city across the bridge below. They were the heads of miscreants and frauds, left out to rot until three full tides had passed.

George and Innes had already barely survived the crossing from Holland: a sudden storm had risen up and threatened to wreck the ship. But now, alive and in sight of their goal, they had more worries.

—*You must prepare*, Innes would hiss. Your language—*you must prepare it.*

Still, they could not have arrived at a better time. London—filthy, fetid, royal, teeming with money and vermin—had just surpassed Paris to become the largest city in Europe. It was the pool to which the swirling dregs of an empire drained, and its inhabitants held a conquering nation's moneyed fascination with the curious, the bizarre, the passing strange. Walking past Painter's Coffee Shop, George could peer at a giant eel on display; the proprietor offered a money-back guarantee if a patron could "say that he has seen a greater." George was an altogether better catch: a natural curiosity that could speak, and write, in impeccable Latin.

PSALMANAZAR WAS BROUGHT forward to greet the bishop and presented him with a sheet of paper. It was the Lord's Prayer written in Latin, and then rendered again in George's native Formosan. Scholars puzzled over the document, and agreed—the savage's words made no sense, but the grammar was so regular, so logical, that it must be a real language. The Formosan, it seemed, was every bit as real as Innes's letter had promised. Soon every noble's door in the city was opened to the chaplain and his noble savage.

Psalmanazar liked to shock his hosts.

—*In my land, men are permitted to kill and eat their wives.*

Forks dropped onto plates.

"But only if they suspect adultery," he added.

When asked if he thought this barbaric, George would demur.

Perhaps eating people is an uncivilized custom, he would admit, but it is not expressly forbidden in the Ten Commandments.

While George entertained London's upper crust, elsewhere in the city lay one of the only men who could prove him a fraud: Father Fountenay, a Jesuit missionary returned from China. Inevitably, the two had to meet; Hans Sloane, the brilliant polymath of the Royal Society, had invited them both to a Society meeting on February 2, 1704. The evening began with the usual matters natural and unnatural, and the examination of some ovarian cysts and a possum penis topped the list. Then, the secretary noted, "A letter was read from Mr. Collins concerning a person who pretended to life without food."

Meanwhile, Psalmanazar cheerfully spoke gibberish to the assembled astronomers and botanists as Father Fountaney glared at him.

"You are a fraud," Fountenay began, "for this simple reason: you say that Formosa is a province of Japan. It is not. It is a province of China."

"You are wrong," Psalmanazar replied flatly.

Fountenay sputtered on, but he faced an insurmountable problem: nobody else had been to Formosa. Every detail he gave, Psalmanazar calmly contradicted. And then the impostor delivered a *coup de grâce*: it was the Jesuits who kidnapped me from my native land. What would you expect from them except an attempt to discredit me?

Fountenay left in defeat; Psalmanazar was asked back the next week to dine with Sir Hans Sloane and other worthies of the Royal Society. Worse still, when the French priest was asked to venture what land Psalmanazar—who was probably from France himself—came from, Fountenay couldn't even guess. He'd never heard such an accent or language in his life.

BUT NOT EVERY Society member was convinced. Later that evening in a tavern, one member approached Psalmanazar and asked him: How long does twilight last in Formosa this time of year? George gave the question little thought. But his questioner had given it a great deal of thought indeed, because with this simple question of astronomy he could detect the fraud. George would hardly have even known who his questioner had been: Sir Edmund Halley, the astronomer.

Halley and a few other members of the Society began to put it about town that perhaps Psalmanazar was not all that he appeared to be. But George now had powerful defenders like the Bishop of London and some of the members of the Royal Society. And Psalmanazar's most powerful defender, bar none, remained . . . George Psalmanazar.

"We have an annual sacrifice of children on the island," he told one assemblage. "Eighteen thousand eight-year-old boys are sacrificed at the altar."

The group gasped, appalled.

"But surely," someone would point out, "Formosa's population cannot support such an annual massacre?"

George shrugged.

"Our god demands it."

On no point could he be made to retract or alter his claims. Ever. It was, he later revealed, a deliberate strategy:

There was one maxim I could never be prevailed upon to depart from, viz. that whatever I had once affirmed in conversation, tho' to ever so few people, and tho' ever so improbable, or even absurd, should never be amended or contradicted in the narrative. Thus having once, inadvertently in conversation, made the yearly number of sacrificed infants to amount to eighteen thousand, I could never be persuaded to lessen it, though I had been often made sensible of the impossibility of so small an island losing so many inhabitants every year, without becoming at length quite depopulated, supposing the inhabitants to have been so stupid as to comply.

George's many friends and defenders, irate at the whispers of fraud, published ads daring anyone to prove such an assertion—even offering cash if they could do it. No one appears to have taken them up on the offer. But perhaps it was only a matter of time.

Two months had already passed since George and Innes had arrived. Innes, sensing that a counterattack was needed, had already goaded George into producing yet another document in Formosan—a rendering of the catechism. But now the bishop and his other allies wanted more, Chaplain Innes told George. They wanted the entire history of the island.

George didn't know the faintest thing about Formosa.

"You have two months," Innes said.

STRANGE TO REFLECT, but it was easier three hundred years ago to get a book published quickly than it is today; Psalmanazar's book was finished in March and in London bookstalls by mid-April. Scarcely three months had passed since Innes had suggested the project.

Psalmanazar may have been an indifferent student and an unprincipled fraud, but he was also a maniacally driven writer. In February and March of 1704, in the moments he could squeeze away from the tables of local nobles and clergy, he worked frantically on his manuscript. At his side sat a copy of Varneius's 1646 history *Descriptio Regni Japoniae et Siam*, from which he freely stole, and which, just to be contrary, he pointedly contradicted. As fast as Psalmanazar could produce the pages, his Latin manuscript was "Englished" by Oswald, his translator. In the space of two months, Psalmanazar produced a 288-page book and sketched out dozens of plates and illustrations. The result, *An Historical and Geographical Description of Formosa*, might have the most insolently ironic opening sentence in English literature: "The Europeans have such obscure and various Notions of Japan, and especially of our Island Formosa, that they can believe nothing for Truth that has been said of it."

Psalmanazar did more than create a dreary recounting of royal lineages and politicians; he conjured an entire world. Writing over a century later, the antiquarian Isaac D'israeli was still so flabbergasted by the book's audacity that he was reduced to sputtering:

If the reader is curious to examine this extraordinary imposture, I refer him to that literary curiosity, "An historical and geographical Description of Formosa . . . by George Psalmanazar, a Native of the said Isle," 1704; with numerous plates, wretched inventions! of their dress! religious ceremonies! their tabernacle and altars to the sun, the moon, and the ten stars! their architecture! the viceroy's castle! a temple! a city house! a countryman's house! and the Formosan alphabet!

Not content with that, Psalmanazar also included interlinear translations from Formosan to English of the Lord's Prayer and the Ten Commandments, buttressed by fold-out plates of the Formosan language and a chart of the Formosan numerical system. These he followed with botany, zoology, gastronomy—both plants and human body parts were eaten raw—and an account of the island's history replete with conquests, emperors, and daggered intrigue. He even reproduced a letter from the King of Japan to the King of Formosa, though where exactly George could have got such a document nobody seems to have thought to ask. But such errors are easy to find. Psalmanazar had also included a detailed accounting of the island's mineral resources, which apparently included two brass mines—a sight that any metallurgist would certainly be most interested in seeing.

THE MOST SENSATIONAL part of the book related to the island's religious practices. Psalmanazar conjured up two founding fathers of the Formosan religion, the philosophers Zeroaboabel and Chorhe Mathcin:

> They Demonstrated, by many Arguments, that there is one Supreme God, who is above all the visible things in the World. . . . But if they would Worship him according to his mind, in an acceptable manner, they should Build him a Temple, and in that they should make a Tabernacle, and an Altar, and upon the Altar they should Burn 20000 Hearts of young Children, under 9 Years of Age.

Not surprisingly, the Formosans drove out the two bloodthirsty prophets, at which point a pestilence descended upon the land; it was alleviated only when, in a slight concession to parental anger, God reduced His divine quota a little and let girls off the hook:

> Ye shall begin the Year from this day, which is the first day of the Month Dig, and the first of the Festival of 10 days, and at this Festival ye shall Sacrifice to me every Year the hearts of 18000 young boys, under the age of 9 Years. . . . every month ye shall Sacrifice in all your Temples 1000 Beasts, viz. 300 Bulls, 400 Sheep or Rams, and the rest in Calves or Lambs.

This annual loss of children, Psalmanazar claimed, was more than made up for by the institution of polygamy on the island. And even with the occasional mass roasting of children's hearts, George was quick to assure his readers that Formosa remained "one of the most Pleasant and Excellent of all the Asiatick Isles."

Some critics, however, were unimpressed. It wasn't Psalmanazar's bizarre description of Formosa that caused problems. It was that he had tacked a rather conventional theological treatise onto the second half of the book. Critics were suspicious of how a recent immigrant from Formosa could knock out an abstruse hundred-page essay on Christianity—and he a nineteen-year-old. Worried by these complaints, Chaplain Innes began to quietly bump up George's age in conversations. Psalmanazar was, he now claimed, actually twenty-two years old.

But the objections of critics hardly mattered, at least at first. London booksellers, clamoring for months for Psalmanazar's book, could barely keep copies in stock; Innes pressed him to write an expanded second edition, even as the first was being translated and rushed into print in French, German, and Dutch editions. And soon Psalmanazar received word that Bishop Compton, his new mentor, had arranged for him to spend a semester attending his old alma mater—Christ Church College, at Oxford University.

———

WHEN YOU WALK into Christ Church, you have arrived.

In the early morning, there is a mist on the quad, through which you can see the carved statue of Mercury; beyond that, there is the towering spire of the cathedral, and the looming stone and wood of the quiet dormitories. Then there is the great Meadow, on which scarcely a moving form can be seen at such an early hour.

It is the focal point of an empire: that space in which the most promising minds are concentrated for a brief moment in their lives, before being refracted outward across the spectrum of British society. Sir Christopher Wren built the college cathedral not long before Psalmanazar's arrival, and John Locke had prayed in it as a student; a century hence, Lewis Carroll would be crossing the college quad with his math students. This, the most imposing college of the empire's greatest university, was where Bishop Compton had sent George Psalmanazar, alleged Formosan and actual theology dropout.

Psalmanazar settled into his college room, and lay in his new bed and looked about in contentment—after years of military barracks and borrowed beds, his new home looked enormous to him. Like many of his fellow students, he was enjoying the first apartment of his own that he had ever had.

Although there had been some notion of his tutoring Oxonians in the Formosan tongue, George assiduously avoided any would-be linguists on campus. Instead, he spent his days sitting in on classes on logic, poetry, divinity, and Newtonian philosophy—what today we would call physics. He loved divinity class, where he could soak in his beloved theological arguments and occasionally bask in attention when the instructor asked him questions about the Formosan religion. But he was bored out of his mind by math class, and "history, especially ancient chronology &c., appeared so dark, intricate and liable to such insurmountable difficulties, that I never expected to meet any satisfaction in them." George's dismay is understandable. After all, he had just written a spurious best-selling history himself.

His attendance in all his classes was rather poor. Instead, he spent his days hiking around campus, usually with a pronounced limp. He was faking an attack of gout, because "my pretended lameness gave me a kind of gravity, which I was not willing to part with." Concerned patrons sent him to a spa for a cure. Not surprisingly, when he returned to campus his limp was as bad as ever.

George was truly at his happiest in the cathedral, singing with the college's choir. The choir, he later recalled, "was the main thing that captivated my vain, roving fancy, and took up most of my spare hours." He may not have been the finest singer in the choir, but he was probably the most sober. He was appalled that many of his classmates attending choir stumbled in smashed from pre-rehearsal pub warmups at the Turf or the Bear, ready to slur and belch their way through "Ave Maria."

In the evening, after a long day of skipping classes, limping around the quad, and singing pleasant hymns, George was faced by a dilemma: how could he work on the second edition of his book, goof off, and still look like a good student? After his years in the army, he hardly needed to use a bed to catch up on his sleep, and so he soon hit on an admirable solution:

> I used to light a candle, and let it burn the greatest part of the night, to make my neighbors believe I was plying of my books; and sleeping in my easy chair, left the bed often for a whole week, as I found it to the further surprize of my bed-maker, who could hardly imagine how I could live with so little sleep.

All in all, it was splendid semester—although he didn't learn very much. At the end of it he had finished a second edition of *Description of Formosa*, with even more outlandish plates than before, gorier details on sacrifice and cannibalism, and thundering denunciations of the critics who had dared to doubt the truthfulness of his first edition. He returned from Oxford to London, manuscript in hand, and disembarked from his carriage at Pall Mall, where he and his mentor Innes had taken lodging.

He's not here anymore, he was told. Innes was now chaplain-general to the English forces in Portugal.

BANVARD;

OR THE

ADVENTURES OF AN ARTIST;

A Biographical Sketch.

LONDON:

PRINTED BY REED AND PARDON

PATERNOSTER ROW.

JOHN BANVARD (Collection of The New-York Historical Society, negative number 73828)

WILLIAM HENRY IRELAND (Shakespeare Birthplace Trust)

JOHN CLEVES SYMMES, sketched by John James Audubon
(Collection of The New-York Historical Society, accession number 1864.4;
negative number 7216)

ROBERT W. WOOD (The Ferdinand Hamburger, Jr., Archives of The Johns Hopkins University)

RENÉ BLONDLOT (Jean-Loup Charmet)

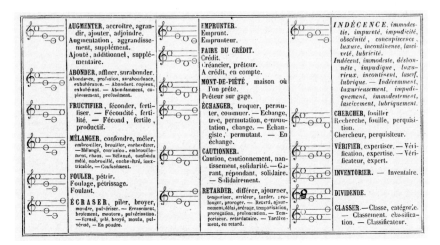

A page from *Langue Musicale Universelle.* Note the correction inked by hand, probably by Madame Sudre (United States Library of Congress)

EPHRAIM BULL (Courtesy of the Concord Free Public Library)

GEORGE PSALMANAZAR (Courtesy of the Bancroft Library,
University of California)

The Battersea pneumatic transport (Science, Industry, and Business Library, The New York Public Library, Astor, Lenox, and Tilden Foundations)

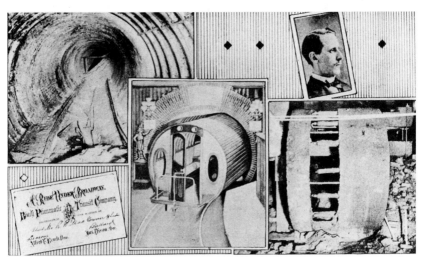

Clockwise from top right: **ALFRED ELY BEACH; the excavating shield as found in 1912; the pneumatic train; the invitation to the 1870 grand opening; the tunnel in 1912.**
(General Research Division, The New York Public Library, Astor, Lenox, and Tilden Foundations)

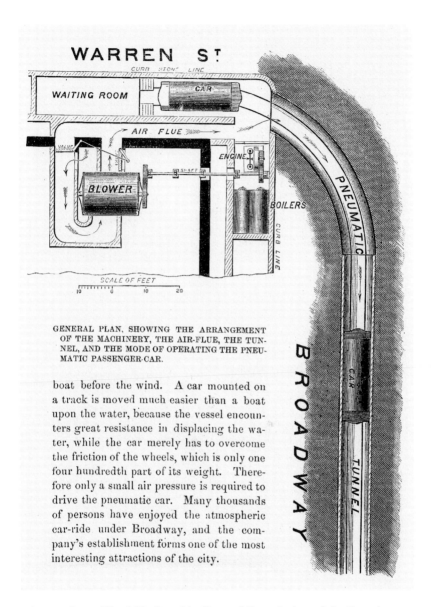

GENERAL PLAN, SHOWING THE ARRANGEMENT
OF THE MACHINERY, THE AIR-FLUE, THE TUN-
NEL, AND THE MODE OF OPERATING THE PNEU-
MATIC PASSENGER-CAR.

boat before the wind. A car mounted on
a track is moved much easier than a boat
upon the water, because the vessel encounters great resistance in displacing the water, while the car merely has to overcome
the friction of the wheels, which is only one
four hundredth part of its weight. Therefore only a small air pressure is required to
drive the pneumatic car. Many thousands
of persons have enjoyed the atmospheric
car-ride under Broadway, and the company's establishment forms one of the most
interesting attractions of the city.

A page from Alfred Ely Beach's *General Description of the Broadway*
Underground Railway (Science, Industry, and Business Library, The New York
Public Library, Astor, Lenox, and Tilden Foundations)

MARTIN FARQUHAR TUPPER (Courtesy of the Doe Library,
University of California)

ROBERT COATES (Courtesy of the Doe Library,
University of California)

GENERAL AUGUSTUS J. PLEASONTON, as spoofed by John Carboy
(This item is reproduced by permission of The Huntington Library,
San Marino, California.)

BLUE GLASS IS NOT A BLISTER!

In a moment he felt like a man around the corner. The effect was miraculous. He threw up the catalepsy and an undigested monkey-stew which he had eaten three months before.

BLUE GLASS CURES CONSTIPATION OF THE OBITUARY ORGANS!

Two panes upset the last stage of consumption, regulated the pulsations of his liver, started the growth of a new pair of lungs with brown-stone trimmings, gave a high stoop to his shoulders, dried up the creek in his neck, enabled him to draw a long breath upon a sheet of brown paper without dropping a tooth, and pitched the roof of his mouth so that it no longer leaked.

The General, in order to benefit the entire human race in the first heat, will send two panes without charge, to any one, upon the receipt of one dollar and four stamps for postage.

Blue will put a head on a bile in five minutes!

All letters containing money will be held strictly confidential.

Beware of imitations without color. *None genuine unless the genuine Blue is blown in the pane.*

A liberal discount to Clubs and Sunday-schools.

THIS IS A HORSE THAT WAS RESTORED TO HEALTH AND A 2.10 GAIT BY THREE PANES OF BLUE GLASS.

From *Blue Glass a Sure Cure for the Blues* (1877)

(This item is reproduced by permission of The Huntington Library, San Marino, California.)

IT REMOVES COLOR FROM NOSES. MR. THE SECOND APPLICATION.
TOSTER TRIES IT.

THE GLORIOUS RESULT.

Even the old women were afflicted with the fever, and hid their ancient occulars behind Blue Glass spectacles.

One old farmer wrote to the General and wanted to know what it would be the probable cost of Blue Glass enough for a hot-house to put up over his garden, and if he put it up in December whether it would raise a crop of "gardening truck" inside of two or three weeks.

The General answered the letter at once. The General informed him that properly applied, if the weather was clear, a medium-tinted Blue Glass hot-house would bring up in December all the vegetables he wanted in one week's time. In fact, through an agent of his sent expressly for that purpose, he had

From *Blue Glass a Sure Cure for the Blues* (1877)

(This item is reproduced by permission of The Huntington Library, San Marino, California.)

Copyright 1888, by Theodore Bacon.

Very gratefully yours
Delia Bacon,

DELIA BACON (By permission of the Folger Shakespeare Library)

Thomas Dick.

THOMAS DICK (Science, Industry, and Business Library, The New York
Public Library, Astor, Lenox, and Tilden Foundations)

Standing in a London street, Psalmanazar was for a moment the man he had claimed to be all along: a stranger in a strange land, without a true friend in the world.

FOR A WHILE, the absence of his stage manager scarcely affected George. The second edition of *Description of Formosa* was a hit once again, and he continued his ruse by publishing a 1707 theological tract titled *A Dialogue Between a Japanese and Formosan*. He wasted months on end lolling about with London bohemians and noble patrons, indulging their endless appetite for novelty and details of quaint savage customs. Women, too, seemed strangely drawn to the celebrity cannibal, though George was privately so mortified with shyness that he rarely took advantage of adulterous advances made to him. "Hardly any man," he admitted later, "who might have enjoyed so great a variety, ever indulged himself in so few instances of the unlawful kind as I have done."

But eventually Londoners tired of their freak, and those who had never believed him much to begin with grew bolder in their attacks. By 1710, skeptical voices were becoming so loud that George's benefactors felt obliged to publish a defensive tract, *An Enquiry Into the Objections Against George Psalmanazar of Formosa*. But it was too late, as any reader of the *Spectator* could see when it ran a spoof announcement in its May 16, 1711, issue:

> On the 1st of April in the theatre on the Haymarket an opera will be performed with the title "The Cruelty of Atreus." N.B. The scene in which Thyestes eats his own children will be played by the famous Mr. Psalmanazar, recently arrived from Formosa; the whole meal will be accompanied by kettle-drums.

Psalmanazar was becoming a joke.

PSALMANAZAR HAD SPENT most of his life—and all his adulthood—in deep disguise, and could hardly go back to the child he had once been. There was nothing left for him, it seemed, but life as a citizen of country and culture that existed nowhere but in his own mind.

Years of dallying about London had left him completely broke, and by 1712 he had been unemployed for so long that his job prospects were grim indeed. But then, one day, an inventor named Pattenden came calling. He'd developed a new white liquid japan—a variety of lacquer that was all the rage among Orient-bedazzled artisans in London. Pattenden had tried selling it, but was meeting with little success. And then he thought, why not hire a Japanese to tout liquid japan? "His proposal," Psalmanazar admitted, "was that I should father and introduce it, under the notion of my having learned and brought the art from Formosa; in which condition, and my putting now and then a hand to painting, he offered me a considerable share in the profit."

George Psalmanazar, washed-up celebrity, had found his first product endorsement. The pair hawked Psalmanazar's White Formosan Work shamelessly, plugging it to anyone who would listen.

—As a japan it is exceedingly white!

—Marvelously hard-drying, gentle friends!

—And unaccountably smooth!

In truth, it wasn't a bad lacquer. But Pattenden became enthralled by his own hyperbole. Whenever he saw a potential sale, he would praise the product outrageously, and then demand so much money for a jar of it that he drove all the customers away. It didn't take long for the whole venture to go bust.

George was left in a deep depression, and with a nagging feeling that dishonest business was something that he could not stomach anymore.

HE TRIED TO go straight; although still halfheartedly maintaining his Formosan habits and accent, he sought out work as a tutor. The problem was, his education had been so lackadaisical that his attempts to teach "empyrical physic" and modern languages met with only the barest success. Fortunately, a London lawyer took notice of him and hired him as a full-time personal tutor to his children. The eldest son, though, was hopeless at Latin, and George cast about in vain for a topic that he knew anything about that the boy might show some ability at. He became desperate.

Today we will build a berm.

And so the Latin and rhetoric texts were set aside for George's half-remembered teenage classes in military fortifications.

Eventually the job came to an end. The lawyer wasn't very good about paying his tutor fees, and George already had old debts hanging over him. He drifted back into an army regiment in 1715, and followed it around the country. He still cut an unusual figure in the regiment. As noble a savage as ever, he was nicknamed Sir George, and the more gullible soldiers in the outfit actually came to believe that he really had been knighted.

His discharge in 1717 left him in Bristol, out of work once again. He longed for an honest living, and recalled how well his instinctive abilities at illustration had served him before—in lavishly illustrating his *Description of Formosa*, even in outlandishly embellishing the Japanese "hymnal" he kept as a teenager. Perhaps, he thought, he could turn an honest living at painting decorative fans. His friends encouraged his work, and soon he set himself to it. But like many an artist, he found he could not live by his brush. "I lived with a good family almost gratis," he sighed, "and was early and late to work, yet I found it almost impossible to get a bare competency at it."

A kindly local man of the cloth, who had heard of George's tales but not of his critics in London, earnestly took up a collection in his parish to support the stranded Formosan. The money was good, twenty pounds per year, but George felt sickened when he accepted it. His fellow parishioners were giving money for a man they believed to be a needy Christian convert from savagery, not for the fraud that he knew himself to be. And so George Psalmanazar, a man who could invent entire languages from thin air, pocketed the money and set about polishing his Latin and other languages. Perhaps at the end of it all he could make an honest living as a translator of actual languages.

YEARS PASSED, AND Psalmanazar moved to London, where he gained more and more work from printers as a translator. By the 1720s he'd slowly allowed the charity payments to lapse. He never turned down the payments, but when contributors died off, he didn't bother to seek replacements. Eventually he found himself earning his own way through the world. Friends, though, still delighted in knowing a real Formosan, and they continued to pester him for stories about his homeland. It made George heartsick—he could never admit the ruse to them, and so he dejectedly muttered Formosan sentences to hosts when asked, but he would just as soon that everyone forgot about it. He felt irredeemable, doomed.

And for a while, he very nearly was doomed. In 1728 he became deathly ill, and was sent to a friend's country home to rest. He was already over forty now, and as he lay in his deathbed he saw his life as an awful waste. He was, for perhaps the first time in his life, ready to be converted; and one day during his infirmity, it finally happened. The instrument of conversion was a volume titled *Serious Call to Devotion*, just published by John Law. Its words struck at Psalmanazar's heart:

> What numbers of souls there are now in the world, in my condition at this very time, surprised with a summons to the other world; all seized at an hour when they thought nothing of it; frightened at the approach of death, confounded at the vanity of their labours, astonished at the folly of their past lives. . . .
>
> God Almighty knows greater sinners, it may be, than you are, because He sees and knows the circumstances of all men's sins, but your own heart, if it is faithful to you, can discover no guilt as great as your own; because it can only see in you those circumstances, on which the great part of guilt is founded.

Psalmanazar, unutterably weary from illness and a lifetime of secret guilt, took in each word as if it had been directed at him personally. But Law did offer hope—through a genuine and heartfelt conversion, and the living of an ascetic, penitentially laborious life.

George did not die that day, nor the next. In fact, to his great surprise, he lived for four more decades to be a very old man indeed.

WHEN PSALMANAZAR HAD recuperated and returned to London in 1728, he was a changed man. He lived simply and sparsely, and wrote from seven in the morning to seven at night, taking on grueling literary hackwork, contributing to weighty shelf-breakers like *A General History of Printing* (1732) and the massive multivolume *Universal History* (1736–50). When he contributed an anonymous article on Formosa to Emanuel Bowen's *Complete System of Geography* (1747), it was to attack the frauds of . . . George Psalmanazar. By then he was refusing any sort of byline; he did not want his name before the public anymore.

Decades passed. The man who had once been an idle impostor became a beloved fixture around his lodgings on Ironmongers Row, with children and adults alike greeting the pious old man as he stepped outside each day. He had become so steeped in theology and translation that he taught himself Hebrew, and visited synagogues around London in order to stay in practice. He also tried his hand at "a tragi-comic piece, entitled *David and Michal*, in Hebrew verse." But though he was a master of fiction in his identity, the piety of his old age left him with surprisingly little talent in printed fiction. Shortly after Samuel Richardson published *Pamela*, one of the first successful novels in the English language, George eagerly sent him a chapter for a sequel volume. It was pretty poor stuff, stuffed with religious sentiment; the manuscript, which still survives, includes Richardson's comment "Ridiculous & improbable" scrawled in the margins.

George also made one truly appalling error in his old age. Like many people of his time, after taking a nightly tincture of opium as a curative during a painful illness, he found himself hopelessly addicted to it. Searching desperately for a cure, he found a tract published by one Dr. Jones, titled *Mystery of Opium*. Experimenting with its recommendations, Psalmanazar found he could "strip the opium of all its pernicious qualities" of addiction by boiling it in a solution of juice squeezed from Seville oranges, along with a few alkali powders mixed in. The acid and alkali would react and bubble up in a scummy froth; skim it off, and you were left with opium that was healthy and wholesome. Psalmanazar recommended it heartily to his friends and fellow churchgoers, and soon they were enthusiastically juicing oranges and cooking up.

After a while, Psalmanazar was back to his daily habit of ten spoonfuls of opium. He never did manage to shake it. The orange juice hadn't worked, of course. And with great chagrin, the God-fearing old man realized that he'd got his friends and neighbors hooked on it as well.

TAKING A BREAK from his long hours of writing, George would re-pair to an alehouse on Old Street, where he'd meet with a prom-ising young writer friend named Samuel Johnson. In later years, Johnson told his biographer Boswell that he preferred Psalmana-zar's company above anyone else's in London. "George Psalmana-zar's piety, penitence and virtue," he commented to another friend, "exceeded almost what we read as wonderful even in the lives of the saints."

Johnson, like Psalmanazar, had been deeply moved by Law's *Se-rious Call to Devotion*, and the two found a common bond in their religious belief. But sometimes Samuel could not contain his curiosity about George's past.

—About Formosa . . .

And George would give him such a deeply pained look that Sam-uel would immediately stop his sentence. "I should as soon think of contradicting a *Bishop*," he later told Boswell.

On another occasion he ventured one more question.

—Why do you keep the name Psalmanazar, if it is not your real name?

Psalmanazar's pained look returned.

—Because, he explained, I deserve no other name other than that of an impostor.

Psalmanazar was nearing eighty by now; nearly everyone that he had cheated of sympathy and alms was now long dead. He needed no forgiveness from them, as they'd died blissfully unaware of his deception, and content in the knowledge that they'd helped a poor Formosan traveler. But Psalmanazar himself had been sentenced to a long life, and he had never forgiven himself for what he had done.

AFTER PSALMANAZAR'S DEATH in 1763, a bundle of papers was discovered in his desk; included in them was one bearing this title:

THE LAST WILL AND TESTAMENT OF ME A POOR SINFUL
AND WORTHLESS CREATURE COMMONLY KNOWN BY
THE ASSUMED NAME OF
GEORGE PSALMANAZAR

In it, he left all his possessions to his faithful housekeeper, Sarah. He also directed that some money be set aside to publish the memoir that he had left in his desk; he said it would provide a full accounting of his misdeeds.

Then, George begged to be consigned to oblivion:

> I desire that my body, when or wherever I die, may be . . . conveyed to the common burying-ground, and there interred in some obscure corner of it without further ceremony or formality than is used to the bodies of deceased pensioners where I happen to die, and at about the same time of the day, and that the whole be performed in the cheapest and lowest manner. And it is my earnest request, that my body not be enclosed in any kind of coffin, but only decently laid in what is called a shell of the lowest value, and without lid or other covering which may hinder the natural earth from covering it all around.

He was to be laid in the earth like a pauper, the grave unmarked. Nobody knew where George Psalmanazar had come from. Now, nobody was to know where he had gone. It would be as if the man had never existed.

———

TWO YEARS LATER, his *Memoirs of* **** were published; they have never been reprinted since. In them, he admits everything. But there was one secret that the man who called himself George Psalmanazar took to his obscure grave, one that more than three centuries have failed to prize from his grasp.

His real name.

THE PNEUMATIC UNDERGROUND

Cryptic invitations arrived at the City Hall offices of Boss Tweed and his cronies earlier in the week:

UNDER BROADWAY RECEPTION

*To State Officers, Members of the Legislature, City Officials,
and Members of the Press:*

You are respectfully invited to be present on Saturday, February 26th, 1870, from two to six o'clock P.M., at the office of the Beach Pneumatic Transit Company, 260 Broadway, corner of Warren street.

JOSEPH DIXON, *Secretary*   A.E. BEACH, *President*

Those looking out their windows at City Hall would have good reason to be puzzled. The corner of Warren and Broadway was not far up the street, and there was scarcely any sign of activity—nothing, that is, other than the usual cacophony of plodding delivery vans, packed horse-drawn trams, and yelling street urchins. The building in question was a mere clothing store; it could hardly fit the mayor's staff, let alone the entire city's press corps. And underground . . . well, there *wasn't* any underground.

Was there?

That Saturday afternoon, when the first journalists and politicians arrived at the premises of Devlin & Co. Clothiers, it didn't look like much of a place for a grand reception. But they were quietly ushered down the back steps, into what had been the cellar of the store.

It was not a cellar now. An amazed reporter for the *New York Herald* described the scene that unfolded before him: "Descending an ordinary basement 'dive' under Devlin's clothing store, visitors found themselves in a comfortable office, and a few steps lower there was *a kind of Aladdin's cave opened to view. . . .*"

The crowd filed through a doorway to find a reception room, 120 feet long and ablaze with gaslit chandeliers, spread out before them. Fine paintings hung upon the walls, lavish tables of champagne and hors d'oeuvres had been laid out, a fountain glittered with its stock of goldfish, and sumptuously upholstered couches awaited the visitors; in one corner a piano was playing, its notes echoing through the subterranean lair. But the crowd could also hear the distant rumble of traffic—for twenty-one feet over their heads was Broadway, where thousands of New Yorkers traipsed and drove by, utterly unaware of what was right under their feet.

Beyond the edge of this cavernous room, brilliantly lit up, lay something that no New Yorker above or below had seen before: a subway car.

THEIR HOST WAS ready for them. He was a dapper fellow in his mid-forties with a carefully groomed mustache, and instantly recognizable: Alfred E. Beach, the owner and publisher of *Scientific American* magazine. He patiently guided the bewildered elite of the city around the cavern. What you see before you, he explained, is an atmospheric railway: "The Pneumatic Dispatch consists of a railroad track enclosed in a tube, the cars being driven by atmospheric pressure. The car, in effect, is a piston, moving with the tube."

He showed the crowd a single handsomely built railway carriage; the tracks that it sat upon disappeared into a brightly lit and whitewashed circular tunnel that gently curved away into the distance, into the bowels of the Manhattan earth. A keystone over the tunnel bore a carved inscription:

PNEUMATIC TRANSIT.
1870.

But where was the locomotive?

"A tube, a car, a revolving fan! Little more is required. The ponderous locomotive, with its various appurtenances, is dispensed with, and the light aerial fluid that we breathe is the substituted motor."

Those still scratching their heads at this were led up a few steps to view a massive machine housing festooned on the outside with elaborate frescos. The Aeolor, Beach called it. A glance inside revealed its purpose: it was a gigantic steam-powered fan. It was all very simple, really—the subway car they had seen in the cavern below fit snugly into a tunnel in which it was pushed along by the force of wind, just like a sailboat. Only, as Beach pointed out, "a car mounted upon a track is moved much easier than a boat upon the water, because the vessel encounters great resistance displacing the water, while the car merely has to overcome the friction of its wheels."

The return journey was easily arranged. Just run the fan in reverse, and the resulting vacuum drew the car back again.

More guests showed up as the afternoon progressed, each emerging dazed through the doorway into the cavern now filled with the city's elite, all chatting and drinking, and leaning upon the piano in an enormous space that should have been nothing but thousands of cubic feet of dirt and rock. Alfred Beach was the center of attention, leading his guests all around the subway station that he had built entirely in secret. Guests were amazed and delighted; champagne glasses were raised and, as the *New York Times* wryly put it the next day, "the 'health' of the tunnel was not forgotten."

After a while, Beach gathered his first adventurous group of passengers together. Holding on to their champagne glasses and their hats, the crowd watched as the Aeolor wind machine built up to a roar, the doors closed on the tunnel tube, and the car slid out of sight. The first subway in America had officially gone into service.

THE RIDE TOOK only seconds; at the end of it, the passengers stepped out to find themselves at another subway station. They were now by the corner of Murray Street.

At this point, it might have started to dawn on the passengers just what Beach had really done. Not only had he built a subway without telling anyone, *he had run it beneath City Hall.* It is hard enough today to imagine what an insane enterprise this was: how, working in the dead of night and without permits, could one man build a working subway line under Manhattan's busiest street, right next to City Hall itself, and all without a single neighbor ever catching on to it?

But Beach had done it.

He was not the first to build an atmospheric railway, though. That honor belonged to others an ocean and a decade away.

ALTHOUGH IT HAS undergone a renaissance of late, Battersea is not the most scenic of London locations; it was no accident that Pink Floyd once chose it for the grim postindustrial cover art of their album *Animals.* During the Industrial Revolution, though, there was no better place to build a power station, a massive smokestack, or any other hulking behemoth of iron and brick to grab a capitalist's fancy. Where else, then, for the Pneumatic Dispatch Company to lay down a quarter mile of cast-iron pipe?

Readers of the July 19, 1861, issue of the London *Mechanics Magazine* were treated to this description of the strange goings-on by the Thames riverside:

> On Wednesday last some experiments, on a rather large scale, were made on the right bank of the river . . . with a view to testing the efficiency of the novel mode of transmitting goods and parcels. The mechanical arrangements in connection with the experimental line of cast iron tubing—which, like a huge black snake, stretches for more than a quarter of a mile along the river side— are few and simple.

It was, like Beach's subway, essentially a giant peashooter. This straw was a yard high and built of cast iron, the pea weighed about half a ton, and the breath propelling it was a giant pneumatic ejector fan spinning at 200 rpm.

The carriages, low-slung and rather sporty-looking, stood less than three feet high—far too short for passengers. But the directors of the Pneumatic Dispatch Company gathered at the riverside that Wednesday watched with satisfaction as workers loaded a carriage with one ton of cement bags. The carriage was pushed into the end of the tube, the hatch shut with a clang, the signal given, and— *whoosh*—fifty seconds later a ton of metal and cement came banging out the other end, a full quarter mile away.

The company directors were delighted.

More tests were run, with the little carriages merrily zooming back and forth through the tube, around sharp curves and up and down steep grades, every time without a hitch. The crowd watching all probably had the same thought by now: *Who will ride in it?*

And then their eyes settled upon, in the rather unkind words of *Mechanics Magazine*, "a living passenger in the shape of a dog, not very handsome." The hapless pooch was tossed in along with some bags of cement and sent rocketing off. Word came back from other end—the dog was fine. Now the real question came up. Would a *man* climb in?

It being London, there were a couple of likely lads happy to oblige. A mattress was thrown into a carriage, a saddle blanket found to tuck in the adventurers, and in they went, lying flat on their backs and staring up at the sky. The carriage was rolled forward and enclosed in the utter darkness of the iron tube. The signal was given and, with a mighty blast of air, the two felt themselves thrown forward.

Fifty seconds later the two emerged at the other end, the lucky recipients of a bizarre joyride. But the company directors watching had more than amusement in mind. They now knew their tube could carry mail, heavy cargo, even passengers—and it could carry the Pneumatic Dispatch Company all the way to the bank.

PNEUMATIC TRANSIT HAD been tried even before then. In 1810, the London inventor George Medhurst published a curious pamphlet titled *A New Method of Conveying Letters and Goods with Great Certainty and Rapidity by Air*. Using air forced through a tube, Medhurst thought, goods could be shot along at up to 100 mph. Soon he expanded his vision to passenger lines, and he spent the next two decades perfecting his ideas, at one point issuing shares for the building of an atmospheric railway line. He had few takers.

Others followed, though. In the 1820s and 1830s, John Vallance and Henry Pinkus both took cues from Medhurst's later work and developed passenger railway designs that kept the compressed air but dispensed with the all-enclosing and claustrophobic tubing: instead, their tubes of compressed air would be built into the trackway, with the carriage riding atop it in the open air. Pinkus even claimed that farm plows could be driven by laying these pneumatic rails across fields. Vallance managed to attract the attention of officials from the Russian embassy, who examined his designs with a view toward building their own atmospheric line from St. Petersburg to the Black Sea.

But these inventors were far ahead of the public's imagination and the technology of their day. Both floated stock to finance their designs, and both went home empty-handed. By the 1840s, though, there were enough improvements in these open-air designs that investors started taking more notice. One inventor built a working model across a London cricket pitch. Not too far away, near Wormwood Scrubs Prison, another team of inventors built a full-scale experimental rail line that carried seventy-five passengers and could reach 40 mph when empty.

There was a boom in atmospheric railway building for the next few years, and for good reason: the trains were quiet and clean, and they could stop and start with astonishing speed. One unwary tester on a Dublin atmospheric line accidentally hit 84 mph, which may well have made him the fastest man on earth for a time. Lines were built in France, Austria, Ireland, and England. Stock offerings were legion, and in England extensions were planned all the way down to Cornwall.

But the system remained a bit dodgy. The materials at hand just weren't reliable enough: air pistons leaked and cracked in the cold, and rats nestling in them were shot out like furry bullets as the train approached. Many designs only allowed trains to go in one direction at a time, so that if a train overshot a station, all the passengers had to get out and push it back to the platform. Tracks could not be merged or crossed. Worse still, the compressors of the day lacked sufficient power for long rail lines. Timetable inspectors found that breakdowns were a constant problem on some lines, and—most humiliating of all—sometimes a steam locomotive had to be hauled out to do the job. By the late 1840s, investors had decidedly had it with atmospheric rail.

POPULATION DENSITIES IN London, Paris, and New York became intolerable in the 1860s; city planners knew they needed to expand outward with worker housing, but they lacked transportation for a daily commute to work. In the meantime, downtown street traffic was becoming increasingly dangerous and grindingly slow.

Amid these traffic jams, surface rail lines looked less appealing now, at least inside cities, and so attention naturally turned to subways. But coal-fired locomotives, which spewed cinders and smoke into passenger compartments even aboveground, were doubly undesirable in a confined tunnel system. Inevitably, the massive propeller blades of pneumatic motors began to turn once again—and now, thanks to engineering developments during the 1850s, they could spin in reverse, so that cars could be pushed forward and pulled back within the same tube. Telegraph offices in London started installing small-bore tubes to send messages from stock exchanges to central telegraphy offices, and by 1858 there was over a mile of tubing under London. Large-bore tubes for cargo and passengers were the next logical step.

After the success of the Battersea line, in 1863 the Pneumatic Dispatch Company built cargo lines in London for the post office,

including a half-mile pipe from Euston Station to Eversholt Street;
by 1865 the company had extended it another two miles, through
Tottenham Court, New Oxford Street, and finally to the central
General Post Office at 245 Holborn Street. It was not unknown for
workers to take joyrides in the mail carriages, getting shot through a
massive iron tube across two and a half miles of metropolitan London
in a matter of a few minutes. The Duke of Buckingham, who happened to be the chairman of Pneumatic Dispatch, was fond of personally showing off his thrill ride. One pneumonaut recalled:

> The sensation at starting, and still more so upon arriving was not
> agreeable. For about a minute in each case there was a pressure
> upon the ears suggestive of a diving-bell experience, a suction like
> that with which one is drawn under a wave, and a cold draught of
> wind upon the eyes, having almost the effect of falling water.

But as long as the passengers kept their heads down, no one seemed
to be worse for the experience. *Frank Leslie's Illustrated Newspaper*
announced that "the air in the tube was by no means foul or disagree-
able," though "here and there a strong flavour of rust was encountered."

Inventors became ambitious again. In the Crystal Palace Exhibition of 1864, the public boarded a quarter-mile-long line set up by
the Pneumatic Dispatch Company and overseen by the company's
chief engineer, T. W. Rammell. Afterward, Rammell proposed a huge
London system of atmospheric subways, running thirty trains an
hour. The sum of £135,000 was raised from investors, and groundbreaking was held on October 25, 1865.

Pneumatic postal schemes met with even greater success. Lines
snaked between London post offices and businesses, and over the next
thirty years, ninety-four lines with more than thirty-four miles of
tubing crisscrossed the city. The London *Times* sunnily predicted that
"between the pneumatic dispatch and the subterranean railways, the
days ought to be fast approaching when the ponderous goods vans
which fly between station and station shall disappear forever from the
streets of London."

Pneumatic systems roared to life in every major city in Britain, as well as in Berlin, Paris, and Vienna. One was even proposed across the Swiss Alps. None, though, were being built in America—at least, not at first. But that was about to change.

BEFORE HE LAID a single foot of railway track, Alfred Beach had seen an even faster and cheaper means of transport: pigeons.

The pigeons belonged to his father, Moses Beach, owner of the scrappy tabloid the *New York Sun*. One of Moses's first acts as a publisher was building a massive pigeon house on the roof of his building; his winged legions carried news back from Albany and Washington, D.C., giving him a slight edge in a publishing world so rough-and-tumble that *Sun* and rival *Herald* newsboys would knock each other down in the streets.

Alfred inherited his father's publishing savvy, but he was also deeply interested in sciences. And so in 1846, at the age of twenty, he and prep school roommate Orson Munn bought out a failing magazine called *Scientific American*. Early on, Beach had a masterful insight: he added a patent law business to the magazine offices. With nearly every New York inventor passing through his doors, Beach had an endless supply of breaking technology news. He had patent papers to write stories from before the Patent Office examiners in Washington had even seen them.

Beach traveled down there every month to Patent Office hearings, and was the best friend that inventors in this country had. It is easy to see how this empathy arose. Beach was a brilliant inventor himself, having designed one of the first working typewriters when he was only twenty-one years old. His greatest passion, though, was reserved for atmospheric railways. He pored over London papers and magazines as they came off arriving boats, saving any article mentioning the successes of pneumatic transit. Soon, the idea began to germinate within him: why not build one in Manhattan?

IF YOU STOOD in just the right spot on 14th Street on September 16, 1867, you could see the future. It had arrived in Manhattan with the opening of the American Institute Fair, and it had visitors craning their necks to look heavenward: suspended from the ceiling of the Armory was a gigantic wooden tube, 107 feet long and six feet wide, with an open carriage sliding back and forth inside. Delighted visitors clamored to get aboard, a dozen at a time, and by the end of the exhibition it had carried more than 100,000 Manhattanites.

Near the train was another exhibit, an ingenious postal pneumatic system consisting of street-level lampposts with built-in mail slots for letters bound uptown and downtown. A letter dropped in would waft down to a bin far below the street. This bin hung just over a pneumatic tube; a car roaring by would smack open the bin, dumping out its contents into the mail car, which then rocketed onward with the cargo. It was to be far cheaper than conventional Manhattan haulage: for what was spent each year on cargo horses in Manhattan, the pneumatic system could be laid down in every street three times over.

Presiding over these wonders was Alfred Beach. The passenger line had been built in just six weeks by Beach, and it was already unlike any train ever seen before. For one thing, *you could hang it from a ceiling*. A new laminating process used by Beach meant that the tube was only a one-and-a-half-inch thick wooden shell, light and strong enough to be hung almost anywhere, and flexible enough to be bent into outlandishly arcing and curving designs.

Beach had fantastic visions on offer to exhibition visitors—of a future landscape of pneumatic trains burrowing into the depths of Manhattan, and then rearing up aboveground to lace the urban airspace, arcing out in gentle curves to hang from the sides of buildings, even passing on stilts right over the rooftops. The metropolis would be a writhing mass of silent, slithering tubes, pulsing with encapsulated citizenry hurled along at up to 100 mph. Passengers embarking from City Hall could arrive at Jersey City in just five minutes, Central Park in eight minutes, or Harlem in fourteen minutes.

"Almost anything is possible to modern engineering," marveled one bedazzled reporter from the *Brooklyn Daily Eagle*, "providing money enough is furnished."

WITH THIS GREAT truism in mind, Beach spent much of 1868 lobbying the legislature in Albany, exhorting readers in the pages of his magazine, and issuing *The Pneumatic Dispatch*, a lavishly illustrated booklet describing his dreams for the city. But Beach was not the only one making plans. His father's old rival Horace Greeley was also lurking the halls of the capitol; he and Cornelius Vanderbilt, among others, had hatched their own railway scheme for the city. Vanderbilt and his minions were to be sorely disappointed, though, for not only did the legislature turn them down, it also gave Beach permission to build a small pneumatic mail line by City Hall.

Beach was going to get his chance to prove himself at last. He hurriedly drew up a charter and scrambled to issue $5 million in stock, and on August 1, 1868, the Beach Pneumatic Transit Company was born. And then, for a while . . . nothing happened.

Or so it seemed. Beach knew he had to move very carefully. Vanderbilt and others were waiting to pounce on him at the first sign of actual construction, ready to halt work with court accusations of disruptions in water and sewage service. And the teamsters at the stagecoach and cargo companies, furious at their looming obsolescence, would love nothing better than to crack a few heads at the construction site while cops pointedly looked the other way.

There was no groundbreaking ceremony, then—quite the opposite. Beach had assembled his team in the basement of a clothing store and sworn them to utter secrecy as they burrowed down into the earth. The telltale piles of dirt they excavated were whisked away in sacks in the dead of night. Tons of brick, marble, and wood and an entire piano were all smuggled down through the store's basement, all without a soul on the street knowing it.

It helped that the team had something of a secret weapon. The ever-inventive Beach had designed a special tunneling shield for them, a massive honeycombed metal disk propped up with hydraulic jacks; under pressure, the shield extruded dirt out the back, which was then dug out and carted away. By cranking up the pressure of the jacks on either side, the excavators could make the tunnel curve to the left or right. The Beach shield was to become standard excavating equipment years later, but right now, Beach's workers were the only people in the world to have one—and they couldn't even tell anyone about it.

Even those in on the secret, though, might have noticed something puzzling about the proceedings. The bill passed by the legislature had allowed Beach to build two fifty-four-inch tubes under Broadway, a limit that effectively ruled out passenger traffic. What Beach was laying track down for, though, was a single tunnel with a 108-inch bore—which just *happened* to be big enough to carry passengers.

Explaining this decision to the public afterward, Beach held up the smallest of fig leaves:

> The quickest and best method for construction for the two tubes was to . . . erect a masonry shell large enough to enclose both of the fifty-four inch tubes. It is a portion of this outer tunnel that has been erected; and as it has proved to be strong enough and large enough for the transit of passengers, the company laid down therein a railway track and provided a passenger car, for the purpose of *temporarily* illustrating, by an actual demonstration, the feasibility of placing an actual railway under Broadway.

As an explanation it was, like the rail line itself, marvelously convenient.

BOSS TWEED WAS not amused.

Today William M. Tweed is a byword for machine politics and unbridled corruption. It is a reputation that is richly deserved: Tweed had his fingers in every pie in New York City, and in the space of a three years he and his minions siphoned away up to $200 million from city coffers, single-handedly tripling the city's debt burden. So even as the city and state dallied over the implementation of a mass transit plan, Tweed's men were sure that, whatever the outcome, they would all get their cut of the action.

Would-be railway companies eyed the city hungrily. Building New York City's light rail would be the largest public works project in U.S. history, and the rail construction contracts alone would be worth hundreds of millions. Tweed, who had already installed himself on the boards of a local railway company, a gas company, a bank, and the Brooklyn Bridge Company, all while still serving as the mayor, had an unbeatable inside track to landing any construction contracts.

But then came *Beach*.

New Yorkers loved Beach Pneumatic Transit. City luminaries eagerly boarded the plush carriage for their 321-foot ride of the future, and visiting dignitaries came down to Warren Street to marvel at the station. Newspapers throughout the city were almost unanimous in their praise of Beach, and wondered if the solution to the city's transit problems had been found at last.

Tweed was appalled, and then flabbergasted, and then utterly furious. He and his men had stood to gain astronomical sums from rail contracts, and now some delicate-boned egghead publisher had yanked the rug out from underneath all of them. And, just to rub it in, Beach had dug out his illegal subway almost underneath Tweed's City Hall lair—a place already in danger of sinking into the earth under the weight of all its plundered loot.

Beach seized the moment, and the 1871 session of the state legislature saw him pushing a bill to allow him to extend pneumatic lines from the tip of Manhattan all the way up to Harlem, down to Jersey City, and out to Brooklyn. At first, there was little Tweed could do to directly block Beach. Pneumatic rail was tremendously popular, and even a rapacious despot like Tweed knew that the public's fancy would not tolerate a frontal assault. Residents of both the East-Side Association and the West-Side Association had voted their support of the Broadway Underground Railway bill and circulated petitions around the city. Newspapers also supported the bill, and the *Journal of Commerce* made much of its most startling feature in a February 15, 1871, editorial: *"There can be no good objection to the passage of the bill*—one of the chief merits of which is, that the company *ask no subsidy from the city*, but are willing to pay the whole cost out of their own pockets." Not only was Beach's company scooping up the most important contract in the city's history, it was making every other company look bad in the process. Beach Pneumatic Transit had already spent $350,000 of its own money, $70,000 of which came out

Beach's wallet. The company was not, unlike nearly every other railway builder in the city, busy lining its pockets.

The opposition consisted of the usual suspects: Tweed, Astor,
Vanderbilt, and an assortment of Broadway residents who feared for
their mansions. They were, Beach complained, "an organized clique
of opponents to this beneficent measure, consisting largely of rich
men, who ride in their carriages, and don't want to be disturbed by
fast railways." And, as with any major undertaking, a few naysayers
were simply crotchety old men. "I have fought steam railroad projects
in Broadway for the last twenty years," snapped one at a reporter,
"and I mean to fight them for twenty years more."

This kind of reasoning carried little weight in Albany, and on
March 17, 1871, the assembly passed Beach's bill by a staggering
margin of 102 to 11. Not long afterward, the senate passed it by 22
to 5. Now it was only up to Governor Hoffman to sign the bill into
law. A hearing was set for March 30, and Beach showed up to plead
his cause.

He was walking into a trap. Tweed was prepared all along; the
governor was already in his pocket. That day, citing the possibility
of damage to houses along Broadway, Governor John T. Hoffman
dutifully bowed to his dread master the mayor of New York, and
vetoed the bill.

SURELY NONE OF those at the offices of *Scientific American* could have
imagined for long that they could take on Boss Tweed and simply
get away with it. And yet, they *had* dared to imagine it.

Beach—a sober and industrious man who never took a day off
work in his life—would not be put off so easily by the infamous
diamond-bedecked mayor. He and his railway company pushed the
legislature into approving the bill again the following year, and the
company now wielded a fistful of engineering reports asserting that
no damage would done to any buildings. But Boss Tweed had his
own kept man: Edward Tracy, the chief engineer of the Croton
Aqueduct Works. Tracy issued a dire report on the Beach bill, pre-
dicting that sewer lines would need to be torn up, tunnels would

flood, buildings would sink, and fifteen massive ventilators would have to project out of the street for every mile of pneumatic subway.

Citing Tracy's report, Hoffman vetoed the bill once again on May 1, 1872. Amazingly, he claimed that much of the route in question didn't even need mass transit, accusing Beach of seeking "possession of the valuable portion of Broadway . . . where the facilities for transit are already many, making the great question of Rapid Transit through the whole length of the city secondary." Any Manhattanite not utterly appalled by Hoffman's reasoning would have found this claim hilarious.

And then came help from another funnyman—a cartoonist. Although a number of citizens appalled by Tweed's dirty dealings helped topple the mayor, Thomas Nast's cartoons for the *New York Times* effectively revealed to the world the vast scale of the extortion and skulduggery employed by the Tweed Ring. Tweed fell under indictment and was ultimately convicted for his myriad crimes; at one point, he even fled to Spain to avoid prosecution. There was a change in power in Albany, too: power passed from Governor John Hoffman to Governor John Dix.

This time, when the bill came up for vote again in the 1873 session, both the legislature and Governor Dix approved it. Beach's dream, it seemed, was to come true at last. But the very feature that buoyed the bill—all the money would come from the company, and none from the public—also cruelly sank it. The year ended with a massive financial crash, the Panic of 1873; investment money dried up, and suddenly Beach and his company were left stranded.

When Boss Tweed finally died in 1877, the new mayor stubbornly refused to lower City Hall's flags to half mast. A great evil was now dead. But so was a great good—the Beach pneumatic line. And neither was ever coming back.

PNEUMATIC LINES BACK in Europe were faring little better. As steam and electric trains improved, the advantages of pneumatics looked less overwhelming. Some mail lines collected seepage at the bottom of inclines, so that carriages rocketing through them would hit puddles that dashed water all over the mail inside. Air leakage bedeviled the systems, and the cost of maintaining them became harder to justify to post offices that, with the advent of instant communication via telephone, no longer had a market in carrying messages with the utmost speed.

Still, a few systems clung to life. Amazingly, the Royal Mail still uses a few of its air-driven lines in London. A vogue for message-bearing "pneus" developed in Paris and remnants of the Prague pneumatic mail system remain in use to this day. One of the few stateside survivors is the tube system in the New York Public Library; it is used to convey book requests from Room 315 to workers in the vast catacombs below.

Pneumatic passenger trains, though, have vanished entirely. The Whitehall & Waterloo passenger line, the offspring of the enthusiastic reception given to the Crystal Palace exhibition, actually did break ground and begin tunneling beneath London. But the venture was swamped by an economic slump in 1866, and the half-finished tunnel was never demolished or filled in. It now sits eternally entombed somewhere beneath the sidewalks of Whitehall.

But occasionally the notion of pneumatic passenger lines is disinterred. Even as pneumatics went out of favor, in 1877 the journal *Nature* carried a hopeful notice for the formation of a company to build a pneumatic railway between South Kensington Station and the Royal Albert Hall. In the 1940s the Nobel physicist Irving Langmuir floated the idea of a 5,000-mph rocket-assisted pneumatic railway running from Manhattan to San Francisco, and in 1965, *Scientific American* returned to its roots by running a plan for a 300-mph intercity atmospheric network. But, like every other pneumatic proposal, these railways in the air had the same terminus: nowhere.

THE BEACH PNEUMATIC Transit Company staggered on for years. The Broadway tunnel was hired out for a while as a shooting range and then a wine cellar, and then simply sealed up. Beach's interest waned with the defeat of pneumatics, and the company went on to abandon air pumps for steam and electric engineering schemes that might actually see some return on their huge venture-capital expenditures. The company became the Broadway Underground Railway Company in 1874, and then the New York Arcade Railway Company in 1885. Each name change reflected a vast new engineering scheme, and hence a new round of lobbying and debilitating lawsuits from rivals in the railway business.

Alfred Beach died in 1896, and the next year his old company gave up any pretension to winning contracts to build passenger service—it would now be the New York Parcel Dispatch Company. It struggled feebly for the next decade to secure any sizable business, and failed utterly.

In 1912, long after the contests of Boss Tweed's days were forgotten and the Beach line but a distant memory, the city of New York announced plans to build a new subway station at City Hall. From out of the void, a letter arrived at the subway commission's office:

New York City, February 19, 1912
Notice is hereby given that the tunnel under Broadway from Warren Street southward about two hundred and ninety-four (294) feet in the Borough of Manhattan, City, County, and State of New York, is the property of the New York Parcel Dispatch Company, that anyone molesting or interfering therewith will be proceeded against as a trespasser and that the rights of the owner will be enforced in the courts.

New York Parcel Dispatch Company
EUGENE W. AUSTIN, PRESIDENT

But nobody knew or cared about Beach anymore. And so with the shattering of brick and the splintering of wood, one day the subway sandhogs came crashing and stumbling through the darkness and into a pitch-black recess.

It was Beach's old tunnel.

Lights were brought in, and the awed workers looked around. The tunnel had been sealed for forty years now, and yet all was ready for another run. Workers shining their electric lights into the sumptuous parlor found that it lay untouched and entombed in a layer of dust, its soft divans still awaiting the impress of the next visitor's body. Nor had the tunnel leaked or caved in, for the air inside it was warm and dry. At the far end of the tunnel was Beach's wondrous excavating shield, still waiting its next push, ready to go all the way across the city and under the East River. Its wooden frame disintegrated to the touch.

And farther back, inside the tunnel, a vehicle awaited its next run. The pneumatic train, decomposed with dry rot, was still sitting on the tracks, waiting for a rush hour that would never come.

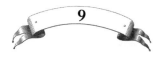

9

HE BEING DEAD YET SPEAKETH NOT

Predicting literary reputations is a tricky business. When I was a student at the College of William and Mary, a conservative student newspaper ran a dismissive article headed:

MAYA ANGE*WHO*?

Visiting Poet Hardly a Household Name

About a year later, Angelou intoned her poem "On the Pulse of Morning" at President Clinton's inauguration. The poem became a best-selling book, and she became . . . well, a household name.

THERE IS A problem with being a household name, though, and that is that sometimes the household disappears. When we peruse modern editions of old literature, we are not reading literature as people of that time experienced it. We are only reading it as *we* experience it. To understand the literature of an era as it was known by its own inhabitants, you need to leaf through the actual physical objects of the era, the crumbling acid-rich paper of old books and periodicals.

Read the contents pages of these literary magazines, annuals, or book catalogs. It is a bewildering experience. You might not see any names you recognize; the authors that today we consider the geniuses of an age may have been unknown in their own time, while others who were then considered the pillars of an era have toppled into the dust. History has not changed, but what we wish to remember from it has.

So were you to think on one of the best-selling poets of the nineteenth century—a man who sold upwards of 1.5 million copies, and was proclaimed by Britain's *Spectator* as having "won for himself the vacant throne waiting for him amidst the immortals . . . adopted by the suffrage of mankind and the final decree of publishers into the same rank with Wordsworth, Tennyson, and Browning"—you might think of Coleridge, Keats, or perhaps Longfellow. They have all passed into worthiness, to be engraved into library cornices and published in cheap student editions. Yet the poet we seek was not any of these men. He is not anybody at all, as far as most readers are concerned, for his works have been out of print for over a century now. It would have been hard for him or anyone else to believe this, for he once seemed unassailable in his position as the most beloved poet in Britain.

MARTIN FARQUHAR TUPPER was not meant to be a poet. Born in 1810, the son of a successful London physician, he was groomed from an early age for a respectable career as a clergyman or a barrister. First he was sent to the petty tyrannies of boarding school at Charterhouse—"Slaughterhouse," his disgusted classmate Thackeray preferred to call it—where he was exposed to both the classics and the sight of a sadistic schoolmaster "smashing a child's head between two books in his shoulder-of-mutton hands till his nose bled." From Charterhouse he was packed off to Christ Church College at Oxford, where he could enjoy much the same view over the quadrangle as George Psalmanazar once had over a century before.

Tupper immersed himself in his studies, spending his spare time pondering theology and poetry, and taking earnest stands like refusing to eat any sugar "by way of somehow discouraging the slave-trade." He was an unusually industrious and sober student, so much so that the young Duke of Hamilton delighted in torturing his pious Christ Church classmate by always using Tupper's name when he signed in late after carousing. But then Tupper was always surrounded by classmates who, though more cavalier in their studies, seemed marked out for greater destinies. In his course on Aristotle his classmates were three future bishops, three future governors general of India and Canada, a future chancellor of the exchequer, and future Prime Minister William Gladstone. One simple problem held Tupper back from dreaming of a fate as lofty as theirs.

He could not utter an intelligible sentence.

TUPPER, GROOMED FOR professions that required a mastery of rhetorical skills, faced this cruel irony: he could scarcely speak. Stuttering had plagued him from an early age, and it had been immeasurably worsened by the beatings he received at Charterhouse. Tupper pursued his training for the clergy in the forlorn hope that perhaps someday, somehow, the stutter would go away.

But what Tupper could not speak aloud he could express fluently upon the written page. He had already edged out his friend Gladstone for a college prize for writing, and ever since his days at Charterhouse he had filled composition books with his own verses. As early as 1828 he had tried longer efforts, such as versed proverbs on marriage for the benefit of his cousin Isabelle. "A letter was too light, and a formal Essay too heavy," he later explained, "so I thought I would convey my sentiments in the manner of Solomon's proverbs." His young mind plumbed the topics of wifely duties, children, and, of course, Love:

> *Hath a seducer known it? Can an adulterer perceive it?*
> *Or he that seeketh strange women, can he feel its purity?*
> *Or he that changeth often, can he know its truth?*

He mailed the verses off to his cousin and then forgot about them.

In 1832, at the age of twenty-two, he published his first collection of poetry, *Sacra Poesis*. It received little notice, but it still encouraged Tupper to continue writing. That same year, his final term at Oxford, he realized that his stuttering had become hopeless. He could not take a First degree, for it required an oral exam that he was incapable of taking. His fondest hope, of becoming a man of the cloth, drifted further and further away; who would want a preacher who could not preach?

Disappointed, Tupper graduated and moved into his own lodgings, where he pondered what to do with the rest of his life. As determinedly idealistic as ever, he took up vegetarianism, and bought an enormous wheel of Cheshire cheese to live off of. He spent two months eating through part of the wheel until, weakened by this attempt at virtuous living, he gave up and gratefully tore into a mutton chop. Then, like any unemployed college student with an empty larder, he did the sensible thing: he moved back in with his parents.

The young man's first priority was to cure his stammer, and so his physician father brought in an array of the best specialists to "help" his son:

> In a purposely monotonous note and syllable by syllable, with a crutch under my tongue, I have read all through in a loud voice Milton's whole *Paradise Lost* and *Regained*, and the most of Cowper's *Poems*! That was the sort of tongue-drill and nerve-quieting recommended and enforced for many hours a day. . . . [I was prescribed] emulcents, and then styptics, and was fortunately prevented by my father from some surgical experiments on the muscles of the lip and tongue!

His father, despairing of a cure, sought out a legal job that would allow his son to work silently, and Tupper went to work at twenty-one in Lincoln's Inn, copying deeds and conveyances and studying for the bar exam. He passed the exam on his first try and, assured of a respectable profession, got married the very next day to his cousin Isabelle. His near-total lack of clients hardly seemed to matter, since his wealthy father was happy to support him and Isabelle. But sitting in his empty law office, Martin could scarcely help wondering whether the moral purpose of his life had somehow been lost.

He would soon have his answer. Martin Tupper's true calling had been lying in plain sight all along, in the advice poems he had written for Isabelle years before they had married. They were worthy of an entire book, he now realized. One day in August 1837 as Tupper was leaving the house of an acquaintance on Hampstead Road, the opening lines of his book unfurled in his mind; as the street traffic and pedestrians passed him on the corner, Tupper scrawled on the back of an envelope. Back at his offices, the lines grew, and ten weeks later, he was ascending the dingy staircase of the London publisher Joseph Rickerby, manuscript in hand. It was titled *Proverbial Philosophy*.

IT IS AN extraordinary document. Tupper, without seeming to realize it, had kicked down the fence between poetry and prose. He did not actually call *Proverbial Philosophy* poetry—indeed, he claimed to be surprised when one reviewer described it as such—and yet the lines clearly were not your usual essay ramblings. They were too rhythmic, too parallel in their cadences. But Tupper's invention was as old as the hills. His lines were modeled on the King James Bible, which in turn had been crafted to reflect the content and the form of the Hebrew and Aramaic scrolls that formed the Bible's source documents. These had been meant to be sung, invoked rhythmically.

And so in Tupper we find lines such as these in "Of Hidden Uses," a prescient paean to the ecosystem:

Of the stored and uncounted riches lying hid in all creatures of God:
There be flowers making glad the desert, and roots fattening the soil,
And jewels in the secret deep, scattered amongst groves of coral,
And comforts to crown all wishes, and aids unto every need,
Influences yet unthought, and virtues, and many inventions,
And uses above and around, which man hath not yet regarded. . . .

Not too long to charm away disease hath the crocus yielded up its bulb,
Not the willow lent its bark, not the nightshade its vanquished
* poison . . .*
Even so, there be virtues yet unknown in the wasted foliage of the
* elm,*
In the sun-dried harebell of the downs, and the hyacinth drinking in
* the meadow,*
In the sycamore's winged fruit, and the facet-cut cones of the cedar;

And the pansy and bright geranium live not alone for beauty,
Nor the waxen flower of the arbute, though it dieth in a day,
Nor the sculptured crest of the fir, unseen but by the stars;
And the meanest weed of the garden serveth unto many uses. . . .

Search out the wisdom of nature, there is depth in all her doings;
She seemeth prodigal of power, yet her rules are the maxims of
*   frugality:*
The plant refresheth the air, and the earth filtereth the water,
And dews are sucked into a cloud, dropping fatness on the world:
She hath, on a mighty scale, a general use for all things;
Yet hath she specially for each microscopic purpose:
There is use in the prisoned air, that swelleth the pod of the laburnum;
Design in the venomed thorns, that sentinel the leaves of the nettle;
A final cause for the aromatic gum, that congealeth like moss around
*   a rose;*
A reason for each blade of grass, that reareth its small spire.
How knoweth discontented man what a train of ills might follow,
If the lowest menial of nature knew not her secret office? . . .

Man doeth one thing at once, nor can he think two thoughts together;
But God compasseth all things, mantling the globe like air:
And we render homage to his wisdom, seeing use in all his creatures,
For, perchance, the universe would die, were not all things as they are.

Such work earned Tupper respectful if somewhat puzzled notices in British newspapers and magazines—the *Spectator* called *Proverbial Philosophy* "a quaint and thoughtful volume," while the *Atlas* lauded it as "one of the most original and curious productions of our time." The January 1838 debut of the book was a modest enough financial success that Tupper was inspired to write a second edition later that year. But Tupper's appeal seemed limited; a third edition was so unsuccessful that the publisher shoveled off the unsold stock onto American booksellers. Americans scarcely knew what to make of it at all; one of the few stateside reviewers to read *Proverbial Philosophy*, the powerful editor N. P. Willis, was so perplexed by the form of the book that he guessed it to have been written some time before . . . in the seventeenth century.

Over the next several years, Tupper dallied with a few volumes of more conventional poetry, as well as essays on scientific inventions and morality. It took time for *Proverbial Philosophy* to soak into the fabric of Victorian culture, and a second series of the book did not appear until 1842, when the London publisher Hatchard issued it. But for those around Tupper who read the manuscript, there was no question: this volume was his life's work. The author's father, no longer young, read the new poem "Of Immortality" with his own fate much in mind:

> *I live, move, am conscious: what shall bar my being?*
> *Where is the rude hand, to rend this tissue of existence?*
> *Not thine, shadowy Death, what art thou but a phantom?*
> *Not thine, foul Corruption, what art thou but a fear?*
> *For death is but merely absent life, as darkness absent light;*
> *Not even a suspension, for the life hath sailed away, steering gladly*
>   *somewhere.*
> *And corruption, closely noted, is but a dissolving of the parts,*
> *The parts remain, and nothing lost, to build a better whole.*

His father was, Martin later recalled, "seriously affected" by the lines, and pressed £2,000 upon his son, enough for him to continue writing for some time without fear of poverty. But success was just around the corner for the younger Tupper. The elderly Hatchard family patriarch, wise after many decades in the publishing business, may have been the only one to see it coming. Meeting his young author for the first time, Grandfather Hatchard placed his hand upon Tupper's dark hair. He had tears in his eyes.

"You will thank God for this book when your hair comes to be as white as mine."

THE 1840S WROUGHT an astonishing transformation. *Proverbial Philosophy* went through nine editions in that decade alone; the following decade saw twenty-eight more editions—and this did not include the innumerable pirated editions. Tupper, the man whose speech infirmities seemed to render him Least Likely to Succeed of his Oxford class, saw himself turned into a de facto poet laureate of Victorian Britain. For an era of moralizing—as every era is, in its own narrow and hopeless way—Tupper's truisms were a comforting balm. He was not a mad, bad, and dangerous-to-know Romantic poet; he could be safely pressed into the hands of any young person or spouse in need of Lessons in Life. During the 1840s and 1850s, *Proverbial Philosophy* appeared in a bewildering variety of guises—cheap reading editions, gilt gift books, even lavish presentation editions meant to be given to young couples on their wedding day. Copies were given on the birth of children, on anniversaries, on any occasion of importance at all.

Ramble through the Highgate cemetery and you soon come face to face with Tupper—or rather, less disconcertingly, with his words. The man whose thoughts served to mark so many births and marriages also became the poet of eternity, whose words on immortality and divine intention were chiseled into headstones and burial vaults.

It was no small help that Tupper was the Queen's favorite poet. Things had not started so auspiciously; when Tupper was preparing the second edition of his book, he had asked if he might dedicate it to the Queen. His request was graciously denied by the Court with a letter explaining that "the Queen cannot permit a *Second Edition* of any work to be dedicated to her Majesty." Still, Tupper's book made its way into the royal quarters, and Victoria and Albert often read it to their children. And as the Queen did, so did her subjects.

Even the country's official poet laureate, Wordsworth, had a copy of Tupper's work; in his declining years he might have wondered whether this young man was to be his successor. And after Wordsworth's death in 1850, Tupper very nearly was the next poet laureate—but, in the end, Alfred Tennyson just barely edged him out. This hardly affected Tupper's stature. In one typical clothing store ad of the day, a lineup of the latest fashions is pictured on a pantheon of the greatest living authors: Browning, Hawthorne, Tennyson, Longfellow . . . and Martin Tupper.

Inspired by the Crystal Palace exhibition hall being erected near his home, Tupper made the grandest of poetic gestures in his contribution for the Great Exhibition of 1851: "The Hymn of All Nations." This was a simple hymn, but Tupper had contracted scholars to translate it into thirty languages, including everything from Latin to Arabic to Ojibway:

Moonedoo ke ween e gook
Noos ke de nah goo me goo . . .

As the public's regard for Tupper expanded, so did the author's ambitions. Tupper poured out a steady stream of patriotic songs, including a Liberian national anthem, moral fables like "The Crock of Gold," essays on subjects ranging from human-powered flight to opium abuse, translations of old English poetry—and, of course, sheaves of his own poetry.

YOU ARE A success in the eyes of the world when everyone wants to steal from you—and by that measure, Martin Tupper was the most successful man of his generation. Pirate editions of *Proverbial Philosophy* sprang up like mushrooms, particularly in America, where the weak laws of copyright made English authors irresistible to publishers. Although the British publications brought Tupper a steady if not magnificent income every year, the only money Tupper ever received from America was $400 from the one Philadelphia publisher who was his official publisher. But scores of knockoff editions were printed in every city; Tupper was amused and a little chagrined to constantly receive in the mail from some admirer yet another unauthorized edition of his own work, and he added each of them to the groaning shelf of Tupper editions in his library.

If Americans had at first been puzzled by Tupper, they now threw their arms around him. On New Year's Day in 1848, a *Literary World* writer marveled at the poet's ubiquity across the land:

The circulation which the works of Tupper have had in this country, is truly astonishing. A circulation, not confined to cities, towns, or villages, but embracing the entire population. The

> *Proverbial Philosophy* is found upon the centre-table of the metro-
> politan, in the scanty library of the student, and has gone hand-
> in-hand with the *Farmer's Almanac*, into the dwelling of the
> humblest tiller of the soil.

One of the poet's most ardent admirers was an eccentric Long Island
newspaper editor named Walt Whitman, who enthusiastically re-
viewed Tupper's books in the *Brooklyn Eagle*. Tupper's weighty orac-
ular pronouncements, the breadth of his far-ranging and hypnotic
catalogs of flora and fauna, and his free-flowing lines that defied the
conventions of poetry and prose alike—these all struck a chord deep
within Whitman, who later commented that were it not for *Proverbial
Philosophy*, his own *Leaves of Grass* would never have been written.

We can also thank Tupper for some of Whitman's worst poetry.
Whitman's masterpieces are mixed in with poems of dreadfully boor-
ish nationalism; and indeed Tupper could be both jangling and jin-
goistic when the occasion demanded it:

> *Stretch forth! stretch forth! from the south to the north!*
> *From the east to the west,—stretch forth! stretch forth!*
> *Strengthen thy stakes, and lengthen thy cords,—*
> *The world is a tent for the world's true lords!*
> *Break forth and spread over every place,*
> *The world is a world for the Saxon Race!*

As appalling as these lines sound to us now, they did capture the
spirit of an era; even without his nationalism, Tupper was still capable
of whipping up his reading public with such chest-thumpers as
"Cheer Up!" and "Never Give Up!"

Thanks to the dubious magic of copyright piracy, such works
achieved an even greater circulation in America than in Britain. It has
been estimated that in Tupper's lifetime about 250,000 copies of his
work were sold in the United Kingdom, while 1.5 *million* copies were
sold in the U.S. It became clear to Tupper that he would simply have
to visit America personally, and so in 1851 he arranged a tour of the
country. New York City's major newspapers, nervously anticipating

his arrival, kept readers updated of the expected arrival time of the Great Poet, and they primed readers by reprinting his work in the papers. In the meantime, Tupper, essentially traveling incognito and pacing about the decks on the voyage over, discovered a copy of *Proverbial Philosophy* in the ship's library; and after listening to fellow passengers murder its recitation, the poet revealed his identity.

His arrival in New York was a whirlwind of meetings with the great and the famous—dinner with the Astors, meetings with the mayor and the city's leading journalists, and personal introductions to nearly every major writer of the time. Amusingly, he did not care much for the one great Anglophile of the lot, James Fenimore Cooper, whom he found "a cold unpleasant mannered man, and in every way a great contrast to warmhearted Washington Irving."

Tupper was amused by the American obsession with the famous. Hit with constant requests for newspaper interviews (rare in Britain, except for political figures of actual importance), Tupper could open the morning papers in New York and find that "one's extorted opinions on all matter of topics—social, religious, and political—were published by tens of thousands in conflicting newspapers." Americans, too, had an odd fixation on autographs. These were a little more trying on his patience: "At a party my perhaps too exacting hostess put a large pack of blank cards into my hand, posted me to a corner table with pen and ink, and flatteringly requested an autograph for each of her 100 guests!"

Moving on to Philadelphia, home of his official publisher, he found his popularity even greater. Several times he encountered young women who, scissors in hand, were hoping to shear off one of his locks as a keepsake. He avoided any mishaps until, one particularly hot day, he wandered into a tiny barber's shop to get his hair cut. Passing by the next day, he found a MARTIN TUPPER sign in the window, surrounded by gold lockets for sale. Each contained hairs hurriedly swept up from the floor after the author had left.

Tupper took a particular interest in America's reform institutions, and he visited youth houses, schools for the deaf and the blind, and lunatic asylums. Upon his arrival, inmates would crowd around him— at an institute for the blind, he wrote his children, "they flocked about me like bees to touch me." On one such visit in Philadelphia, he discovered just how far his writing had penetrated into the soul of the hopeful and the hopeless alike: dropping in unannounced on the vast local lunatic asylum, he found his poem "Never Give Up!" posted on every single door. His name did not appear on the poem, though, and he asked the head doctor if he knew who the author was. The doctor didn't—he had simply clipped the anonymous verse one day from a newspaper.

—It is I, Tupper told him.

The doctor was amazed.

What happened next still astonished Tupper four decades later: "He asked if I would allow the patients to thank me; of course I complied, and soon was surrounded by kneeling and weeping and kissing folks, grateful at the good hope my verses had helped them to." In his old age, Tupper would pass over his meetings with mayors and tycoons fairly quickly in his reminiscences. But he remembered the insane asylum.

BACK HOME, TUPPER'S popularity continued unabated through the 1850s, and he settled into the life of an author patriarch, presiding over a brood of artistic children who would stage amateur theatricals in the living room and miniature concerts in the parlor. Three of his ten children had died, a not uncommon ratio for that era. But one tragedy hit Tupper especially hard: the death of a daughter afflicted with spinal ailments at the age of two and half. After her death, all he had of her was a marble statue of her sleeping, modeled in life and then sculpted after the child's death. In the midst of his great fame, there is something heartrending in the accounts of Tupper sitting alone with his little sculpture. And yet Tupper was, in many ways, an utterly optimistic soul. He would show the statue to visitors not out of morbidity, but to marvel at the beauty of the child that had once been his to love. He was a man of truly unaffected emotional simplicity.

Had he cared for the world's opinion, he'd have found his simplicity vulnerable to scorn. Nathaniel Hawthorne, who was as reserved as Tupper was gregarious, penned a detailed and yet offhandedly devastating account of his visit to Tupper's house in his journal on April 2, 1856:

> I felt in an instant that Mr. Tupper was a good soul, but a fussy little man, of a kind that always takes one entirely aback. He is a small man, with wonderfully short legs, fat (at least very round), and walks with a kind of waddle, not so much from corpulence of body as from brevity of leg. His hair is curly, and of an iron-gray hue; his features are good, even handsome, and his complexion very red. A person for whom I immediately felt a kindness, and instinctively knew to be a bore. . . .
>
> Tupper is really a good man, most domestic, most affectionate, most fussy; for it appeared as if he could hardly sit down, and even if he were sitting he still had the effect of bustling about. He has no dignity of character, no conception of what it is, nor perception of his deficiency. . . . He is the vainest little man of all little men, and his vanity continually effervesces out of him as naturally as ginger-beer froths. Yet it is the least incommodious vanity I ever witnessed; he does not insist upon your expressing admiration; he does not even seem to wish it, nor hardly to know or care whether you admire him or not. He is so entirely satisfied with himself that he takes the admiration of all the world for granted,—the recognition of his supreme merit being inevitable. I liked him, and laughed in my sleeve at him, and was utterly weary of him; for, certainly, he is the ass of asses . . . if it were not irreverent, I should say that his Creator, when He made Tupper, intended to show how easily He could turn a gifted, upright, warm hearted, and in many ways respectable person into a fool and laughing-stock even for persons much inferior to himself.

Years later, when Julian Hawthorne published his late father's journals, Tupper was deeply hurt by this account of what he had innocently imagined to be a pleasant visit. And yet Hawthorne, in his final lines at least, was absolutely correct in his judgment.

WHEN YOU OPEN a window upon your soul, idiots are prone to come along and throw rocks at it. And so Martin Tupper, whose very simplicity and sincerity in verse made him beloved by one generation, was soon to find himself the target for the next. It is hard to know exactly when the transformation from Great Poet to crashingly boring fogy occurred in the mind of the public. In Tupper's earlier days, his very youth in conquering the States was held by Oliver Wendell Holmes in his *Autocrat of the Breakfast Table* as something of a liability:

> These United States furnish the greatest market for intellectual green fruit of all places in the world. . . . The demand for intellectual labor is so enormous and the market so far from nice, that young talent is apt to fare like unripe gooseberries,—get plucked to make a fool of. Think of a country which buys eighty thousand copies of the *Proverbial Philosophy*, while the author's admiring countrymen have been buying twelve thousand! How can one let his fruit hang in the sun until it gets fully ripe, when there are eighty thousand such hungry mouths ready to swallow it and proclaim its praises?

But by the 1860s, with the author entering his fifties, there were plenty of countrymen ready to pick up Tupper's now-overripe fruit and fling it right back at him. The children who had once received gift book editions of Tupper for their birthdays were heartily sick of the man.

Tupper, unlike many poets, hadn't conveniently gone away. Rather than getting borne off in his glamorous youth by a bout of consumption, he had aged and stayed very much alive. He could always be counted on for a poem when any sort of national or local commemoration called for it, and was happy to dedicate a poem or two to a good cause or a benefit show. He was particularly keen on promoting kindness to animals, "for I believe in some future life for the lower animals as well as for their unworthier lord." Furthermore,

Tupper's visage was everywhere—even on soapboxes and tobacco ads, though Tupper detested advertising.

His very generosity and omnipresence worked against him. By the 1870s, each week began to bring fresh pummelings by clever young men in humor magazines like *Punch*, *Figaro*, and *The Comic*. One particularly nasty attack was penned by H. C. Pennell:

> *"Off! Off! thou art an ass, thou art an ass,*
> *Thou man of endless words and little sense,*
> *Of pigmy powers and conceit immense—*
> *Thou art a Donkey!—Take a bit of grass?"*
>
> *Oh Martin! Oh, my Tupper!* thus *exclaims*
> *A grov'ling Age, grown envious of thy fames,—*
> *Thou boundless sonnets; and Proverbial bays. . . .*
>
> Yet *will I breathe my pleasant Poems forth*
> *Innumerable. Hundreds more—ay tens*
> *Of thousands! Sweet ethereal rhymes,*
> *I hold ye here! and hug ye—all the lot;—*
> *A monstrous pile of quintessential ROT!!*

It is little wonder that Walter Hamilton, writing on Tupper in the 1889 volume *Parodies of the Works of English and American Authors*, was taken aback by how many writers went "to hunt most mercilessly to death his *Proverbial Philosophy*." Critics wishing to smear a new author would simply call him "a Tupper." Tennyson, who had also lived to an old age, was chagrined to find himself lumped together with Tupper by hostile critics. In fact, so many poets were tarred this way that a new insult, "Tupperian," entered the language. It can still be found in the eternal rest of dead verbiage, deep between the covers of the *Oxford English Dictionary*.

Even less aggressive attacks—like a parody of *Proverbial Philosophy*'s opening lines, altered to "BEER, hath entered my head / And peopled its inner chamber"—had the cumulative effect of a snowdrift slowly covering up the body of Tupper's work. But Tupper pressed still onward, forced by dire finances—for he lost most of his money in bad investments, an insurance swindle, and in bailing out his dissolute son Martin Jr.—and released two expanded editions of *Proverbial Philosophy* in the late 1860s. His old friend Gladstone, now Prime Minister, quietly diverted some government funds to his ailing classmate; and, showing that his sympathetic comments on Tupper's fame were no mere pose, Oliver Wendell Holmes also pledged a few guineas to him.

Sales of the new editions were modest but respectable. But even Tupper could now see that his publishing career was slipping into the past. A return tour of America in 1871 was met with enthusiasm in Philadelphia and Manhattan—Tupper noted with satisfaction that in New York auctions his autograph fetched $3.50, while Dickens's went for just fifty cents—but toward the end of his tour, he was facing half-empty houses. And when his old classmate Thackeray, also on tour, was asked by an American what they thought of Tupper back home, he replied crushingly:

"They do not think of Tupper."

TUPPER SPENT HIS old age in his usual tireless way. He dabbled in such inventions as improved horseshoes and glass screw tops for bottles, and contrived a curious proportional voting system; the proportions were of morality, with extra votes being doled out to voters who had met certain criteria of worthiness:

SURPLUS CLAIMS—ONE VOTE EACH
For the Victoria Cross
For the Albert Medal
For faithful domestic service in one family [for] twenty-five years
For field work on the same farm [for] thirty years
As a famous self-taught naturalist

And so forth. In-person voting bothered Tupper to no end. "It is a barbarism and an anachronism," he admonished, and imagined that thanks to the modern postal system, soon all voting would be done by mail.

His last few years were as a convalescent, attended to by his many children. The occasional letter still came from America asking for an autograph, and his devoted daughters always read to him from the paper each day. But they did not tell him of the family's declining finances, or that his writing no longer brought in any money at all. When he died in 1889, even the London *Times* was inclined to temper its criticism in its obituary: "That he enjoyed a strange and unique position in literature is beyond question. This is a tribute to the British heart rather than to its intellect."

AMAZINGLY, TUPPER'S WORKS have been out of print for over a century now. He had approached twenty-six publishers in 1875, hoping to publish a *Collected Works*; everyone turned him down. An illustrated 1881 edition of *Proverbial Philosophy* sold so poorly that his publishers, the Cassell brothers, took to taking swipes at each other in the columns of the *Times*. Since then, there has only been silence on the topic of Tupper.

It's an ironic fate for a man whose headstone reads, *He being dead yet speaketh*. Quite to the contrary: Tupper speaketh not. Even as we still read Tennyson and Browning, Tupper has vanished from anthologies and literary histories. Scholars in English literature pass through both an undergraduate and graduate education without ever hearing of the man. This may be because anthologies create a vast gulf between the value of those who are remembered and those who are not, and the effect feeds upon itself: can this writer be important, a reader may assume, if I have not heard of him before?

When the *Times Literary Supplement* published a brief retrospective on the man in 1938—one of the few articles written about him in the entire twentieth century—its writer could only conjecture, "Whenever a poet arises who can say what all of the people are saying, and say it all the time, we may see an explanation of the once world-wide popularity of the *Proverbial Philosophy*; and an explanation of its complete disappearance." And indeed Tupper's poetry did express the morality of his day. When his day passed, so did much of his writing.

It didn't help that Tupper was also capable of writing poems like "The Toothache":

A raging throbbing tooth,—it burns, it burns!
Darting its fiery fibres to the brain,
A stalk of fever on a root of pain,
A red hot coal, a dull sore cork by turns,
A poison, kindred to a viper's fang,
Galling and fretting: ha! it stings again!

And yet not all of Tupper's poetry is so ludicrous, nor all his moralizing so moth-eaten. Tupper still has his charms for the patient reader. But scholars and readers are not always patient people; when they do not see an immediate use for an old writer, they do not file him away or look more closely at their own idea of "usefulness." They simply forget him.

It is a mark of Tupper's utter obscurity today that buying an original Tupper manuscript is cheaper than paying the photocopy fee for his work from a library. There is, in my household, a small space kept for one such autographed manuscript page. It would please Tupper no end to know that even now, he might still reach a growing child or two to impart his proverbial wisdom.

A babe in a house is a wellspring of pleasure,
    a messenger of peace and love;
A resting-place for innocence on earth; a link
        between angels and men:
Yet is it a talent of trust, a loan to be rendered
        back with interest;
A delight, but redolent of care; honeysweet,
        but lacking not the bitter.

Martin F. Tupper.

March 11. 1857.

Manuscript of a poem by Martin F. Tupper. (Author's collection)

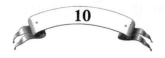

10

A DEDICATED AMATEUR OF FASHION

It is hard to achieve greatness, but harder still to have the passions of greatness without the talents to realize them.

For those lacking great skill, the London stage during the reign of George III was a cruel and unforgiving place, as William Henry Ireland was once unfortunate enough to discover. Yet just a few years after that teen prodigy's spectacular flameout, there appeared on the boards of Drury Lane another doomed soul—a man both so seemingly bereft of talent and so monumentally confident of his abilities that he created an entire thespian tradition all to himself. This one lone soul had, in his middle age, the courage not only to move to a foreign land and reinvent himself as an actor, but to pursue this acting career through a driving hail of ridicule and spite—sustained only by his utter and unrequited love for the theater.

LIKE ANY FASHIONABLE trend in 1809, the Amateur of Fashion made his first appearance not in London, but in the wealthy resort spa of Bath. He was hard to miss. The residents of the opulent York House hotel could scarcely fail to notice the dark-skinned and queerly attired man who started showing up at morning breakfast and afternoon tea. He was so deeply tanned that it was difficult to tell whether he had been entirely white to begin with; the exotic hue of his skin, in a room filled with ladies who had rendered themselves so fashionably pale with arsenic that their lips had turned blue, was only heightened by his attire: he was entirely covered in expensive furs and wielded a thick cane with a large diamond set into the top of it. At night, he would dress resplendently in a vaguely Hessian uniform and stud his entire outfit with diamonds: diamond buttons on his shirt, diamond buckles on his shoes, and the ever-present diamond cane. He was borne about town in a huge, gleaming carriage built in the shape of a scallop shell and emblazoned with the coat of arms of a crowing rooster. Written beneath the brazen fowl was this motto:

Whilst I Live I'll Crow

A pair of expensive matched white horses led the procession.

The nobles whispered among themselves in the breakfast room, trying to decipher the fellow, who all the while sat happily unaware in a corner of the room, scarfing down a hearty morning provision of muffins and eggs. Some thought that he might be an Eastern prince, a traveling rajah. Upon discreet inquiry, though, they discovered his name was Robert Coates. But nobody was quite sure who he was or where he had come from.

ROBERT COATES WAS determined to soak in the world of Fashion, for it had already been denied to him for far too long. He was born on a sugar plantation in Antigua in 1772, where his father, Alexander, possessed twenty thousand acres of land and vast wealth; one time when His Majesty's representatives sheepishly asked for a £5,000 loan to protect the island from an impending Spanish and French raid, Alexander Coates blithely sent them away with a pledge of £10,000.

For all his wealth, Alexander was helpless against the appalling mortality rate among children of that time. Parents back then might wait months before even naming their offspring, and with good reason—it was not wise to pin too many hopes on the survival of any one child, not in a land racked with malaria, dysentery, and yellow fever. And so it came to pass that all of Alexander's nine children died in infancy or early childhood . . . except for one. It would not have been untoward for Robert Coates to think that, surviving against such odds, destiny had mapped out a special fate for him.

Alexander Coates dutifully sent his one remaining son back to the Old World at the age of eight so that he would receive the classical education expected of any young gentleman of means. The effect of this change for little Robert was absolute and permanent. Although his father had accompanied him on the way over to London, there was nothing else familiar about the land before him. Robert had grown up among the sunny, fertile, and endlessly vast plantations of an island thousands of miles away. But he was now in the world's most densely populated city, mingling with boys who were classmates in both senses of the word—for beneath their childish fancies lurked the future aristocracy and governance of the country. He grew to love the sophistication and artistry of this new land, and was deeply unhappy to be recalled to Antigua upon the completion of his education.

After making the long and perilous voyage back home, Coates was asked by his father what he wished to do in life. Young Robert had a ready answer: he wished for a commission in a British regiment, so that he might serve alongside the Duke of York. Europe was engulfed in war at this time, though, and Alexander could not bear the thought of his only remaining child being mere cannon fodder, or even of his simple absence for yet another decade back in Britain. Instead, he sent him off on a shorter tour—just a few years, this time—of Britain and then the United States, so that his education might be complete.

Settling back down in Antigua by the turn of the century, Robert felt the provinciality of the place press upon him, and he eagerly grasped at any twig of culture or outside civilization that floated by. Among the island's thin fare of entertainments was a theatrical company composed of a few islanders, an orchestra drawn from soldiers from the island's British garrison, and any stray actors that happened to be passing through the colony. Coates joined this company and became an enthusiastic participant in its productions of Shakespeare. The audiences of islanders and soldiers liked their Shakespeare rare and bloody rather than well done, and the troupe excelled at putting on crudely staged, high-body-count tragedies like *King Lear*, *Macbeth*, and *Romeo and Juliet*.

Coates spent years devoted to such pursuits, giving extra zeal to learning the part of Romeo, while assiduously avoiding any hint of gainful employment. But he didn't really need any: he was his father's son, and there would be a job open for him when his father died. When his father's end finally did come, though, his son found that he had absolutely no inclination to oversee the family business. With a fortune now at his disposal—£40,000 a year, an astronomical sum back then—he decided to leave management of the plantation to an underling; after a suitable period of mourning for his father, he boarded a vessel bound for his true homeland: England.

ONE GUEST AT York House, Pryse Gordon, finally did gather up the audacity to acquaint himself with the strange inhabitant of the breakfast room:

> He shortly attracted my notice by rehearsing passages from Shakespeare during his morning meal . . . I could not help complimenting him on the beauty of his recitations, although he did *not always stick to his author's text*. On one occasion I took the liberty of correcting a passage from *Romeo and Juliet*. "Aye," said he, "that is the reading—I know, for I have the play by heart—but I think I have *improved* upon it."

This stranger, Gordon discovered, was so devoted to the character of Romeo that he kept a character costume packed with him on all his travels. Then why not, Gordon asked him, play the part of Romeo here in Bath?

"I am ready and willing to play Romeo to a Bath audience, if a manager will get up the play and give me a good Juliet," Coates said grandly. "My costume is superb and adorned with diamonds."

Gordon gave him the address of a local theater manager and offered himself as a reference. Coates hurriedly tucked in his breakfast, invigorated by the prospect of treading the boards once again, and set off in his grand coach. But when he reappeared an hour later, he was clearly outraged.

"That fellow," he huffed, "has treated me in a manner I am not accustomed to . . . I will show him I can play *Carte and Tarte!*"

Snapping up his diamond cane like a fencing sword, he thrust and cut it straight at the heavy wooden door into the dining room, driving

his point home with an earsplitting crack against the baize that sent
an old man jumping out his seat.

Perhaps a flash of the diamond scepter was all that was ever
needed, for soon afterward the Bath Theatre made an announcement to the public that the next week, on February 9, 1809, would
bring them

ROMEO, BY AN AMATEUR OF FASHION

The Bath Theatre was sold out that night; ladies of fashion and
rascals alike had packed the seats and boxes to peer at the lavish man
whose every detail seemed to be known to one and all—save for who
he was and where he'd got his money from.

When, late in the first scene, Coates swept upon the stage, there
was an eruption of applause and perhaps a gasp of consternation. He
was indeed, one witness recalled, wearing his very own Romeo costume, and moving in his own unique way:

> He came forward with a hideous grin, and made what he consid-
> ered a bow—which consisted of thrusting his head forward, and
> bobbing it up and down several times, his body remaining per-
> fectly upright and stiff, like a toy mandarin with a moveable head.
>
> His dress was outré in the extreme: whether Spanish, Italian, or
> English, no one could say; it was like nothing ever worn. In a cloak
> of sky-blue silk, profusely spangled, red pantaloons, a vest of white
> muslin, surmounted by an enormously thick cravat, and a wig à la
> Charles the Second, capped by an opera hat, he presented one of
> the most grotesque spectacles ever witnessed upon the stage.

For full effect, his hat was topped with ostrich feathers and a
liberal sprinkling of diamonds; still more diamonds were sewn into
his pantaloons and his shoe buckles, and gold spangles had then been
slathered onto the leather of these shoes. The whole glittering costume was so tight upon his body that his limbs bulbed out like sau-
sages, and he jerked across the stage in a tight-wrapped transport of

delight. Every word he pronounced was wrong—histrionically rising and falling, with the wrong emphasis, and apt to simply dispense with the Bard's script altogether. Coates would occasionally turn to the audience with a ghastly grin, glorying in the moment.

And then his pants burst.

It was something that only a few in the front row might have noticed at first, but Romeo's pants were so tight that the seat blew out. Audience members watched in disbelief at "the sudden extrusion through the red rent of a quantity of white linen sufficient to make a Bourbon flag, which was visible whenever he turned around." Ladies in the crowd were scandalized, and then, when it became clear that Coates had no idea what had befallen him, it became increasingly difficult to suppress the giggling.

And so the crowd watched in a sort of horrified fascination for all the first act, until finally some miscreants began to yell at him.

"Off! Off!"

Apple cores and orange peels, the favored weapons of theater ruffians, rained down from the balconies and onto the stage. A hissing filled the room.

Coates paused from his scene, still blissfully unaware of his bunnytail of undergarments, and glared witheringly at his critics Then, undaunted, he finished, and allowed the curtain to fall. He continued on, lurching through until he reached the climax of the play.

Juliet appeared dead, and so he, the grieving Romeo, was to pick her up and carry her in grief away from her tomb. Coates picked up the unfortunate actress like a sack of laundry and tossed her aside. Then, whipping out a handkerchief from his pocket, he carefully dusted the floor of the stage, and gently took off his massive sparkling hat and set it on a convenient pillow. Only now was he, Romeo, ready to die; but for reasons known only to Coates, he decided to address his entire dying soliloquy in a whisper to a single box by the stage.

Here's to my love! [He drinks the poison.] *Oh true apothecary,*
Thy drugs are quick! Thus with a kiss I die.

His speech may have been inaudible to the puzzled patrons of the theater, but Coates was not a man to let his hero die without a fight. He took minutes to die—gasping and grimacing over and over again as he lay writhing on the floor, groaning his way through every stage agony imaginable. The crowd began to shriek with laughter now, and one wag's voice rose above the din:

"Die again, Romeo!"

Coates, lying sprawled out on the stage, decided this was a splendid idea. And so he miraculously resurrected himself to a full standing position, took another swig of the prop vial of poison, and then proceeded to die *all over again*.

No sooner had Romeo completed his final death-shiver than another cry went up.

"Die *again*, Romeo!"

Delighted, Coates stood up again, and would have gone through it a third time, had not his costar, Juliet, so appalled that she rose up from her grave as well, stepped in to put a stop to it. The tumult in the audience became deafening. Arguments were arising on all sides, and the panicked manager let loose the stage weight so that the curtain came crashing down on the scene, never to rise again.

Patrons sat stunned, unable to decide whether what they had witnessed was comically tragic or perhaps just tragically comic. It was certainly unique.

The Bath Theatre exploded in applause.

ODD REPORTS OF Coates's appearances surfaced over the next couple years: a show in Brighton, and dazzling recitations to assemblages of noble friends at dinner parties. When Coates finally arrived in London and took up lodgings in the Strand, it could only be a matter of time before Drury Lane fell before his diamond cane.

Coates soon became as famous on the streets of London as he had been in Bath, jaunting about Pall Mall and Bond Street in his blue scallop-shell chariot, glittering from head to toe with diamonds. His passage was marked by the shouts of onlookers as he a passed by: "*Cock-a-doodle-doo!*"

Coates, as proud as ever with the cock logo on the side of his carriage, was very pleased by all this. Local papers gossiped and jested over the man they called "Romeo Coates" and "Diamond Coates," and he developed a crowd of hangers-on, many of whom would have been glad to have but a single diamond button pop off his shirt and into their pockets. Coates lent them money freely, rarely expecting to see it back. The more desperate their straits and the less likely that a loan would ever see any gain to Coates's social standing, the more generous he was. In the back-stabbing world of London social climbers, Coates was guileless.

When a poor widow came to him to ask for help, there was but one action he could take: a benefit play. But first he had to warm up, and that meant playing off-Soho: in Richmond, to be precise. He held a one-night stand at the Theatre Royal on the night of September 4, 1811, reprising his role of Romeo. His reputation much preceded him; ladies in the audience came prepared to defend their glamorous hero, and drunken young bucks arrived with pockets stuffed with fruit ripe for throwing.

Coates was ready for them. There was the usual fracas during Romeo's death scene, with supercilious young men sniggering ironically at Romeo's prolonged death throes. But Coates concluded his show by strolling to the center of the stage and reciting a poem to his audience:

BUCKS, HAVE AT YE ALL

Ye social friends of claret and of wit,
Where'er dispersed in social groups ye sit.
Damn me, I know you, and have at ye all . . .

If you with plaudits echo to renown,
Or urged with fury tear the benches down,
'Tis still the same, to one God ye prate,
To show your judgment and approve your taste.

'Tis not in nature for ye to be quiet.
No, damn me, Bucks exist in but a riot.

*For instance now—To please the ear and charm the adoring
    crowd,*
Your Bucks of the boxes sneer and talk aloud,
To the green-room next with joyous speed you run.

Hilly ho! ho! my Bucks! Well, damn it, what's the fun?
Though Shakespeare speaks, regardless of the play
Ye laugh and loll the sprightly hours away
For to seem sensible of real merit,
Oh! damn me, it's low, it's vulgar, beneath us lads of spirit!

You Bucks of the pit are miracles of learning,
Who point out faults to show their own discerning;
And critic like, bestriding martyred sense,
Proclaim their genius and vast consequence.

The actor wheeled and pointed straight into a theater box of his greatest tormentors:

Ye Bucks of the boxes there, who roar and reel,
Too drunk to listen and too proud to feel!

The theater leaped into an ovation. With this one speech Romeo Coates, the most outlandishly bad actor in existence, had shamed his detractors. For he had something that scarcely anyone else in the theater has had before or since: complete sincerity.

BY THE TIME Coates gave his benefit performance at the Haymarket Theatre, his fame had grown so that well before the six-thirty curtain call, more than a thousand Londoners were turned away at the door; the theater was already packed. Desperate ticket seekers pounded on the stage door and offered bribes of much as £5—an enormous sum for a ticket in those days—just to sneak in through the back door. They too were turned back.

Inside the theater, trouble was already brewing. The young men who had come to pillory Coates were hooting and hollering at Coates's friends as they filed in; the rest of the audience fidgeted as six-thirty came and went and as the clock ticked past seven. At long last, the curtain rose, and when eventually Coates strolled onstage, the Haymarket resounded with whistling, applause, and shouts of *Cock-a-doodle-doo!* Coates wore a grand mantle of pink and silver silk, jewels flashing throughout his person. His hat was once again topped with high plumes of white feathers, and his shoes sported large diamond buckles. The audience came to such an uproar over him that the curtain came down during the fourth act.

The next day, on December 10, London papers attacked the performance with a disdain that Coates could not ignore; cartoonists feasted upon his outrageous dress, and there was much sniggering about the dark-skinned and gay Romeo. His country of origin was a tempting target: darkened by years in the sun, Coates's skin was a little like that of a black man—and indeed, some whispered, maybe *was* that of black man.

His enemies had a point. Given the secret bloodlines of slaveholding islands like Antigua, the only real surprise might have been to find that Coates was *not* somewhat black. And as for the suspicious dandiness of his apparel, which was outlandish even for 1811, the following day a letter in Coates's hand arrived at the offices of the *Morning Herald*, the one paper that all of fashionable London was sure to read:

> In regard to the innumerable attacks that have been made upon my lineaments and person in the public prints, I have only to observe, that as I was fashioned by the Creator, independent of my will, I cannot be held responsible for that result, which I could not control.

Coates would neither confirm nor deny anything. But whatever he was, he would also never apologize for it—for like Quentin Crisp over a century later, he didn't know how he could be anything else.

COATES APPEARED IN only one more performance the following year, but by 1813 he was reinvigorated, and in the first four months of the year he headlined at least half a dozen shows. Some patrons arrived primed to heckle him, and others to shout on his ever-increasing flights of histrionics. So when an appearance by "the Celebrated Amateur of Fashion" was promised after a performance of *Othello*, curious audience members waited past the end of the play to see just exactly what was promised to them.

The curtain rose to reveal Coates sitting at a table set upon the stage, a decanter before him, drinking his wine contentedly. He looked up and smiled at his audience, and then strolled over to the edge of the stage, glass in hand, where he "drank to the health of his enemies, whom he desired might live to see him prosper." He then launched into a poetic recitation.

The strange sight before them—a single actor onstage drinking wine and inviting the audience down for a drink, as it were—was unlike any stage performance seen at the Haymarket before. Whatever was left of the fourth wall of drama was gone now, with Coates simply refusing to recognize it, and addressing the audience as if he were having a drink with each one of them personally.

The crowd roared its approval, and when he exited, it begged for him to return. Coates, however, had vanished.

THE PUBLIC HAD embraced Coates, but it was his dearest wish to be close to royalty. Despite his friendships with dukes and barons, including some he had known since his childhood, Robert had gone all these years in England without securing a meeting with the Prince of Wales. His hopefulness that such a meeting would take place was touching, even pathetic, and could hardly fail to be noticed by those around him.

That spring of 1813, an engraved invitation card arrived at 38 Craven Street, addressed to Coates. Upon opening it, he could scarcely contain himself: he was invited to a royal party the following night! The next day was a whirlwind of activity, as he spared no expense in fitting himself out for the royal bash. He bought new diamond buttons, a diamond brooch, and a diamond ring for the occasion; his personal tailor was set to work assembling a new outfit of the finest silk, and a bootmaker brought in to create a new diamond-buckled creation.

As Coates made his way to Carlton House that fateful night in his magnificent carriage, the Prince's entourage, courtiers, and officers had already made their way inside, through the vestibule and up the crimson-carpeted staircase, and into the grand salon where the Prince was holding court. A steady procession of military officers, court officials, posh dandies, and ruffled ladies arrived.

As the Prince amused himself by listening to a performance by the court musician, a member of his staff came forward bearing a card tray.

"What is it, Bloomfield?"

The Prince picked up the invitation card from the tray and peered at it through a gold eyeglass.

"A manifest forgery!" Eyebrows rose in the room. "Someone has taken an unpardonable liberty in concocting this."

Guests drifted forward to look at the spurious card.

"Do you know this person, Brummell?" asked the Prince of one court dandy as he passed the card to him.

Brummell gave a look of horror.

"*I* know him! Why, he makes sugar and sells coffee—in short, he is a sort of grocer. How could I know such a man?"

The card was passed to another court dandy.

"Do *you* know him, Alvaney?"

"Is it the black fellow who played *Romeo*?" Alvaney passed the card along. "Of course, I don't know him in the least."

"Is he a friend of yours, Sherry?"

"Not that I know of. But were it possible for the poor man to patronize me handsomely, I couldn't be so hard-hearted as to object to his presence."

The assembled crowd had a good laugh at Coates's generous ways, whereupon Sherry turned serious.

"The person is not presentable; that style of thing cannot be permitted here, positively."

The Prince, though perhaps a little sorry for the fellow waiting at his gate, had to agree.

"I do not like this affair at all."

He summoned Colonel Bloomfield.

"Go to this gentleman, and undeceive him in a way not to hurt his feelings—taking care to express the extreme regret of the Prince of Wales that such an accident should have occurred."

And so Bloomfield glided out to dispatch Romeo Coates, who, still waiting patiently to enter Carlton House, was imagining the grandeur that awaited him.

AT SEEMINGLY EVERY block on his way home, Coates's magnificent coach was halted by the wave and *Hallo!* of some fashionable man about town.

"My dear sir! Let me congratulate you on your well-deserved distinction! Of course you found His Royal Highness a most charming host?"

"Oh, there was some irregularity . . . I do not understand what. But the Prince sent a most kind message. I have no doubt that His Royal Highness will speedily set it right."

And as the Amateur of Fashion passed onward, each man sniggered. It seemed that everyone but Coates knew that he had been the victim of cruel hoax. Or rather, it *would* have been cruel had its intended victim ever come to realize what had happened. But Coates never seemed to entertain any such notion. He was not a man who imagined the worst of the people around him, though he might have been justified to do so with London's aristocracy. Instead, he truly believed that there had been some sort of misunderstanding, and that sooner or later his proper invitation to meet His Royal Highness would come.

Days and weeks passed without an invitation, and still he did not suspect.

HIS RIDICULE AND fame increased with each month. *At Home*, a spoof of Coates's acting, was already running nightly at the Covent Garden Theatre, and this travesty of a travesty actually inspired a thoughtful defense of Coates and his work by a most unlikely ally, the magazine *The European*. An essay in its March 1813 issue featured an engraving that gives us one of the few portraits of Coates that is not a comic caricature. It followed with this spirited defense of his work:

However we may esteem MR. COATES for the liberality with which he has, upon many trying occasions, come forward to succour the distressed, we are not yet such dupes to our *credulity* as to believe that he would, or could, have braved the horrors of a series of *theatric storms*, or smiled at the illiberal absurdities of a series of *theatric imitation*, had he not been strongly possessed with the *histrionic passion*; but as this, although, *unprofessionally*, perhaps, not a very *laudable* propension, is certainly, when applied as he applies it, very innocent; therefore, when exercised in the cause of humanity, it ought rather to have been *praised* than *censured*. . . .

We will venture to say, that Mr. Coates, as an actor, is infinitely more amusing than the generality of any of these critics. He is, in his way, quite as accomplished an artist; and infinitely more disinterested.

This hardly silenced audiences. They were now coming to the theater expecting, even demanding, to see *Romeo and Juliet* fall apart before their eyes. The motive was still so inchoate that nobody even had a word for it yet, but we certainly do today.

Robert Coates had, in utter innocence, invented Camp.

THOSE AROUND COATES did not bear the brunt of this new artistic experience with such panache. At the April 23 benefit performance, the beneficiary, Miss FitzHenry, had agreed to take on the part of Juliet; after the marriage scene she was almost reduced to tears by the crowd's booing and hissing, and she fearfully threw her arms around a stage pillar.

A few weeks later, during the May 10 performance, one wag in the audience smuggled in a rooster under his coat; just as the duel between Romeo and Tybalt was about to begin, the clucking and flapping fowl was tossed up on the stage, where he strutted around the scenery amid shouts of *Cock-a-doodle-doo!* Coates at long last lost his patience—he turned to the patrons of one offending box and shook his sword at them, a clear provocation to a duel. They bawled out angry demands for an apology, which he would not give. Orange peels proceeded to rain down upon him and the other actors. Then the hecklers dispensed with the courtesy of peeling altogether; after the death scene of Paris, one patron whipped an entire orange across the theater and belted the slain Paris on the nose, whereupon the "dead" man stood up, angrily pointed at the offending fruit, and stormed offstage. When Romeo's turn to die onstage came, his famous histrionics kept getting preempted by yelling from the boxes:

"Why don't you *die?*"

Such words simply rolled off Coates. But later that year, his sincerity was thrown into question. This was the one thing he could not bear to hear, and it hurt him so badly that he never entirely recovered. An army widow had beseeched Coates for help, and so he helpfully planned out a benefit show for her on December 1. He was to play the role of Belcour in the play *The West Indian.* After the last few shows, Coates had wisely inserted this statement into the evening's playbill:

A Reward of £5 will be paid by the gentleman who plays "Belcour" on conviction of *each* offender throwing anything on the stage to annoy the performers.

But as the show began that night, a young man stood up in the audience and demanded to be heard. There was a serious accusation to be lodged against Robert Coates, he said gravely: "Ladies and gentlemen, the charge against Mr. Coates is that he does not act upon a principle of philanthropy, but directly or indirectly gives his services for remuneration."

The crowd erupted in a tumult, with shouts for proof. The young man described how the young woman benefiting from that night's show had fallen into dire straits. "Having heard of Mr. Coates's generosity in these matters," he continued, "she applied to him, through the medium of Mrs. Lyall, that gentleman's landlady. . . . Aid was persistently refused, until the benficiary agreed to give Mrs. Lyall *forty pounds* for the amateur's services."

He then produced a copy of the receipt. The crowd was outraged and broke into an uproar. Coates, for once in his life, was struck dumb with horror at their jeers.

IT IS HARD to know what might have appalled Coates more—the idea
that he was acting from less than sincere motives, or the imputation
that a man of his enormous wealth would be extorting such trifling
amounts from people. But after the show he threw himself and his
money into an investigation of the matter, and found to his disgust
that it was all true. His landlady at his Craven Street lodgings, Mrs.
Lyall, was collecting payment from the straitened widows and or-
phans that he had been performing for, all the while claiming that
she was doing it under Coates's orders. Coates marched Mrs. Lyall
over to the offices of the mayor of London and had her issue a full
written confession, witnessed and notarized by the mayor himself. He
had the confession set into type, and then printed and distributed
widely, but it was too late; the damage had already been done to his
reputation among Londoners.

Yet theater managers and needy widows in other cities were still
beseeching him for help, and so in 1814 he began playing outer cities
like Birmingham—these crowds were delightfully unironic, simply
enjoying the spectacle of Coates repeating the death throes of Lo-
thario and Romeo. But his high point was in Stratford-on-Avon that
December, playing his beloved Shakespeare in the Bard's own home-
town. One patron of the barnlike Stratford theater, Charles Matthews, watched on in bemusement:

> That darling Fancy's child of Nature—Coates—acted here, and
> was advertised in the character of Romeo.
>   After he had acted, he was determined to have a procession all
> by himself, a minor pageant . . . and walked, dressed as Romeo,
> from the barn to the butcher's shop where Shakespeare was born.
> Here he wrote his name on the walls and in the book kept for
> that purpose, called himself the illustrator of the poet, complained
> of the house, said it was not half good enough for the divine bard
> to have been born in, and proposed to pull it down at his own
> expense and build it up again, so as to appear more worthy of such
> a being!

But few of Coates's grand plans came to pass anymore; his plantations on Antigua suffered reversals, and he slowly found himself with less and less income to flaunt. Over the next couple of years his star faded from the British stage; his fans moved away from him and on to the next bright and shining object. Coates, still devoted to his Bard, was left alone again.

Without his public, and entering his fifties, Coates sought companionship. He found it in Miss Emma Robinson, and married her in 1823. The two became devoted helpmates and produced a son and a daughter. But Coates, who alone had escaped childhood death from among his many siblings, was not so lucky with his own children—neither lived to see adulthood.

Humbled by his shrinking fortune and domesticated by marriage, Coates decamped from London to Boulogne-sur-Mer, where tapped-out English nobility and misspent capitalists retired to ponder their financial exile. Sometimes, when a visitor recalled the old days in London, the Amateur of Fashion could be coaxed into giving one of his famous recitations. But no matter how many times he was asked, he refused to take to the stage again.

DECADES PASSED, AND memories of the strange actor faded into oblivion. But one day in 1843, a member of a London gentlemen's club happened to be looking out the window when he spied a strikingly odd figure making his way up St. James's Street. It was an elderly man, dressed in Hessian boots and clothes that were thirty years out of date.

Then it dawned upon the watcher.

"It's Romeo Coates!" he shouted.

Club members rushed to the windows. The old man had continued walking past the club, but the distant memory of the shouted phrase arrested his step. He turned around and returned to the club's window, where he politely doffed his hat.

"My name, gentlemen, is *Robert* Coates."

He then walked onward with perfect elderly gravity, and disappeared into the crowd.

Coates and his wife had moved back after decades away, and taken up lodgings at 13 Portman Street. Coates could be seen in his haunts once again now, though an observer of this seventy-one-year-old man could scarcely have thought him capable of the famed histrionics of his youth.

Visiting old friends in the city, he was sometimes goaded into performing, particularly for younger men and women who had not seen him thirty years before. Watching Coates, they were mystified: why had he been so reviled by critics? During the long decades of Coates's absence, the theater had embraced melodrama; what was once histrionics was now artistic passion. Coates, it seemed, hadn't been born to the wrong style of acting at all. He had simply been born to the wrong era.

RETURNING TO LONDON meant that Coates could indulge in his one great passion again, which was going to the London theaters. And so he died as he lived: by the theater. On the night of February 15, 1848, after attending a show at Covent Garden Theatre, Coates was departing in his carriage when he remembered that he had left his opera glasses on his seat in the theater. He clambered down from the carriage and out onto crowded Russell Street, and into the path of another speeding carriage. He was knocked down; the wheel went over his head.

The carriage sped away, and its driver was never found. A crowd gathered around the bleeding and broken old man. The theater was steps away, just out of his reach.

11

A. J. PLEASONTON'S BLUE LIGHT SPECIAL

Just off the corner of 19th Avenue and Lincoln is a typical San Francisco house, a white Victorian set back slightly from the avenue. It is easy to miss, wedged as it is between a Chevron station at one end of the block and a Shell station at the other, a house on what is not really a residential block at all; this part of 19th Avenue is, technically, a stretch of US 1, and there is a continual hiss of traffic pouring out of a hole punched into Golden Gate Park.

This house has nothing to distinguish it from innumerable others in the city save for one modification: a front porch that has been glassed in to form a sort of sunroom that one must pass through to enter the house proper. Though there's nothing too strange here—walk around an old college campus back East, like Mount Holyoke's, and you'll find these quaint old sunrooms fading genteelly off at the edge of the old dorms.

But now look *up*. The top panes of this sunroom are not consistent. They alternate between clear glass and ancient panes of velvety cobalt blue. It's not much of a design statement, frankly, and yet as the sun slants in through the westward panes in the late afternoon, it does cast the whole sunroom in a rather pretty blue glow.

During the day, when the world is at work, there is little sign of life in the house; it is hard to know anything about its present inhabitants from the outside. But one thing can be known for certain: in the late 1870s, sitting in that sunroom and watching the horse-drawn traffic on the old avenue, someone sat waiting for a cure to what may have been a grave illness. And, perhaps, they waited in that very sunroom until they died.

THE SECOND HALF of the nineteenth century was a miraculous time for medicine; our era merely gilds its lily. Some of the most basic notions of modern medicine were being formed during this time, and mortality rates went into a free fall as a result. Ether eliminated the agonizing pain of surgery. Forceps lowered death rates in childbirth. Hospitals, where cures had often been more fatal than the ailment, changed dramatically: the theory of sepsis meant that doctors and nurses began to clean their hands and their instruments between operations. French medical professors Xavier Bichat and Charles Louis introduced an empirical approach to examining the effectiveness of medical treatments, and a roaring trade in medical cadavers gave a rising new generation of medical students an actual understanding of the functions of internal organs.

But where there is hope, there is also false hope. The triumphant march of medical progress left the public believing that nearly anything was possible, and quacks and charlatans sensed an opportunity. Thanks to the rise of a national parcel post, and the ad pages crammed into the backs of the women's and sporting magazines now distributed across the country, you no longer had to work from town to town as a medicine show, always worrying about getting tarred and feathered and run out on a rail; now you could operate anonymously from the huge new urban centers, placing ads and fleecing suckers with impunity from thousands of miles away.

Useless pills and ointments proliferated, often with thinly veiled promises to desperate consumers. A young woman who had—well—made a mistake could find in the back of women's magazines ads for Chichester's Pennyroyal Pills. Pennyroyal is an abortifacient, though there is no mention in the ad of that—no mention, in fact, of what these pills were for at all. But every woman knew what pennyroyal meant.

There was just one problem: there was no pennyroyal in the pills. And so, inevitably, as the pregnancy came to term—assuming the woman hadn't perished in the meantime from a botched illegal abortion—she could buy herself a bottle of Mother's Friend, which, as the Bradfield Regulator Company of Atlanta promised, "shortens the duration of labor" and "will assist in the safe and quick delivery." The actual ingredients of this secret elixir? Oil and a little soap.

Not only did false nostrums thrive, but so did entire fake medical practices, for diploma mills and shoddy medical schools had sprouted up around the country. One of the most notorious and most durable was the American Health College, run for decades from a building in downtown Cincinnati by an old-fashioned quack named John Bunyan Campbell. After years of granting worthless diplomas, the picturesque old rogue was finally hauled before a judge. The prosecutor's cross-examination of Campbell is ludicrously evasive. ("You have no histological laboratory?" "No, not exactly.") Further examination revealed one by one that every member of the school's faculty was retired or on leave—that, in fact, Campbell was the *only* faculty member—and that his "vitapathic" treatment largely consisted of applying copper plates to the feet of patients so as to *draw the poison out of them.*

The cross-examination of Campbell culminated in this masterful display of circular logic about the origins of disease:

Question.—Within the last few years of your practice of vitapathy, what class of cases have you treated?

Answer.—Well, mostly pulling out poisons on our copper plate. We ain't curing disease at all; the person may not have any disease. He is simply full of poison, don't you see?

Question.—What do you consider poisons, doctor?

Answer.—Well, calomel is poison; strychnine is poison; iron is poison.

Question.—Would you consider disease germs poison in the same case?

Answer.—Well, I have a different idea of germs from most everybody else.

Question.—How would you destroy disease germs in the patient?

Answer.—My idea is the germ is not the cause of the disease at all, but the disease is the cause of the germs. You will never get any germs in anybody until there is a separation or decomposition there, something. Put that down, you old doctors, as a fact, that germs don't make disease!

Question.—What would cause the disease, doctor?

Answer.—They didn't have the disease; they simply had the poison, and I pulled it out.

Question.—You say the disease was the cause of the germ?

Answer.—Yes, sir.

Question.—What causes the disease?

Answer.—Well, persons are liable off-hand to disease the world over, of course.

Would-be doctors, some truly and naively well-intentioned, traipsed over to the American Health College to get these pearls of wisdom from Campbell.

The old quack may not have had any lab, or an operating theater, or medical instruments to work with, but he did have an office. In that office, one recruit recalled, was a rather unusual feature:

In the doctor's little office was a pane of red glass and a pane of blue glass. I was curious to know what that was for, and the doctor explained it by saying they would vitalize the remedy they were to give the patient, or sometimes food, depending entirely on the nature of the disease; it would be placed beneath the red glass or blue glass.

And there, thousand of miles away, we see it again: that mysterious pane of blue glass in the window.

Why?

TO UNDERSTAND THE blue glass in San Francisco and Cincinnati, first you must travel yet again, this time even farther east to Philadelphia, to the backyard of Brigadier General Augustus J. Pleasonton, the officer in charge of Union forces defending the state of Pennsylvania. In 1861, as the Civil War erupted around him, Pleasonton found himself in the backyard of his Spruce Street home one day, planning and undertaking a mission of massive import to his country, and to the world around him:

He was planting grapes.

To be fair, Augustus already had a respectable military career behind him. Born in 1808 and an eager West Point cadet by the age of fourteen, he spent his youth bouncing around the country in the infantry, then in the artillery, then in helping to map the Western frontier. He resigned his army commission at the age of twenty-eight, studied law, and founded a practice in Philadelphia. There he rose quickly through the ranks of local respectability, briefly serving as the state's paymaster general in 1839, and then as the president of a local railway company. Nor did he ever entirely leave the military behind. He stayed on as a brigade major in the Pennsylvania Volunteer Militia, and was rewarded for his loyal service by a musket ball to his groin, courtesy of an armed mob that he helped to quell in Philadelphia in 1844.

When not catching bullets in his shorts or filing court briefs, Pleasonton had one overriding passion—he read, and read voraciously. He was fascinated by books on physics, galvanism, natural science, and geology. He built up an extensive library, and one well-thumbed volume in particular was Professor Robert Hunt's *Researches on Light: An Examination of All the Phenomena Connected with the Chemical and*

Molecular Changes Produced by the Influence of the Solar Rays (1844). Hunt had just a few years before published *A Popular Treatise on the Art of Photography*, the first English work on the subject, and his research into the action of light on inorganic chemicals like silver nitrate placed him at the cutting edge of a new medium. But although he is remembered today as a founder of photography, Hunt's work interested Pleasonton for a very different reason: for his other chapters, on how light affected *organic* materials. Hunt had dug up accounts of experiments that, to Pleasonton, showed that different wavelengths of visible light could accelerate or retard the carbon dioxide production, and the growth rate, of plants. Blue light, it seemed, was especially good at speeding up growth. And it was easy enough to procure blue light, Hunt noted—all you needed was blue glass.

The idea appealed to Pleasonton. For all his civic respectability, he had always been a sky-gazing sort of fellow, someone prone to staring out into the blueness of the sky above and wondering what it all meant. "For a long time," he later recalled, "I have thought that the blue color of the sky, so permanent and all-pervading . . . must have *some* abiding relation and intimate connection with the living organisms on this planet."

Pleasonton set himself to designing his own experiment in blue light agriculture, one on a far greater scale than the few straggling seedlings that had been observed in Britain and France. He planned out an enclosed grapery, a sort of greenhouse for his backyard. At more than two thousand square feet in area and sixteen feet high, it would be hard for his neighbors not to take some notice of his work. Ground was broken in the autumn of 1860, and by March the grapery was ready. It looked like a typical large greenhouse, save for one feature—every eighth pane in its roof was of blue glass. This would be, he reasoned, enough blue light to stimulate the plants, but not so much as to lower the temperature of his greenhouse.

That April, like innumerable other gardeners in the city, he planted his vine cuttings, and he tended anxiously to them over the months that followed. All he could really do was prepare, wait, and see what grew out of it.

EVEN IN THE midst of Civil War, General Pleasonton was always ready to make some time for his backyard experiment. One day in September 1861, he received a most important visitor: Robert Buist, a horticulturist and owner of a local plant nursery. It was Buist who had sold the general his vine cuttings that spring, and now he wanted to see how they were coming along. Pleasonton led Buist out into his backyard and opened the door to the grapery; his visitor walked inside and, after some hesitation, carefully examined the vines. Pleasonton watched the expression on the horticulturist's face. Buist was awestruck.

"I have been cultivating plants and vines for the last forty years," Buist marveled. "I have seen some of the best vineyards and conservatories in England and Scotland. But I have never seen *anything* like this growth."

Buist kneeled down to measure the thickness of the vines near the ground, and then measured their growth from one end to the other. *Forty-five feet.*

"I visited last week," he continued, "a new grapery near Darby, the vines in which I furnished at the same time as yours. They were of the same varieties, of like age and size, when they were planted as yours. When I saw them last week, they were puny spindling plants not more than five feet long."

Pleasonton was delighted, and when Buist visited again one year later for the general's first harvest of grapes, he was astounded yet again by the luxuriant growth of thick vines all around the greenhouse. He examined the vines again and sized up the grapes on them; then, taking out a pencil and pad, Buist did a few quick calculations.

"Do you know," he turned to Pleasonton, "you have *twelve hundred pounds* of grapes in this grapery?"

—I had no idea, the general responded.

"You have indeed that weight of fruit, but I would not dare publish it," Buist mused. "No one would believe me."

EACH YEAR THROUGH the 1860s brought thicker and heavier harvests from the greenhouse. Pleasonton leafed through his volumes of Hunt and Becquerel and began to wonder—if animals were built from many of the same basic organic compounds as plants, wouldn't they too stand to benefit from blue light? But how would you test something like that?

In the fall of 1869, Pleasonton built himself a piggery on an outlying farm, arranging the barrows so that on one side a litter of pigs would grow up under a clear glass window, while on the other side another litter of pigs would mature under a pane of blue glass. Under clear glass, four pigs that weighed a total of 203 pounds fattened up in a few months to 530 pounds; under the blue glass, four scrawnier pigs, weighing a total of 167 pounds, fattened to 520 pounds: still lighter, but a significant closing of the gap. Encouraged by these results, Pleasonton took an ailing newborn calf and put it in a chromatic pen, and sure enough, it grew rapidly into a fine specimen.

Word got out among Philadelphians of the strange experiment being conducted by their garrulous neighbor, and Pleasonton was always quick to recommend that others try it—he soon had one neighbor raising chickens with blue light. Inevitably an invitation landed on his doorstep.

1390 Walnut St.,
April 27th, 1871

MY DEAR GENERAL:
Will it suit you, and will you do us the favor to explain your process of using glass in improving the stock to the Philadelphia Society for Promoting Agriculture, on Wednesday next, the 3rd of May, at eleven o'clock A.M., at their Room, S.W. corner of Ninth and Walnut Streets (Entrance on Ninth Street)? You were kind enough to express to me, in conversation, your willingness to give us the result of your experiments.

Yours, very truly,
W. H. DRAYTON, PRESIDENT

The members of the society got a little more than they'd bargained for; when Pleasonton showed up at their offices the next week, he had a speech that ran to about twenty dense pages.

But as his speech wore on, Pleasonton turned to his audience and launched into another topic that fascinated him just as much: electricity. He had developed some theories that were . . . unique. By Pleasonton's reckoning, just about every natural phenomenon relied on electricity at some level. Diamond formation, planetary rotation, all heat and weather, and all organic processes were directly based on it, as far as he was concerned.

"What do you suppose has produced the giant trees of California?" the bearded old man roared at his startled listeners. "Electricity!"

This is not entirely untrue; any chemical compound relies on a transfer of electrons in order to bond, but this could be called an electrical phenomenon only on the most minute level. Pleasonton was a big-picture man: he was talking about very large amounts of electricity. And, not coincidentally, it turned out that blue light and electricity were intimately connected. Pleasonton explained that light hitting blue glass at 186,000 miles a second, upon which all colors but blue and indigo were stopped, generated a tremendous amount of power:

> This sudden impact of intercepted rays on the outer surface of the blue glass with this inconceivable speed, produces a large amount of [electrical] friction. . . . This current of electromagnetism, when allowed to fall upon the spinal column of an animal, is conducted by its nerves to the brain, and thence is distributed over its whole nervous system, imparting vigour to all the organs of the body.

And if such electromagnetic benefits could accrue for plants and dumb beasts, who could imagine the effect on humans?

For a country that had just lost a sizable portion of its young men, General Pleasonton offered a blue future of vitality renewed: a race of true *giants*, strapping in strength and boundless in energy.

> The result would prove to be one of the greatest blessings ever conferred on mankind. What strength of vitality could be infused

into the feeble young, the mature invalid, and the decrepit octo-genarian! How rapidly might the various races of our domestic animals be multiplied, and how much might their individual portions be enlarged!

Pleasonton walked away from the society meeting with a greater sense of purpose than he had ever had before. He went to the printers and immediately had the speech set into type and printed up as a pamphlet; when it was ready, he carpet-bombed the intelligentsia of the country with copies.

Cases began to pour in. That same summer a friend's wife became gravely ill with a wasting illness. His friend, a doctor, was despondent. Pleasonton went up to see the wife and talk sense into her. What you need, he said, is to go to French, Richards & Co., buy yourself a big pane of blue glass, and put it right *there* in your parlor window. And then you need to sit under it for at least two hours a day.

She gave it a try.

When Pleasonton came back a week later, he met a changed woman, as he later recalled:

[She said:] "Do you know that when I put my naked foot under the blue light, all my pains in the limb cease?" I inquired, "Is that a fact?" She assured me that it was, and then added, "My maid tells me that my hair is growing not merely longer on my head, but in places there which were bald new hair is coming out thick."

Her husband was ebullient, and pronounced it as "the greatest stimulant and most powerful tonic that I know of in medicine"—and then wondered aloud whether it might work on cholera.

It certainly was a panacea, for soon afterward, Pleasonton's own son was suddenly lamed by a nerve injury to his hip. The young man was made to sit out under a plate of blue glass each day, bathing his hip and his spine in the cool rays. Three weeks later, he was healed.

The old general was now emboldened enough by his success that his next step became clear: *he would patent visible blue light.*

PLEASONTON SENT HIS letter to the Patent Office at the Department of the Interior on August 14, and waited patiently for the patent examiner to come visit his experimental garden. Finally, late in the month, Professor Brainerd of the Patent Office arrived in Philadelphia on the one-o'clock train. He examined the general's fabled grapery and went out to his farm to see his piggery and his wondrously restored calves and lambs. It was rare enough for an examiner to pay a personal visit to an applicant, but Brainerd was so impressed that he stayed three days as Pleasonton's guest. The last day he had three agricultural professors reexamine the grapery with him.

"General," Professor Brainerd said as he prepared to leave for Washington, "everything you have alleged on this subject of blue light is confirmed."

Pleasonton swelled with pride.

"If my investigation should establish the verity of your statements, you have made the most important discovery of this century—transcending in importance even that of Morse's Telegraph, which, at best, furnished only a means of communication with distant places, while your discovery could be brought home to every living object on the planet. . . . Your patent would be one of the most valuable that had ever been issued in the United States."

And with that, he left.

On September 26, 1871, General A. J. Pleasonton of Philadelphia was awarded U.S. patent #119,242 for Improvement in Accelerating the Growth of Plants and Animals.

PLEASONTON'S PATENT PAPERS for a "cerulean process" were passed around the Patent Office with great interest; the commissioner read over them and passed them along to the Board of Public Works, which was planning to build a grapery for President Grant. Pleasonton had already published an article on blue light in the August 1871 issue of *Gardener's Monthly*, and a reader in France was so impressed that at the next meeting of the Académies des Sciences he had an extract of the article printed in *Comptes Rendus*; a pirated and unattributed French translation of the Philadelphia Society for Promoting Agriculture speech turned up soon afterward. Requests to Pleasonton for his English-language pamphlet soon came from as far away as South Africa.

But the first enthusiastic adopters of the blue light cure were Pleasonton's fellow Philadelphians. One after another, they traipsed down to the glaziers at French, Richards & Co., requesting blue glass to be fitted into their front parlors and sitting rooms. One man set a lemon tree under the glass, but failed to place it in the full view; the branches that were blue-lit grew lush and heavy with fruit, but the branches that were not withered and died. Another man's ailing canary had stopped singing; placed under blue glass, it commenced singing more strongly and sweetly than ever before. Chickens and lambs raised under blue grass grew faster and fatter than before; friends wrote to Pleasonton telling him of how blue glass had rid them of rheumatism. Pleasonton himself found that a mule, which he discovered after a horse trader had fleeced him to be profoundly deaf and arthritic, could be cured by a few months in a stable with blue glass and clear glass in the transom. "The removal of this deafness," Pleasonton propounded in another speech in 1874, "was produced by an electro-magnetic current, evolved by the two lights upon his auditory nerves and exciting them to healthy action."

What topped it all off was a letter attesting that a premature infant, born paralyzed, had gained the power of movement after being set for long periods under some blue glass. Another infant, a one-month-old girl under the care of Dr. William McLaury, had a "tumour about the size of a robin's egg"; after one hour of blue light on the tumor a day, McLaury found that it disappeared in six weeks.

Pleasonton was now convinced that the public at large needed to know about blue light. It was one thing to explain blue light to neighbors and in specialized horticultural magazines; it was another to bring it to the attention of the world. That would require nothing less than an entire book.

A. J. PLEASONTON'S 1876 volume *The Influence of the Blue Ray of the Sunlight and of the Blue Colour of the Sky* is one of the most striking medical texts ever written—it is visually arresting, with an appropriate powder-blue binding. Open it up, and you'll see why Pleasonton's long-suffering printers in Philadelphia, Claxton Kensen & Haffelfinger, found their author to be something of a challenge. Pleasonton demanded the entire book be printed on tinted paper in light blue ink—because, as he patiently explained, it would "relieve the eyes of the reader from the great glare, occasioned by the reflection of gas light at night from the white paper usually employed in the printing of books." Whatever was used to tint the paper, it oxidized badly over the years—readers today will squint hard to read the faint blue ink stamped on what appears to be wet beach sand.

But it does make for very interesting reading.

Only the first quarter of the volume's 230-odd pages deal directly with blue light; these pages are largely reprints of Pleasonton's lectures, as well as a selection of letters from both astonished colleagues and beseeching invalids. But the rest of the book is filled with speculations on electricity and its effect on everything from glaciers to the buoyancy of ships in water. It is the most remarkably eccentric assemblage of hypotheses ever to make it past a copy editor. Take, for instance, the following passage:

> Our sun is simply a huge reflector of light. The gray covering of his nucleus or body is represented in our mirror by the metallic covering we place on the backs of our glasses. . . . rays of light from every luminous object in the universe, mingling together, and reflected from this gray covering of the sun, furnish the white sunlight that illuminates the world.
>
> Heat destroys gravitation . . . Now, if what our astronomers tell us of the inconceivably high temperature of the sun be true, there can be no gravitation towards its centre. . . . Heat disintegrates solids, separates their molecules, destroys their densities, and consequently is opposed to gravitation, which is the attraction

of densities. Alas! for poor Sir Isaac Newton and his theory of centripedal and centrifugal forces!

Nor did Pleasonton limit himself to the earth and sky. Just as Puritans saw the providential hand of God in every stone on the ground and every bird in the sky, Pleasonton sees the force of electricity in every living and dead thing—even in the drunken arguments between spouses late at night:

> The sexes are oppositely electrified—hence their mutual attraction for each other. Now give them the same electricities, and mutual repulsion immediately results. . . . It has been shown that the negative or masculine electricity of the man is reversed, and becomes positive like that of the woman under excitement of alcoholic stimulants—in other words, for the time being, the man becomes a woman. . . . His attributes become feminine; he is irritable, irrational, excitable by trivialities, and when opposed in his opinions or conduct, becomes violent and outrageous, and if, in this mood, he meets his wife, whose normal condition of electricity is like his present condition, positive, they repel each other. . . .

The logical obverse, just exactly who drunk men *would* get attracted to while brimming with alcoholic feminine energy, Pleasonton passes over in tactful silence.

Scholars, to Pleasonton's dismay, did not start chucking out their copies of Newton, and barkeeps did not install galvanic batteries to keep their soused customers properly charged up. In fact, most scientific journals didn't bother to review or list his book at all; as is so often the case, serious scientists simply hoped that the obvious absurdities in it would make it go away.

The entire print run sold out.

PLEASONTON'S TIMING WAS fortuitous. Word of a medical study had just arrived from Italy: there, according to an April 22, 1876, article in *Medical and Surgical Reporter*, one Dr. Ponza had taken violent inmates at his lunatic asylum at Alessandria and placed them in rooms painted either red, blue, or violet. The ones in the red rooms seethed with rage; the patients in the blue rooms recovered. And perhaps, one medical editor speculated, the color of light and inmate clothing chafed at them as sorely as any straitjacket. After all, he added confidently, some people could *feel* color:

> It is a fact that some persons can detect the color of a material by feeling it. Suppose such an one in an insane state irritated by contact with material of a color from which, as the result of a delusion, he has a special aversion: how his case must be retarded unless the very conditions of his mind are recognized, and he is bathed in light of a proper tint.

Such experiments gave Pleasonton's an added luster, no matter how bizarre his theories on electricity sounded—and it is debatable whether any readers even bothered to read that section of his book— his experiments with blue light did seem to have some medical basis.

Indeed, days after Ponza's results were published in Europe, other asylums there followed suit; at the Kent County Asylum in England, one homicidal maniac was locked up into a "blue room" by the order of the asylum's superintendent, F. P. Davies, who reported:

> The first day he was very noisy; he daubed the walls with feces and destroyed his clothes. At night the room was thoroughly cleansed, recolored, and the next day he was again put into it, and acted just as before. Toward evening, though, a change was noticed in him; he was quieter, and, upon being removed, asked not to be sent back there again. However . . . he was put into it for the third time. About noon he begged to be let out of it, complaining of severe frontal headache. . . . From that time he has given us no trouble, and has exercised great control over himself.

The same day as the *Medical and Surgical Reporter* article on European experiments, as chance would have it, the *New York Herald* also decided to run an interview with Pleasonton that gave a glowing account of his blue light experiments with pigs. Articles from the

Herald and other major New York newspapers, then as now, were often picked up by smaller local papers across the country.

Watching this blue light gospel spread, one scientific journal could hold its tongue no longer. On July 1, 1876, *Scientific American* sniffed that Pleasonton's book "is more eccentric than we could have believed . . . beyond the sphere of legitimate criticism, and [we] place it among the many melancholy burlesques of science." And yet even as it sneered at the general's bizarre notions, it had published another article that seemed to demonstrate that blood was drawn into capillaries near the skin at different rates depending on the color of light used. And the most efficacious at imparting a healthy rosy glow to test subjects was . . . blue light.

WHEN THE SECOND edition of Pleasonton's book came out in 1877, claiming that cobalt glass could cure everything from gout and spinal meningitis to paralysis and pulmonary hemorrhages, blue light had become a genuine craze. Homeowners were adding sunrooms onto their homes set with blue glass; decorators were snowed under with requests for blue curtains and blue wallpaper. Fashionable health spas in New York City had to scramble to get contractors and glaziers in: not only were patrons demanding sunrooms, they wanted them to be made *entirely* of blue glass. It was a bonanza for overnight schemes like the Mazarine Blue Glass Company, which sprouted up at 823 Broadway advertising "Imported Blue Glass, Arranged in Frames, Scientifically Constructed According to the Beidler Patent."

H. Mercer Beidler was one of many fellow Philadelphians who had cashed in on Pleasonton's discovery. He'd attempted to patent a striped blue glass pane design, which was then to be "scientifically" set at a fifty-six-degree angle over the user's body. Portable models were available for travelers to use on the decks of ships. Beidler had published his own pamphlet and built a public blue glass parlor at the corner of Ninth and Chestnut, with "Hours for Invalids 10 A.M. to 3 P.M."

Some would-be customers, as a subsequent notice by Beidler in a local paper showed, were not entirely clear on the concept:

We are sorry to disappoint the good people who crowded our
parlours all day yesterday, hoping to avail themselves of the first
opportunity to enjoy our vitalizing and life-giving Blue Glass Sun
Baths; but they will please remember in the future that the Baths
can only be administered when the Earth is bathed in the bright
sunshine of heaven.

But on sunny days, at least, the invalid and the merely languid alike
now spent their afternoons lounging in a blue haze. "It is now quite
common along our streets and avenues," observed *Scientific American*
in April 1877, "to see frames of azure crystals hanging within dwelling
house windows; while, on sunny days, the invalid grandfather or other
patient, may be noticed basking in the ethereal rays, his countenance
filled with hope, though streaked with blue."

Blue light quickly jumped from America to Europe—it was Belgian factories, after all, that still supplied the world with most of its
blue glass. "Blue light baths are, it appears, an infallible remedy for
pains in the bones arising from rheumatism or railway collisions,"
The Times of London enthused. Over in Paris, opticians frantically
made a run on "medicated glass"—blue glass—because their customers didn't want the green or smoke-tinted ones anymore. One com-
mentator hoped that this would only prove to be a temporary visual
aid, since "offensive colored spectacles or goggles so disfigure the
countenance and detract from the natural appearance of our Students,
Lawyers, Doctors, and Clergymen."

Inevitably, blue glass began to show up in popular culture. When
the American humorist Josh Billings issued his yearly collection for
1877, it was titled *Josh Billings' Trump Kards: Blue Glass Philosophy*—
and printed, in a nod to Pleasonton's book, on blue paper. In Philadelphia, the prolific composer Edward Mack published "The Blue
Glass March," complete with a cover illustration depicting invalids in
a sunroom tossing their crutches aside. Mack, as much as anyone, had
a good sense of the pulse of popular culture; he'd previously had hits
with novelty piano tunes that cashed in on the late 1860s craze for
bicycles, "Velocipede Gallop" and "The Cyclopede Waltz."

The height of blue glass giddiness came with the publication of an entire book-length spoof: John Carboy's *Blue Glass a Sure Cure for the Blues* (1877). Carboy, a pen name of humorist John Harrington, was a prolific writer for J. B. Collin & Co., a Manhattan publisher of the cheap humor quickies that sold on railroad platforms and street corners for a quarter each in paperback. Teamed up with his frequent collaborator Thomas Worth, a fine pen-and-ink caricaturist, Carboy gleefully leaped into the blue glass fad.

Like any good satire, Carboy's was based on a thorough knowledge of his subject: he clearly had read Pleasonton's book very carefully, and then proceeded to exalt it to ludicrous lengths. "Blue Glass isn't any of your common quack nostrums, like Jink's Solidified Bug Juice, or Doctor Scrap's Carbonated Extract of Hepisdam," he assures readers. "Blue Glass Cures Constipation of the Obituary Organs!. . . . Cures the Itch Without Scratching. . . . As a table-sauce it has no superior, and for polishing furniture it cannot be surpassed." He then dispenses all kinds of handy household hints for the use of blue glass, such as "Square pieces of blue glass weighing six pounds each may be used for dispersing a cluster of tom cats."

At the center of Carboy's account is one "General Bottleton," who finds that a giant magnifying glass of blue glass makes criminals confess, cures drunkards, vanishes warts, and—most hilariously to Carboy's readers, I'm sure—bleaches black people white.

Carboy could also spoof the testimonial letters in Pleasonton's book with perfect pitch:

DEAR BOTTLETON,

I have been for years afflicted with an amanuensis in the verticle goiture of my left arm, followed by a paragraph of the liver, which left me in a comictoes condition, with a constant suppuration of axminster over the protoxide of my manipulative organs. . . . Dr. Carnochan advised me to have my umbilical cord stuffed, and diet myself upon the farinaccous extract of solidified lightning. I tried his advice; but, alas! my sufferings were in nowise abated. Then, as a last resort, I bought five sheets of Blue Glass. The first sheet brought out my sine qua non, reversed my crustacea, and expanded my cheek-bones, so that I couldn't close my mouth without lifting my shoulders with a rope and tackle. The second, however, remedied, by removing my secretions, and bringing about a general pulverization of my cardigan coagulations. . . . I can now get drunk every day, with no trouble . . . You can publish this for the benefit of all mankind and other afflicted people.

Enriched beyond his wildest dreams by the craze for "bluefied solar rays," General Bottleton soon takes to jaunting about town in a magnificent blue coach, driven by a blue-eyed coachman who lays a blue whip to blue-ribboned horses wearing blue glasses.

In reality, General Pleasonton made very little money from the frenzy that he had sparked. His was an altruistic project, meant to bring the blessings of blue light to all humanity. By 1877, though, seeing quacks and doctors alike profiting off his discoveries, Pleasonton decided to enforce his 1871 patent. He explored a partnership with the Keely Motor Company, which claimed to harness the atomic vibration of water molecules with a "hydro-pneumatic pulsating vacuum engine," a perpetual motion machine invented by founder John Keely in 1872. "The stockholders of Keely Motor," *The Manufacturer and Builder* magazine dryly noted, "have come to the conviction that blue glass is to be the connecting link between solar power and the machine for the perfection of which they had furnished the funds"— in other words, a sort of solar-powered atomic reactor. Not suprisingly, the Keely Motor Company failed to profit anyone much except, perhaps, John Keely.

Undeterred, Pleasonton then had inserts placed into the second edition of his book reminding readers- "Specific licenses can be procured from me, with directions for the use of my discoveries, and for the proper kinds of glass to be used." But nobody paid any attention: the blue glass trend was much bigger than Pleasonton now, and the niceties of patent law were hardly any match for the waves of customers demanding cobalt-tinted glass in every shape, size, and form. In fact, it didn't even have to be glass; his competitor Beidler was now also recommending for consumptives in blue parlors "that the body be denuded to the waist, with a cape of of light *flannel checked with blue and white preferred*, thrown over the shoulder."

Pleasonton, in all likelihood, scarcely saw a penny off his patent.

WHEN THAT RAW medical recruit saw the blue and red panes at the American Health College years later, he was seeing a knockoff of a knockoff of Pleasonton—for as hapless as Pleasonton was at defending his patent, others were all too ready to cash in on blue light. At the height of the frenzy in 1877, Seth Pancoast, a rather colorful figure among medical writers of the time, quickly produced his own guide to light therapy, *Blue and Red Light; or, Light and Its Rays as Medicine* (1877). Like Pleasonton's book, it was published in Philadelphia. Pancoast expanded on colored light treatments—"the source of all the physical and vital forces in nature"—by including some uses for red light; he even one-upped Pleasonton by printing his book in blue ink with a red border.

Pancoast was not a man to let a few failed experiments get in the way of his belief in colored glass:

> Facts are facts; they must and will in the end stand in spite of their defects or faults in the eyes of scientists. Facts are stubborn and do not always yield to "authorities." . . . The "failure" of the most accepted experiments by the most accepted experts, proves absolutely nothing beyond the proof of their failure.

Indeed, for Pancoast the efficacy of light became an article of faith. While Pleasonton made some religious musings in his book, in Pancoast the spiritual element of heavenly light became much more pronounced; by 1883, his medical text had morphed into the theosophical hodgepodge of *The Kabbala: Or, The True Science of Light*. Nor was he the only writer to make this connection, for just a year after Pancoast's *Blue and Red Light*, Edwin Babbitt published the quasi-mystical *Principles of Light and Color* (1878).

Scientific publications, then as now, rolled their eyes at the way the public fervently medicated itself with a hash of quackery, theological hoodoo, and half-understood medical research—following anything, in other words, except the advice of a trained physician. One issue of the journal *Railway Surgeon* took this potshot at women who dabbled in medical fads:

THE SCIENTIFIC HOUSEWIFE

Give me a spoon of oleo, ma,
And the sodium alkali,
For I'm going to make a pie, mamma,
I'm going to make a pie;
For John will be hungry and tired, ma,
And his tissues will decompose—
So give me a gramme of phosphate,
And the carbon and cellulose.

Now, give me a chunk of casein, ma,
To shorten the thermic fat;
And hand me the oxygen bottle, ma,
And look at the thermostat. . . .

And so forth. Others were less inclined to merely laugh at such trends—and as the blue glass mania reached its height, *Scientific American* decided that it had had enough.

WHEN ALFRED ELY Beach and his writers decided to shatter the blue glass fad, it was through an almost unprecedented multipart series of articles in its pages, beginning with the three-part "The Blue Glass Deception" on February 24, 1877. *Scientific American* was a weekly magazine back then, and each week for much of 1877 its readers were treated to public trouncings of the research of A. J. Pleasonton, sometimes two or three times in the same issue.

The magazine immediately hit Pleasonton with the most damning fact of all: standing under blue glass exposed you to *less* blue light than just standing out in the sun, or under clear glass. A piece of common cobalt blue glass merely diminishes all the rays across the visible spectrum; blue and violet are diminished less than the others, but they are diminished. "Prior to these splendid original discoveries of our contemporary," the magazine sneered on February 24, "we ignorantly believed that blue glass only partially sifted out the orange and yellow rays from the spectrum." And given that what Pleasonton had used was only one pane of blue glass to seven panes of clear glass, the net composition of his "cure" was this: very slightly shaded ordinary sunlight.

The drumbeat continued the next week with another installment, this time attacking the supposed cures caused by blue light. Pleasonton's sources of experimental information on electricity and blue light had long been disproved, it pointed out. And as for Dr. Ponza's lunatics, the explanation had less to do with blue glass than with the tendency for people to calm down when placed in any kind of shaded or darkened room.

What curative power blue glass had was, the magazine concluded, derived from that most universal of all panaceas: the placebo effect.

> The cures produced are ascribable to two causes: first, to the healthy influence of the sun bath, and secondly, to the very powerful influence of the patient's imagination. There are abundant cases known where imagination has so powerfully affected the body as to cause death.
>
> Experiments upon criminals have shown that in one instance, where a person was placed in a bed which, he was informed, had just been vacated by a cholera patient (but which had not), he exhibited all the symptoms of the disease. Another person is reported to have shown all the signs of collapse from loss of blood, from the supposition that he was bleeding to death.

There is something to this. Battlefield medics during the Civil War had already discovered that, at least temporarily, they could "cure" pain and shell shock through what amounted to sleight of hand. As Dr. William Hammond describes in his bizarrely compelling 1883 volume *A Treatise on Insanity in its Medical Relations*, the Union colonel Charles May used just such a trick to cure one deranged officer "of the belief that he was inhabited by chicken bones."

But General Pleasonton was no mere colonel, and he certainly was not a charlatan. He struck back within days with angry letters to newspapers. He did not have a particularly good rebuttal to *Scientific American*'s point about the nature of blue glass, but he was indignant that the article was titled "The Blue Glass Deception," for the word "deception" implied that he was some sort of scoundrel. When the third part of the series ran on March 10, the editors offered the backhanded apology that "we believe that General Pleasonton deceives both himself and the public." And as for any further offense they caused, the magazine didn't much care: "Our long experience in dealing with circle squarers, perpetual motionists, Keely motor people, and now blue glass adherents, besides all the other deceptions rife in the mechanical and scientific world, enables us to bear such animadversion with unruffled equanimity."

And that, the magazine said, was all it had to say on the subject. Only it wasn't, really, because as the fad continued to grow throughout 1877, the editors kept inserting new digs at Pleasonton into their pages. In the March 17 issue, this sly poke was inserted as filler at the bottom of one page: "Blue glass will cure a Spitz dog of hydrophobia. Pound it up fine, and mix it with his food." When another medical fad was reported in France the next week—this being the use of Metallotherapy, or the application of cylinders of various metals to cure ailments—the magazine suggested that it might be a good replacement therapy for "when the blue glass believers become tired of their hobby."

Nor did it limit itself to roasting blue glass proponents. A lively trade had started up in urban legends about the dangers of blue glass, as this passage from the *New York Evening Post* shows:

A gentleman in Brooklyn suffering from weakness of sight was recently led by the advice of well meaning friends to use spectacles of blue glass, such as certain opticians are selling just now. The result was that his eyes, already too weak to be used much in ordinary circumstances, were exposed to a terrible glare and heat, which in less than a week entirely destroyed the eyesight of the sufferer. He is now totally blind . . . the dupe of blue glass enthusiasts.

Scientific American, with a sigh, explained yet again in its June 23 issue that blue sunglasses did not focus the rays of the sun upon the eye—to contrary, they merely shaded it somewhat.

In addition to beratements by *The Manufacturer and Builder*, which as early as 1871 had labeled Pleasonton's work "absurd," *Scientific American*'s attacks were followed by a series of publications by Thomas Gaffield, collected in a booklet entitled *The Blue-Glass Mania* (1877). Gaffield had spent years collecting scores of glass panes from around the world and arranging them on the roof of his house in Boston, all in order to observe how different types of glass aged under the sun. He'd already spent fourteen years doing this, and so he understandably considered himself something of glass expert. His *Mania* articles effectively blew apart any scientific foundation that Pleasonton might have thought he was standing on. He was particularly hard on Pleasonton's lack of control groups in his experiments and on his numerous self-contradictions: his claims, for example, that blue light killed houseflies, but also made silkworms grow more quickly. But when the end did come it was not so much due to hard work of critics like Gaffield as to the simple life and death cycle of any fad.

By 1878, blue glass was over.

LIKE ANY GOOD medical fad, blue glass persisted on in various forms and guises for many years afterward, and never with even a nod to its originator. In the 1890s, John H. Kellogg started a run on "light baths"—enclosed wooden sitting boxes lined floor to ceiling with electric lightbulbs—and so a new generation of desperate consumers was primed for the return of the notion that colored light might be useful too.

Professor Niels Finsen continued earnest and rather more careful experimentation with colored light at the turn of the century, with results that occasionally seemed to indicate that blue light could stimulate movement in tadpoles. It was fairly inconclusive, though, and he was soon irritated at how charlatans abused his tests—"My name has been used in a way which could not fail to meet with my disapproval," he griped in his book *Phototherapy* (1901). But under his guidance, doctors were soon dragging powerful marine searchlights into their offices, covering them with enormous blue lenses, and then standing patients in front of them. After a few years with little to show for this, the idea faded away.

The most larcenous of the lot was Dinshah P. Ghadali, founder of the "Spectro-Chromo Institute," who claimed in his promotional materials to have been such a prodigy back in India that he was teaching college mathematics at the age of eleven. His career in the United States, though, seems based largely on the teachings of Rufus T. Firefly. After stints as a "medical electrician," an insurance agent, and founder of the "Anti-Forgery Electric Pen Company," he discovered the panacea of colored light. His intensive courses in "Spectro-Chromo Therapy"—just $100 cash in advance, if you please—taught the "restoration of the human Radio-Active and Radio-Emanative Equilibrium by Attuned Color Waves." It was a medical advance so truly marvelous that in 1925 the federal government rewarded him with a generous term in an Atlanta penitentiary.

The strangest variant of chromotherapy, though, came from Roland Hunt of "the Bureau of Cosmotherapy," with his 1940 book *The Seven Keys to Colour Healing*. The book is a mixture of chromotherapy, Eastern religion, Christian mysticism, and some fairly wretched poetry:

> *In Coolness new, as refreshing dew;*
> *Tone Thou my Speech, O Rays of Blue—*
> *And make It True,*
> *And make it True.*

Hunt's work is directly descended from Edwin Babbitt's earlier *Principles of Light and Colour*, but it goes farther than most in its claims. Blue-tinted water ("Ceruleo"), it turns out, also cures dysentery, cholera, and bubonic plague. "The importance of Blue as a saviour of life cannot be over-estimated," Hunt explains with great seriousness. "In Bombay thousands of lives have been saved from succumbing to Bubonic Plague, by administration of Ceruleo."

AUGUSTUS PLEASONTON HIMSELF died in March 1894, and so he saw few of these travesties of his well-meaning work. He never did give up his belief in blue glass, nor his researches and constant scientific readings; when his estate was auctioned off in Philadelphia, his personal library had grown so large that it needed its own published auction cataloge.

Pleasonton is not an easy man to track down today. There are numerous references in Civil War records to General A. J. Pleasonton . . . except that these are for his gallant younger brother, Albert Pleasonton, who was also a Union brigadier general, but with the Army of the Potomac. Even in his own lifetime, Augustus was always confused with his little brother Albert. Search for *Augustus* Pleasonton, now, and you will find nothing. After all, he only served on the home front. He did not lead any charges, storm any hilltops, or see action at Antietam.

All *he* did was try to cure the human race of its mortality.

And to some extent, he succeeded. Writing in *The North American Review* in 1893, Dr. Cyrus Edson of the New York Health Deparment admitted that "some of the devotees not only declared themselves benefited by the treatment so long as they believed in it, but were unquestionably so benefited." But temporary placebos do not make for undying medical fame, and Pleasonton's 1894 obituary in *The Times* of London only briefly mused on "a craze which for some years held a vast number of people, including many on this side of the Atlantic. . . . Invalids of all classes would sit for hours in the blue light from a window pane waiting for a cure."

Not a word has been written on Pleasonton since. Perhaps the last published comment at all on blue glass came three decades later from Henry Collins Brown in his *Valentine's Manual of Old New York* (1926):

[There used to be] the almost universal belief in the efficacy of blue glass for whatever ailed you. Exactly how this craze began I do not now recall but I do remember that its virtues as a cure-all were on every tongue. The idea spread from a single pane, inserted in the usual window light, till the whole window was blue. . . . The patent medicine men were in a panic. The nostrums which they sold were already guaranteed to cure everything but suicide and a broken neck; but the blue glass crowd went the limit in cures, and made no exceptions whatever.

For years, however, reminders of this strange manifestation remained in the shape of odd looking additions to houses; a lingering pane of blue glass here and there but that was all. . . . The Blue Glass Parlor was undoubtedly the precursor of the light and airy Sun Parlor as we know it today.

The name of Pleasonton had slipped away entirely by now—all that remained were a few enigmatic blue panes. And although all sorts of "heliotherapies" and ultraviolet treatments were pioneered in the early twentieth century to treat rickets, jaundice, and various skin ailments, the use of *visible* colored light faded from medical practice. In the end, Pleasonton's invention lapsed into eternal obscurity for the same reason that most other experimental medical treatments do.

It didn't work.

YOUR GLORIOUS DAY IS COMING

*Our wild Whitman, with real inspiration but choked by
Titanic abdomen, and Delia Bacon, with genius,
but mad . . . are the sole producers that America has
yielded in ten years.*

—Ralph Waldo Emerson, 1857

We do not truly know our own times; at least, we don't know them as our descendants will. A literature scholar reading the above statement today would do a quick spit-take—*no producers?* 1857 ended what is now grandly called the American Renaissance—a period in the mid-1850s that saw the publication of *Moby-Dick*, *The Scarlet Letter*, *Leaves of Grass*, and *Walden*, and Emily Dickinson's first tentative publications of her poetry. And yet the best Emerson can do is half-heartedly endorse the young Whitman and . . .

Who?

DELIA BACON MAY be the most fatally doomed scholar ever to have set a pen to paper. She spent much of her life in poverty and illnesses both physical and mental, every book she published lost money, and her one great magnum opus goes unread even by her editors and biographers.

It is extraordinary that she published anything at all. Bacon was born in a log cabin on the Ohio frontier in 1811, a child of fervent poverty—her father, a missionary, gave everything in his failed attempt at establishing a school. He died when she was but six years old, and Delia's penniless mother had no choice but to farm out the children to kindhearted friends of the family. The Bacon children survived this ordeal to eventually rise to prominence—one grew up to become a crusading New York reporter, another an influential New Haven minister.

And then there was Delia. She landed quite fortuitously in the Hartford classroom of Catharine Beecher, the foremost advocate of young women's education of her time. Like her friend and classmate Harriet Beecher, Delia seemed marked out for achievement. Catharine Beecher later recalled that her "homeless daughter of the Western missionary" was "preeminently one who would be pointed out as a genius; and one, too, so exuberant and unregulated as to demand constant pruning and restraint." Her exuberant genius had one great vulnerability, though—she had, Beecher said, "a morbid sensitivity to criticism."

Bacon proved to have many morbid sensitivities. Her health was always precarious; after leaving Beecher to start a girl's school with her sister, both were stricken with malaria. Delia continued lecturing until, near delirium, she collapsed before her students. Later on she would be nearly killed by an outbreak of cholera; between these near-fatal plagues, she would be struck down for days at a time by recurrences of her malaria and by violently painful migraine headaches.

Yet amid these ills, Bacon's intellect thrived. After her youthful attempt at running a school failed, she moved back to New Haven at the age of nineteen. There she focused on her writing, and one year later had her first publication, the 1831 short story collection *Tales of the Puritans*. Soon afterward, the *Philadelphia Saturday Courier* awarded her $100 for her short story "Love's Martyr." It was a substantial sum of money, and her competitors were no slouches—for unknown to Delia, her closest challenger was a little-known Baltimore writer named Edgar Allan Poe.

BACON SPENT HER twenties teaching private classes to young women in New Haven and then in Manhattan in history, literature, and science. The erudite Bacon crossed disciplinary lines with ease, using each subject to illuminate the other. Her classes were a marvel of progressive education: no exams or textbooks, just lectures followed by intensive reading by each student in whatever field had caught her fancy. This method of research, of pursuing a single question to its utmost limit, was more than just how Bacon conducted learning; it was how she conducted her life.

While in New York, she grew close to Samuel Morse, an eccentric young artist. He earned his living teaching art at NYU, but in his off-hours he pursued a fascination with ciphers, particularly with how they could be applied to that newest marvel of modern life: the telegraph. And codes were a venerable field, Morse pointed out to Bacon—after all, even Francis Bacon had invented a cipher for use in his career as a diplomat. This curious fact occupied her mind long after she left Manhattan.

Life in Manhattan spurred her to try her hand at publishing once again. Her next book was published in 1839, *The Bride of Fort Edward*. It was a closet drama, a play not actually meant for stage. Closet dramas are a hard sell even for an established playwright, and so only 692 copies sold, leaving Bacon stuck with a bill for the 808 remainders. This was a common fate for authors of the time; Thoreau once grimly joked that he owned a large library, the majority of which was composed of unsold copies of his first book. But this was little consolation to Bacon: when she left the city in 1840, it was uncertain whether she could ever earn money as a writer.

BACON SPENT THE next decade traveling the country, becoming caught up in a scandalous ecclesiastical trial, and above all engaged in constant learning. By the time she rose to the Boston lecture circuit in 1850, she was at the top of her form, and the city's female intelligentsia packed her lectures over the next two years. It was an uncanny experience for some: the brilliant Transcendentalist philosopher Margaret Fuller had just drowned in a shipwreck a few months before, and this woman onstage seemed to be her living reincarnation.

Her audiences were indulgent of her brilliance; so what if she occasionally strayed from lectures on Restoration monarchy or ancient Greece to suddenly focus *intensely* on the plays of Shakespeare, and on how such sophisticated literature could not *possibly* have been written by some fourth-rate actor? She was, in fact, convinced that this so-called Shakespeare was nothing but a front for a collaborative effort by Walter Raleigh, Edmund Spenser, and Francis Bacon, and that the plays were a cipher for a political philosophy that, if stated plainly, might have landed the real authors in the Tower of London.

Her friends worried, though. They had already watched her try in 1845 to pitch her brazen theory to the publisher Wiley and Putnam, only to have it fall flat with a heavy thud. Bacon's fixation on the Shakespeare imposture was so embarrassingly unconventional that friends would change the subject whenever she brought it up. One, hoping to keep her friend from becoming agitated, would hide all her copies of Shakespeare before Bacon came to visit.

But one new acquaintance, Elizabeth Peabody, was delighted. It would not be unfair to say that nineteenth-century American literature can be mapped out as Six Degrees of Elizabeth Peabody. First she wrote to her brother-in-law—Nathaniel Hawthorne, conveniently enough—and asked him to look over Bacon's theories. Hawthorne politely declined. Peabody had better success, though, with another good friend—Ralph Waldo Emerson. Emerson had read deeply in Shakespeare and his contemporaries, and Bacon's theory struck him as a brilliant answer to the nagging question of how a mere actor could have written the world's greatest works of literature.

"So radical a revolution should be proclaimed with great compression in the declaration," he advised in his first letter to her, in June 1852, "and the real grounds rapidly set forth, a good ground in each chapter, and preliminary generalities quite omitted. For there is an immense presumption against us which is to be annihilated by battery as fast as possible."

It was good advice—hit hard and fast, and let some later work deal with the niceties and the details. Bacon assured him that she was already in a position to deal some knockout blows: "Confirmations of my theory, which I did not expect to find on this side of the water, have turned up since my last communication to you, in the course of my researches in the libraries here and in Boston." Writing again to him a few weeks later, she coolly announced, "Be assured, dear sir, there is no possibility of a doubt as to the main points of my theory."

But Bacon knew that she would need extensive historical documentation to back up her claims, and there were only two places where she could find the original documents: London and Stratford-on-Avon. After finishing up a final round of lectures on Hindu scriptures, Persian poetry, and Egyptology, she paid a visit to Manhattan banker Charles Butler. He was a well-known intellectual benefactor, having already saved NYU from insolvency and then created its law school. And Bacon was at the top of her form as a public intellectual; in addition to Emerson, a slew of prominent intellectuals like Washington Irving, George Ripley, William Thackeray, and dashing Arctic explorer Elisha Kent Kane had all attested to her intellectual prowess as a lecturer. Butler was suitably impressed, and bankrolled her trip to England for an entire year.

Bacon was ecstatic: her greatest achievement was now within her grasp. She made a pilgrimage up to Concord, where she at last met her mentor Emerson in person and spent an evening conferring in his study. He nodded sagely in his rocking chair as she talked.

"I should give the inductions first," he emphasized again, "and then clinch them with your facts."

"I find the internal evidence more convincing," she insisted. But she admitted, "Of course I am certain I shall find historical proof in England. But, even if I do not, I have already sufficient basis to make the theory at least respectable. In fact, sir, I believe it is irresistible, to a candid mind."

Emerson was delighted at her plans to travel to England. He wrote her a clutch of letters of introduction, including one to his old friend Thomas Carlyle. These recipients were carefully chosen, and would open the doors for Delia to the intellectual life of her new country, and to every major archive in London. Now all she had to do was step through these doors.

On May 14 1853, Delia Bacon left New York Harbor on the *Pacific*, a steamer bound for Liverpool.

ONE OF HER first stops on the way to London was Stratford-on-Avon, the final resting place of "that wretched player," as she called him, "of the sordid play house." She stood in front of Shakespeare's grave in the Church of the Holy Trinity. The wretched player's tomb was certainly gaudy enough, as graves go; while other old tombstones from the time carry chilling messages like *Hodie mihi, cras tibi* ("Today me, tomorrow you"—a spiteful epitaph if there ever was one), the great Bard's monument features a tarted-up painted bust and this odd little burst of doggerel:

Good friend, for Jesus' sake forbeare,
To dig the dust enclosed here,
Blest be the man that spares these stones;
And cursed be he that moves my bones.

Shakespeare, it seemed, was anticipating his visitor—but foolishly failed to extend his curse to women. For Delia Bacon was indeed thinking of doing just such a thing: if Raleigh, Spenser, and Francis Bacon had formed a sort of literary cabal, what better place to hide a confession of their ghostwritten deeds than clasped in the hands of their dead spokesman? But now, amid all these reverent church visitors, was not the time to whip out the spade and crowbar—that would have to wait until later.

Arriving in London shortly afterward, Bacon found lodgings and sent Emerson's letter of introduction to the great essayist Thomas Carlyle. The letter gave Carlyle no clue to what he was in for, only said that his visitor had a *certain theory on Shakespeare*. Ah—but what decent writer didn't? Carlyle invited her over for scones and tea one summer day.

There, in his sitting room, she calmly explained her theory. Francis Bacon in particular fascinated her—his *Novum Organum* had helped to usher in the Age of Reason with its emphasis on scientific method and its underlying skeptical view of cant and unquestioned authority. The political implications of such freethinking were obvious, and dangerous—and they could only be baldly expressed in the history plays of Shakespeare, in which monarchs become less divinely ordained rulers than a tragic collection of human failings. That was why the leading writers of the time had to resort to a doggish hack, suspected by no one of deep thoughts, as their outlet for such revolutionary work.

Carlyle raised his eyebrows.

"Do you mean to say that Ben Jonson, and Heminge and Condell, and all the Shakespearean scholars since, are wrong about the authorship, and *you* are going to set them right?"

"I am. And as much as I respect you, Mr. Carlyle, I must tell you that you do not know what is really in the plays if you believe that that booby wrote them."

Carlyle began to whoop with laughter. "You could have heard him a mile," Bacon later wrote. But once he recovered his composure, he set out for her what she must do to complete her task—she must, by all means, go to the British Museum, and have a look at the Harleian manuscript collection. Hard evidence, he emphasized, was "worth all the reasoning in the world."

After his guest left he could only shake his head at the folly of what she was undertaking. Writing to Emerson, Carlyle lamented:

> I have not in my life seen anything so tragically quixotic as her Shakespere enterprise; alas, alas, there can be nothing but sorrow, toil and utter disappointment in it for her! . . . There is not the least possibility of truth in the notion she has taken up; and the hope of ever proving it, or finding the least document that countenances it, is equal to that of vanquishing the windmills by stroke of lance.

Delia Bacon, in turn, was just as skeptical of Carlyle. She had politely accepted his advice about library research, but she did not follow it. She never made a single visit to the great library; her letters of introduction to the librarians at the British Museum remained sealed. Her one major outing was to the grave of Francis Bacon. Though not actually related to him, she might be able to talk her way into seeing inside his grave, where she thought she would find some papers confessing to the plays. But it was no use: she could not persuade the graveyard beadle to open the tomb.

It did not really matter. She had already decided that she would prove her case on *internal* evidence, rather than the external evidence of historical documentation. All the proof of authorship needed was within the plays themselves, which—like the vast, lonely world around her—were a metaphorical cipher stretching into infinity.

THE NEXT TWO years were a profoundly isolated time for Bacon, spent shut in her quarters reading the plays over and over again—especially *King Lear*, *Macbeth*, and *Coriolanus*. Butler had given her money for only one year abroad, but she had no wish to return home. She belonged *here*, in London, where she would pursue unceasingly the great riddle—*The Shakespere Problem Solved*, she wrote at the bottom of one manuscript, underlining it twice. The manuscript grew, and grew—becoming two, three times as long as it was ever meant to be. *She could not stop writing*.

She dined on crusts, fell behind on rent, lived with scarcely any coals to warm her little lodgings. When the winters grew cold, she wrote in bed, blankets piled over her; it was too cold to write at her desk. She did not speak to anyone—not even her old classmate Harriet Beecher Stowe, who was being regaled about London for her hugely successful *Uncle Tom's Cabin*. Bacon's own fortunes could scarcely have been more the opposite. Despite entreaties by Emerson and Carlyle, one publisher after another in the United States and the United Kingdom rejected her proposed book.

But eventually Emerson managed to land her an offer for a series of articles in *Putnam's Magazine*. Her debut, published in a January 1856 issue, was a slashing attack on the idolatry that surrounded the Bard. The absence of a substantial historical record of the life of this "poor peasant" was almost proof enough to her:

> The two or three historical points we have, or seem to have, at length, succeeded in rescuing from the oblivion to which this man's own time consigned him . . . [and] constitut[e], when put together, precisely that historic trail which an old, defunct, indifferent, fourth-rate play-actor naturally leaves behind him.

Readers and staff reacted with outrage at this attack on the man she derided as "the Stratford poacher," and the *Putnam's* editors quickly rescinded their initial offer to make it a series of articles. Her follow-up articles, they claimed, did not say anything that she hadn't said in her first article.

Bacon was wounded by the criticism—but she took their check for $55. She had little choice. She had already stretched her one-year grant to two years, and was now desperately poor. One evening, her old student Eliza Farrar was roused by a visitor at her lodgings in Bayswater—a woman so shabby that Farrar's elderly mother was afraid at first to let her in. But when she did at last gain entry, Farrar was horrified to recognize . . . her old teacher. Bacon left that evening with £10, enough to tide her over for a little while longer. But when this too ran out, she finally appealed to her last resort, the American consulate. The consul paid a personal visit to her lodgings—governments ran a little differently, back then—but left not really knowing why she had called for him. Face to face with the one man in London who could bail her out and even repatriate her, she had crumpled into silence.

"I TAKE THE liberty of introducing myself to you without introduction," the letter began, "because you are the only one I know of in this hemisphere able to appreciate the position in which I find myself at this moment. . . ."

As the American consul in Liverpool, Nathaniel Hawthorne was used to receiving all sorts of pleas and complaints from Americans who had managed to strand themselves, land in jail, lose their way, and otherwise fall upon hard times thousands of miles from home. And this letter was from London—not his branch consulate's territory, strictly speaking. But he did recognize the name at the bottom, and remembered the strange genius his sister-in-law Elizabeth had spoken so highly of.

She had poured out her theories, her travails, and her hopes for publication to him. Writing back, he marveled at her utter dedication: "Whether right or wrong . . . you have acquired some of the privileges of an inspired person and a prophetess—and the world is bound to hear you, if for nothing else, yet because you are so sure of your mission."

They exchanged friendly letters back and forth, and he paid her

debts and read her essays—but at first she would not see him. The
world of people was no longer hers. The teeming streets of London,
when she ventured into them at all, were filled with inhabitants of a
former world. She was a mere vessel for the Theory that had grown
within her, taking over her bones and muscle, pushing out the blood
and marrow.

Finally, in June 1856, she relented in a note not unlike those penned
by Emily Dickinson to the one writer *she* deigned to show her face to.
It is haunted by the soul of a body that is not even dead yet:

> I hope you will call upon me. The reason I shrink from seeing
> any one now is, that I used to be somebody, and whenever I meet
> a stranger I am troubled with a dim reminiscence of the fact,
> whereas now I am nothing but this work and dont wish to be. I
> have lived for three years as much alone with God and the dead
> as if I had been a departed spirit. And I dont wish to return to
> the world. I shrink with horror from the thought of it. This is an
> abnormal state you see, but I am perfectly harmless. But if you
> will let me know when you are coming I will put on one of the
> dresses I used to wear the last time I made my appearance in the
> world, and try to look as much like a survivor as the circumstances
> will permit.

When Hawthorne visited her, he was surprised. She was not the
haunted being that he had expected at all—"She was rather uncom-
monly tall, and had a striking and expressive face, dark hair, dark
eyes, which shone with an inward light as soon as she began to speak."
The prospect of his visit reanimated her, and brought her enthusiasm
alive again. When he praised the parts of the book that she had sent
him and asked her when she would address finding historical documentation of the literary cabal, she confidently tapped a volume of
Bacon's letters. She would not, she said, try breaking into Francis
Bacon's tomb again.

"Bacon himself showed me my error," she confided to the writer.
"The evidence is in Shakespeare's grave."

SHE WAITED IN the aisle as the sun set, and a gloom gathered in the Holy Trinity Church. She was alone. The pews were empty, and she quietly held a candle the clerk had given to her; its light cast a faint glow on the stones beneath her. Under one of these stones lay the mortal remains of William Shakespeare. Above her stood his bust, staring down at the woman who would dare disturb his bones.

As the church fell into total darkness, she lit her lantern and began sizing up her task. The stones were not so large, and they could be moved with effort. Perhaps there would be a sarcophagus lid to move as well. But not more than a few feet below her, in either case, lay the packet of papers that she believed were hinted at in the letters of Francis Bacon.

She heard a creak far back in the church—the clerk, perhaps fearful of her plans, had hidden himself to spy on his own church. Hours passed, and she could not be sure whether he had left. And so she just stared at the stones beneath her feet, the cool stone beneath her fingers, that somehow lay utterly out of reach. She had neither the strength nor the daring to tear them up from the floor.

At ten o'clock, per their agreement, the clerk returned and let Delia Bacon out of the church. She wandered off into the night.

SHE COULD HAVE done it. But she chose not to, because in that moment of clarity on the floor of the church she knew what she would find—what she would *not* find—in Shakespeare's grave. And her older brother, always her toughest critic, knew it too when he wrote to her:

> Misguided by your imagination, you have yielded yourself to a delusion which, if you do not resist it and escape from it as for your life, will be fatal to you. How to say less than this, I know not. I am now to inform you that your theory about Shakespeare and Shakespeare's tomb and all that is a mere delusion—a trick of the imagination. For five years you have known that I think so. And—O my dear sister—can you not, in God's name, and in the

strength which he will give you, break the spell, and escape from the delusion?

And yet she clung to hope. Her theory could be proved, if only the world could see her book. She continued anxious, frenzied letters to Hawthorne, her sole friend left in the entire country, and the only person left in the world, it seemed, who would still listen to her. When he landed her a publisher—as he finally did in October 1856, with Groombridge and Sons—Bacon and the publisher alike relied on him to provide a preface for the book. He was a famous man. *His* word could get her taken seriously.

But he could not do it.

Or rather, he could, but he would not agree with her. It was a brilliant book in places, yes, but it was turbulent and jumbled, and, well . . . he just did not believe her theory. He finally ground out, with agonizing slowness, a preface that praised her as a dedicated and brilliant scholar. But he refused to affirm her theory.

When Bacon saw it, she was furious. She *was* the Theory now—any attack on the Theory was an attack on her. Her letters turned frenzied:

I have renounced all that I was, every joy and solace in life, to make myself a medium for those spirits that have been waiting so long to give their message. You must not decry my inspiration. You will find the title-page a more perilous place than you thought, if you do, for I shall throw you off entirely. You can not come inside of this book, if you are going to throw doubt on the Oracle. I consider myself a priestess . . . and I dont allow of any scepticism or profane speeches within the lids of this book.

But Hawthorne would not balk. Enraged, Bacon cut Hawthorne off without a word, and never spoke to him again.

The Philosophy of Shakespere's Plays Unfolded arrived at bookstands that April. It was a dense, heavy tome of more than six hundred pages. Copies went to reviewers around the country, and Bacon waited for days and weeks as they read through it. Her vindication was about to begin.

BIOGRAPHICAL ACCOUNTS OF Delia Bacon—Hawthorne's 1863 article in *The Atlantic Monthly*, Theodore Bacon's 1888 account, and the 1959 biography by Vivian Hopkins—all share one striking characteristic. They do not quote from her book. Almost without exception, they talk around her book—describing it in broad terms, quoting from her letters about it, quoting the comments of contemporaries, even venturing a little into her *Putnam's* article or the preface of *Philosophy*, but . . . never into the book itself.

Inevitably, impious thoughts form in the mind of any reader. Did these writers not *read* Delia Bacon's most famous work? And as it turns out, the answer generally is no, they did not. Theodore admitted to his friends that he had never read her book, and Nathaniel Hawthorne has this to say in his own account: "I believe that it has been the fate of this remarkable book never to have more than a single reader. I myself am acquainted with it only in insulated chapters and scattered pages and paragraphs."

How did this come to pass, that a book so widely commented upon should be so little read? The answer, as anyone who picks up a copy of her work soon finds out, is appallingly simple.

It is unreadable.

TO WATCH A brilliant mind unravel into madness is one of the most painful sights imaginable. As the medicines and nostrums fail, and the babble sets in, there comes a time when one gives up on such acquaintances: you cannot hold a conversation with them, because they are simply making no sense. And yet it is not an obvious madness; that is not how the human mind works, nor how it fails. Educated madness retains all the syntax and cadence of rational, educated discussion. It sounds sane. But when strung together, *the words make no sense*.

And so it is in *The Philosophy of Shakespere's Plays Unfolded*. Biographical accounts tend to excuse Bacon's tortured writing and frequent incoherence on the grounds that she was really a lecture hall orator, not a writer. But this claim soon falls apart: well before *Philosophy*, after all, she had written two perfectly readable published works, a novel and a play. Take, for example, this passage from the title story in her 1831 volume *The Regicides*:

> When the subtle spirit of popular superstition is once aroused, it floats not long in unsubstantiated rumor; the airy nothing soon finds a local habitation and a name. So it was in the present instance. The mountain which rears its head about two miles west of the village, was at length declared a favorite haunt of the unearthly visitant. . . . It became, at last, generally reported and believed, that just as the white mist began to break away from the rock, a female form of exquisite, but faded beauty might be seen standing amid the wreathing vapor, and gradually vanishing as it slowly curled from the mountain.

It's a fine bit of local New Haven legend, and prose that would scarcely be out of place in a volume by Washington Irving or Nathaniel Hawthorne. But twenty-six years later in her *Philosophy*, after nearly six hundred tortured pages of endless circling around her claims without ever getting to the point or to actual proof, we find buried in the text this almost ungraspable attempt at summarizing her book's thesis:

> This is the philosophy precisely which underlies all this Play,—this Play, in which the great question, not yet ready for the handling of the unlearned, but ripe already for the scientific treatment,—the question of wrestling forces,—the question of the subjection and predominance of powers,—the question of the combination and opposition of forces in those *arrested motions* which make *states*, is so boldly handled. These arrested motions, where the rest is only apparent, not real—where the yielding forces are only, *as it were*, annihilated, whether by equilibrium of forces, or an absolute predominance, but biding their time, ready to burst their bonds and renew their wrestling, ready to show

themselves, not as subjects, but as predominators—not as states, but revolutions. The science "that ends in matter and new constructions"—new construction, "according to true definitions," is what these citizens, whom this Poet has called up from their horizontal position by way of anticipation, are already, under his instruction, boldly clamouring for. Constructions in which these very rules and axioms, these scientific certainties, are taken into account, are what these men whom this Magician has set upon their feet here, whose lips he has opened and whose arms he has unbound with the magic of art, are going to have before they lie down again, or, at least, before they make a comfortable state for any one to trample on, though they may, perhaps, for a time seem, "as it were, annihilated." . . .

And so a great mind is overthrown. Bacon is desperately wrestling with an idea here, a *coherent* idea. But it is like light trying to pass through several panes of cracked glass—bent through layer after layer, until it is refracted and twisted into a wraith of reason.

PREDICTABLY, THE CRITICS were merciless in their savagery—and those that did not ridicule the book simply ignored it. But it scarcely mattered anymore. By the time *Philosophy* came out, Bacon was almost senseless. She continued to linger in Stratford-on-Avon, a ghostly and deranged presence. She slipped in and out of fevers, accused her kindly landlord of stealing from her and plotting against her, and dragged herself to the doorstep of the mayor of Stratford to complain. The mayor took pity on her and spent months caring for her. When she turned suicidal, and began claiming to be a descendant of Francis Bacon, he had her committed to an asylum.

Just before her committal, though, Bacon had scribbled a cryptic message on a scrap of paper—a letter to herself, perhaps, and an epitaph of sorts to her sanity:

it was a mmrble mmt when you at the Avn. The signs of it are in the strt whether you understand them or not. There reason in those reasons whether you observe them or not. You have forded the Avn. You have untied the spell. Theres reason in the whole. You have crossed the Avon twice. You crossed it in the E. & you crossed it in the West. You crossed the old in the N Haven. The E in the West and you crossed the New, the West in the East. History rest in me a clue & run a right spirit millim me.

Bacon slipped into madness so deep that she could not tend to herself. Friends shipped her back to America, and her brother arranged for her to live in a New Haven asylum that they had innocently walked past many times in her former life.

Her fevers continued on and off for over a year, until one day her brain burned for the last time, and the tortured genius inside writhed no more.

THE FIRST TO give her story to the world was Nathaniel Hawthorne, who contributed the essay "Recollections of a Gifted Woman" to the January 1863 issue of *The Atlantic Monthly*. Much of Hawthorne's essay is a meditation on the town of Stratford itself; he seems unable to turn fully to the story of the ghost that inhabited it. "This is," he sighs, "too sad a story." And Hawthorne had given more to Delia Bacon than she ever knew; without her knowledge, he had secretly pledged to the publisher to cover the losses on her book. This quiet act of friendship, which he stuck to even after Bacon shut him out of her life, cost him £238. The whole affair, he mused, had turned into a sinkhole: "No author ever hoped so confidently as she; none ever failed more utterly."

And yet, at the margins of Shakespeare scholarship, a few still cling to her notions. What began as a metaphorical cipher has become, to some, an actual cipher, with hidden identities and messages to be found in the plays through elaborate numerologies. The height of the approach probably came with the great American eccentric Ignatius Donnelly, who took a break from pondering the lost world of Atlantis to pen the thousand-page Baconian tome *The Great Cryptogram* (1888). And Francis Bacon, who only existed to Delia Bacon as the probable head of a cabal, has become to some the man behind Shakespeare.

Few scholars are impressed.

In 1888, Theodore Bacon put out the family biography of Delia, and it is a fascinating and rare volume. There is a battered copy in the archives of the San Francisco Public Library. Scrawled in ancient pencil near the end of the book, just as her impending death looms in the narrative, is a hopeful cry across the years from a long-gone library patron:

> The ignorance . . . the superficially "cultured" ignorant in their brutal attack upon her published life's work—drove her, beaten and broken into *insanity*. The battle and burden had been too long and too heavy the heart and mind of the noble little woman failed altogether, But, wait! Wait! Delia Bacon—your day, your glorious day is *coming!*

WALKING ON THE RINGS OF SATURN

LUNAR HUMANOIDS
We were thrilled with astonishment to perceive four
successive flocks of large winged creatures, wholly unlike any
kind of birds, descend with a slow even motion from the
cliffs on the western side, and alight upon the plain. They
were first noted by Dr. Herschel, who exclaimed, "Now,
gentlemen, my theories against your proofs, which you have
often found a pretty even bet, we have here something
worth looking at: I was confident that if we ever found
beings in human shape, it would be in this longitude!"

—FROM THE *NEW YORK SUN*, AUGUST 28, 1835

Life on the moon!

It seemed too good to be true—and so it was, in the end. But for a few weeks in 1835, it was as real as the newspaper gripped between every American's hands. Readers could thank journalist Richard Locke for the bizarre account of lunar life; but for the even more bizarre thoughts behind them, they had to turn to a shy, self-taught astronomer from Scotland.

Thomas Dick was not born into the contemplative life. In 1774, science was still a gentleman's profession, well out of reach of the likes of Dick's father, a weaver. But the son of this humble weaver had a revelation in 1782, at the age of eight, when he saw a meteorite flash before him in the evening sky. Soon he was spending his workdays at the loom reading borrowed books on astronomy; at night, he ground his own lenses and constructed crude telescopes with pasteboard tubes. He fell among academics and spent much of his early life teaching, preaching, and promoting, in his words, "literary and philosophical societies adapted to the middling and lower ranks of society." His youthful interest in astronomy was never lost in all this activity; to the contrary, it became the centerpiece of his life-long obsession with marrying religion and science. To Dick, the heavens were God's work made visible on a vast scale to earthly in-habitants.

With successful teaching and writing stints behind him, Dick de-cided at the age of fifty-three to devote himself fully to his lifelong passion. He quit teaching and went to work building a small cottage on a hill near Dundee and fitting it with a library and observatory of his own design. He was by nature a reserved and rather sober man, and the remote perch suited him just fine. By night, he watched the skies, having long since graduated from his apprenticeship of home-made lenses and pasteboard tubes. By day, he wrote books—great masses of them—expounding upon education, prison reform, fire safety, preaching, and most of all astronomy.

He was tremendously popular in the United Kingdom and in the United States, and such luminaries as Emerson, Harriet Beecher Stowe, and William Lloyd Garrison all made pilgrimages to meet him. His massive following came in part because he could write on scientific discoveries for the common man in a way that his learned colleagues never could. But clarity alone doesn't explain his wide popularity. Dick had captured the public imagination with his belief that every single planet, moon, comet, and star was inhabited with intelligent beings. And what was more, he had a fair idea of how to reach them.

WHILE WALKING ACROSS a field, you find a watch on the ground. All the minerals in the earth couldn't have combined together to form a watch on their own; surely this watch must have a watchmaker. Walk-ing farther, you kick up a chunk of quartz. Examined closely, it reveals a fantastic crystalline structure. You assumed the carefully designed watch had a maker; why not the chunk of quartz?

This was the opening argument of William Paley's 1802 work

Natural Theology, which lent its name to the entire field that arose in its wake. Though these ideas had been bubbling for some time, it was Paley who spread natural theology to the intelligentsia.

To a natural theologian, the wisdom and moral perfection of God were evidenced in the compact design and utility of every natural object. Today we might see giraffes as the evolutionary survivor of merciless natural selection, winning over dead-end mutations by virtue of being able to eat lofty edible leaves. But to a natural theologian, a giraffe was evidence of God's kindly hand—creating a plain with high trees, He provided for giraffe welfare by giving their necks a good stretch.

The movement came to a head in the 1830s, when the Cambridge don William Whewell published his *Bridgewater Treatise*, which allowed and even encouraged the belief that a benevolent God would populate other worlds with beings intelligent enough to appreciate the beauty of His creations. This idea also had some currency in the seventeenth century: the theologian Giordano Bruno was burned at the stake for it in 1600, and both the English bishop John Wilkins and the French scientist Bernard le Bovier de Fontenelle advocated it later that century. Now, though, it was to be revived dramatically by Whewell and fellow scientists like Sir David Brewster. But it was Dick, the humble Scottish astronomer, who went farther than anyone else dared to imagine.

TO DICK, THE massive workings of the skies were a means to a magnificent and inscrutable end. For it to be otherwise, a means without an end, would reveal our Maker to be a cruel existentialist. The universe would be, as his book *The Sidereal Heavens* claims, "one wide scene of dreariness, desolation, horror, and silence, which would fill a spectator from this world with terror and dismay . . . without one sentient being to cheer the horrors of the scene." This was clearly unacceptable in a Christian god, as was the "wild hallucination" that our own life was an accident of primordial chemistry. We did not exist as a result of fortunate material reactions—it existed to please us, a conceit now known as the Anthropic Principle. "*Matter*," Dick insisted, "was evidently framed for the purpose of *mind*."

It also followed that having matter anywhere without a sentient being for it to serve would be pointless. Therefore every celestial body must be inhabited. Intelligent life was more than a mere accident of our planet, or of perhaps one or two others: it was the natural state of the universe. To believe otherwise was "impious, blasphemous, and absurd." Writings like *Celestial Scenery* are thunderous on this point: "Let us suppose for a moment that the vast regions on the surfaces of the planets are only immense and frightful deserts, devoid of inhabitants—*wherein does the wisdom of the Creator appear in the supposition?* Would this be an end worthy of INFINITE WISDOM?"

With every world being inhabited, it was natural enough for Dick to first turn his attentions to the moon. By Dick's estimate, if the moon was as crowded as England it would have a population of 4.2 billion. And with every order of life inhabiting every world, he went on in *The Sidereal Heavens* to use this formula to calculate the population of the visible universe:

> There would be the following number of inhabitants in these worlds, 60,573,000,000,000,000,000,000,000; that is, sixty quartillions, five hundred and seventy three thousand trillions, a number which transcends human conception. Among such a number of beings, what a variety of orders may exist, from the archangel and the seraph to the worm and the microscopic animaliculum!

But there is no explanation, sadly, of why a benevolent God would want to make every planet as crowded as England.

Given the magnificent intricacy of virtually any object, Dick's thinking naturally led him to believe that every celestial object was inhabited, including comets and asteroids. "Comets may be the abodes of greater happiness than is to be found on our sublunary world," he marveled, "and may be peopled with intelligences of a higher order than the race of man." These comets might be peopled with rather worldly fellows (or rather, *cometary* fellows), made wise and sophisticated by the vaster and more diverse prospects afforded to them in their long, irregular orbits inside the solar system. He imagined that they might be a race of astronomers, sailing through space in their icy observatory, in eternal contemplation of the planets: "Their movable observatory, cruising from sun to sun, carries them in succession through every different point of view." With keen enough eyes, perhaps these cometary beings could spy upon a whole other order of beings together—the ones, Dick proclaimed, that lived in the interior of the *sun*.

Dick also believed the rings of Saturn to be solid, in the mistaken belief that mere dust debris would have already been flung into space. Given their solidity, and the sublime views of the planet surface below and the heavens above, Dick thought that surely these rings must be populated with "numerous orders of intellectual beings."

These intelligent neighbors were not invulnerable, though. In Dick's time, the asteroid belt between Mars and Jupiter was still a relatively new discovery, and some hazarded the guess that it might be the remains of a planet. In Dick's thinking—since all planets were inhabited—this cataclysm becomes a celestial Sodom: "The fate of the beings that inhabited the original planet must have been involved in the awful catastrophe. . . . Nor should we consider it inconsistent with what we know of the physical government of the Almighty." Some scientists—then, as now—fretted over the possibility of a comet smashing into the earth and snuffing out the human race. But however vengeful this planet-smashing God was, Dick could not imagine that this was the common moral state of the universe:

> The benevolent Father of all did not intend that this moral de-
> rangement should be universal and perpetual. . . . If a world which
> has been partly deranged by the sin of its inhabitants abounds with
> so many pleasures, what numerous sources of happiness must
> abound, and what ecstatic joys must be felt in those worlds where
> mortal evil has never entered, where diseases and death are un-
> known.

A good God meant that most, and maybe all, other worlds were still in a state of innocence. Perhaps, then, it was just as well that we couldn't corrupt them through human contact—a notion that has enjoyed currency among science fiction writers ever since.

In fact, Dick thought that alien intellects and morals might be far more advanced than ours. The distant and irregular motion of the outer planets would demand a superhuman mind in order to make the astronomical observations needed to appreciate God's celestial workings. Comets swooped in irregular orbits, while the inhabitants of the rings of Saturn lived on multiple rings that (by his guess) all moved at confusingly different speeds:

> Intelligent minds exist in the regions of Jupiter, Saturn, and Uranus. . . . Those minds, in all probability, are endowed with faculties superior in intellectual energy and acumen to those of our globe. For the rapidity and complexity of the [planetary] motion . . . require the exertion of [superhuman] intellectual faculties.

And any lunar astronomers had to surmount their initially lunarcentric view of the universe to realize that their role was twice diminished: that is, they were circling another world that was itself circling a sun. But our moon's astronomers, favored with long nights and a thin atmosphere—for Dick refused to believe that the moon lacked any air at all—could at least take solace in crystal-clear views of their earthly brethren.

Better still, he hinted, perhaps these Lunarians didn't even need telescopes to do this. Although our weak earthly eyes might not be able to view them with the most powerful instruments, aliens might have eyes that could spy upon us unaided. Dick's mind also ranged to imagining how the night might look on other planets: "The most splendid object in the nocturnal sky of Venus will be the earth. . . . Our moon will likewise be seen from Mars like a small star accompanying the earth." In fact, Dick could scarcely conceive of blind or dim-eyed aliens. What else is the universe for, he asked, but contemplation by its inhabitants?

All these speculations on interplanetary vistas were easy enough to consider in the abstract, but Dick popularized a grander earthly plan. Reasoning that all alien intelligences spoke the universal language of geometry, in *Celestial Scenery* he proposed the construction of a gigantic geometrical figure on the plains of Siberia:

A correspondence with the inhabitants of the moon could only be begun by means of such mathematical contemplations and ideas which we and they must have in common. They might perhaps erect a similar one in reply. Schemes far more foolish and pre-posterous than the above have been contrived and acted upon in every age of the world. The millions which are now wasting in the pursuits of mad ambition and destructive warfare might, with far greater propriety, be expended in constructing a huge triangle or ellipsis of many miles in extent, in Siberia or any other country.

For many readers, *Celestial Scenery* was their first exposure to this breathtakingly ambitious notion. But variations on this idea—using a giant array of mirrors in Siberia, say, or filling a giant square Saharan trench with kerosene and setting it alight—had been floating around for a couple of decades among similar-minded cosmologists. On a slightly more practical note, Dick envisioned a worldwide corps of thousands of astronomers, each allocated a particular part of the moon to survey for years, all in order to detect any long-term changes in vegetation or topography, either of which might indicate the urban handiwork of an intelligent race.

Even in his era, long before radio, Dick imagined that humans might contrive some better means of reaching out into the ether. "Man is only in the infancy of his being," he mused, for he knew that his monumental proposals were also monumentally unwieldy means of interplanetary communication:

We may conceive that intellectual beings, to whatever portion of the material world they originally belonged, may hold the most in-timate converse with one another, by modes peculiar to their econ-omy, and which are beyond the conceptions of the physical universe; so that distance in point of space shall form no insuperable barrier to the mutual communication of sentiments and emotions.

For a few months in 1835, it seemed that Dick's celestial vision might come true.

IT BEGAN QUIETLY enough. On August 21, 1835, the *New York Sun* reported that astronomer Sir John Herschel "has made some astronomical discoveries of the most wonderful description, by means of an immense telescope." Hyperbole was common to newspapers of the time, so this announcement could have meant almost anything. What it did mean was revealed a day later: in South Africa, the ingenious Herschel had built a telescope so powerful that when the cap was left off during the day, it melted the plaster walls into blue glass, burned a hole through the observatory, and then set fire to a nearby grove of trees. This insanely powerful telescope could magnify objects by an unheard-of 42,000 times, and was promptly turned at the moon the next night to reveal . . . a field of poppies.

As if in an opium dream, the magical images unfolded:

> A beach of brilliant sand, girt with wild castellated rocks, apparently of green marble . . . with grotesque blocks of gypsum, and festooned at the summit with the clustering foliage of unknown trees. We were speechless with admiration . . . [Later we saw pyramids] of monstrous amethysts, of a diluted claret color, glowing in the intensest light of the sun!

If *Sun* readers were stunned by the news, so were the newsagents: the issue sold out, and printers scrambled to keep up with demand for it and the following issue. The *Sun* had scooped every other paper in the country by obtaining the latest copy of the *Edinburgh Journal of Sciences*, which apparently held Dr. Andrew Grant's account of the lunar discoveries. Unable to procure a copy for themselves, competing papers immediately reprinted the story. But even they couldn't have anticipated the next electrifying revelation: *animal life*.

The dawn of August 25 saw New Yorkers sitting down and rubbing their eyes in disbelief. Herschel had discovered herds of small bison living on the moon. What was more, there was a menagerie of bizarre lunar animals that almost defied earthly description:

The next animal perceived would be classed on earth as a monster. It was of a bluish lead color, about the size of a goat, with a head and beard like him, and a single horn, slightly inclined forward from the perpendicular. The female was destitute of horn and beard, but had a much longer tail. It was gregarious, and chiefly abounded on the acclivitous glades of the woods. In elegance of symmetry it rivaled the antelope, and like him it seemed an agile sprightly creature, running with great speed, and springing from the green turf with all the unaccountable antics of a young lamb or kitten.

Looking farther across the lunar plains, they saw palm trees, islands of shimmering quartz, and herds of miniature reindeer, elk, and zebra. Animals ranged in size from mice to a bear with horns, and included—most startlingly—the *biped beaver*. As tall as humans, the beavers walked upright, skating gracefully among their villages of tall huts, which all had chimneys, showing them to be acquainted with the use of fire.

As my more adept readers may have already guessed, there was something missing from this fantastic narrative—an elusive quality that we might call *reality*. For the source of these articles was not Dr. Andrew Grant, but a gang of merry hoaxers at the *New York Sun* led by a certain Richard Adams Locke.

LOCKE WAS A brash young British expatriate, a descendant of the philosopher John Locke, and his schooling at Cambridge in the 1820s would have placed him in a hotbed of natural theology. The phenomenon of Dick and his ilk, whose works were being reprinted and parroted in American periodicals, was just too tempting for Locke to pass up. The 1820s had already brought at least two clumsily executed claims of life on the moon. With his university training, though, Locke was able to imitate his instructors' rhetoric with perfect pitch.

Like any good hoax, Locke's began from reasonable-sounding premises. Dick's and Whewell's writings had already made alien life a plausible and maybe inevitable discovery. Herschel was a respected member of a famous family of astronomers, and he had in fact recently set up shop in South Africa. Still, for all their savvy, neither Locke nor *Sun* publisher Moses Beach (the father of future *Scientific American* publisher Alfred Beach) could have predicted the sensational nationwide impact of their "discovery." The circulation of the *New York Sun* leaped fivefold overnight, and Locke's articles were reprinted by newspapers across the country. Fellow journalists clamored for more details, and enthusiastic astronomers besieged ticket agents to book passages to South Africa. To top this media mayhem would be a challenge indeed—but Locke did not disappoint.

ON AUGUST 28, the *Sun* reported the biggest scoop in the history of journalism: there were people on the moon. Or rather . . . a sort of people:

> They averaged four feet in height, were covered, except on the face, with short and glossy copper-colored hair, and had wings composed of a thin membrane. . . . In general symmetry of body and limbs they were infinitely superior to the orang outang. . . . Some of these creatures had crossed this water and were lying like spread eagles on the skirts of the wood. We could then perceive that they possessed wings of great expansion, and were similar in structure to those of the bat. . . . We scientifically denominated them as Vespertilio-homo, or man-bat; and they are doubtless innocent and happy creatures, notwithstanding that some of their amusements would but ill comport with our terrestrial notions of decorum.

These man-bats lived in a land of towering sapphire pyramids and were accompanied by flocks of doves. In their more relaxed moments, they could be seen picnicking on cucumbers.

Locke now had the nation's ear. In a time when many lands were as yet unmapped, such fantastic claims about another planet could be easily accepted. The *New York Times* even pronounced the claims to be "probable and possible." But really, we might ask, could Locke's fellow journalists have been that gullible? This comment from the *New York Evening Post* stands on its own as a reply:

> That there should be winged people in the Moon does not strike us as more wonderful than the existence of such a race of beings on Earth . . . [such as described by] Peter Wilkins, whose celebrated work not only gives an account of the general appearance of habits of a most interesting tribe of flying Indians, but also of all those more delicate and engaging traits which the author [Wilkins] was enabled to discover by reason of the conjugal relations he entered into with one of the females of the winged tribe.

Not surprisingly, at this point—if not well before—it dawned on Locke and Beach that all this attention could be worth a good deal of money. Following the distinct smell of lucre in the air, they set about printing up the articles in book form. The first printing of *Great Astronomical Discoveries Lately Made by Sir John Herschel at the Cape of Good Hope* quickly sold out its run of sixty thousand copies; pirated editions rushed in to fill the void. Lithograph portraits of Lunarian creatures were sold to enthusiastic lunaphiliacs. The public couldn't get enough of it: congregations began taking up collections for missionaries to preach gospel to the man-bat race, and scalpers sold copies of the coveted book for tidy sums of cash.

Inevitably, Locke's time ran out. Astronomers seeking copies of his sources met with increasingly evasive replies, and they began to get suspicious. Arriving ships showed no sign of the famous article by Dr. Grant in the *Edinburgh Journal of Sciences*. But in the end, vanity did the hoax in. Unable to contain himself, the star journalist revealed his grand prank to a colleague at the *Journal of Commerce*. He had fooled the whole nation!—and, of course, the friend was sworn to utter secrecy.

Locke awoke the next day to screaming headlines. And so on September 16—its chutzpah intact, if not its credibility—the *New York Sun* admitted to the hoax, but excused it on the outrageous grounds that it had performed a public service by "diverting the public mind, for a while, from the bitter apple of discord, the abolition of slavery." But if the *Sun* couldn't be bothered to come up with a better excuse, perhaps it was because Locke and Beach were too busy counting the small fortune they'd made off the whole absurd affair.

DICK WAS UNAMUSED. In a footnote to *Celestial Scenery* he huffs:

> The author of this deception, I understand, is a young man in the city of New York, who makes some professions as to scientific acquirements, and he may be perhaps disposed to congratulate himself.... The *Law of Truth* ought never for a moment to be sported with.... For when untutored minds and the mass of the community detect such an imposition, they are apt to call in question the real discoveries of science.... It is to be hoped that the author of the deception to which I have adverted, as he advances in years and in wisdom, will perceive the folly and immorality of such conduct.

It was a fatherly wheeze worthy of Polonius, but Dick needn't have bothered. Locke merrily hoaxed gullible suckers well into his golden years.

And they *were* suckers, as even Dick was to admit. Any half-educated reader should have realized that a supposed telescope with a magnification of 42,000X would make the moon, a quarter million miles distant, appear about six miles away. "To perceive such objects [as animals]," Dick commented wryly, "it was requisite that they should have been brought within six yards instead of six miles."

Edgar Allan Poe, on the other hand, was quite tickled by the whole affair. Writing in the October 1846 issue of *Godey's Lady's Book*, Poe thanked Locke for having whipped up a sales frenzy that ended up financing most of New York's penny newspaper presses. Poe was no stranger to successful hoaxes, as he had at least three to his credit—his own "Hans Pfall" moon hoax, the bizarre suspended animation of "M. Valdemar," and the past-lives scam of "Mesmeric Revelation." Poe, often quick to accuse competitors of plagiarism, was warm in his praise of Locke.

Nonetheless, for a few years after the lunar hoax, Dick's ideas were quoted in popular periodicals of the day, and they gained a wider (if distorted) circulation through Locke's spoof. He also made his way anonymously into the hands of many unsuspecting readers. As I write, I have before me an 1846 chapbook of Dick's *The Solar System*. It was published in America by the American Sunday-School Union, one of a countless number of tract societies that flooded the American frontier and the British countryside with edifying books on science, theology, and treacly moral tales. Dick's name doesn't appear anywhere on it. Nor does it have any hint of Dick's far-out cosmology: to look at it, you'd think it was nothing more than a nice little guide to the planets put out by a nice little church press. We can only imagine some grizzled dirt farmer in Nebraska scratching his beard as he set his copy down, pondering the building of a Siberian monument to communicate with Lunarians.

Amusingly enough—though not for Thomas Dick, had he lived to see it—Locke's hoax stayed in print longer than the work it spoofed. Dick went out of print not long after his death in 1857, while Locke's *Great Astronomical Discoveries* outlasted Locke himself, with a fifth edition in 1871, the same year that he died.

SO WHY DID Dick's works go out of print first? For one thing, Dick's narrative became almost less credible than Locke's. Presented with evidence that didn't accord with his notion of a wise and kindly God, Dick would reject it out of hand. For example, an apparent glow on the moon had been attributed by some colleagues to lunar volcanoes. Impossible, Dick declared: volcanoes were the result of our fall from grace, and the presence of "such appalling and destructive agents . . . would be to virtually admit that the inhabitants of that planet are in the same depraved condition as the inhabitants of this world." He reacted the same way to correct evidence of screamingly high wind speeds on Jupiter. Such observations, he sniffed, simply showed our ignorance of the planet's indubitably pleasant weather: "A West India hurricane, blowing at the rate of a hundred miles an hour, has blown heavy cannon out of a battery. . . . What, then, would be the force of a gale moving at the rate of a thousand miles per hour? [It is] altogether inconsistent with the idea of a comfortable habitation either for sensitive or intellectual beings."

Natural theology's ensuing death was slow and painful. Its vulnerability lay in its ultimate allegiance to scripture, rather than to scientific methodology. When scripture didn't accord with scientific fact, the resulting reinterpretation of scripture took it farther and farther away from a literal reading of the Bible, and farther out of the grasp of popular understanding. After 1850, in the first glimmerings of evolutionary biology and quantum physics, the link became so tenuous that one may as well be speaking of two different subjects entirely: nature, and theology. Most people did, and so came the end of natural theology.

The only other easy option, an admission that scripture might be *wrong*, was dismissed out of hand by theorists like Whewell: "The results of true geology and astronomy cannot be inconsistent with the statement of true theology." Whewell himself declined in his later years into ineffectual and pathetic attempts to have copies of Darwin removed from his college library.

Dick was spared from these sights; when he died in 1857, the first drops of Darwinism had not yet eroded public belief. Posterity has been less kind to him, though: his once-popular tracts are difficult to find, and have been entirely out of print for well over a century. The 1855 edition of his complete works that I found at UCLA still had uncut pages.

As far as I could tell, I was the first person in 143 years to even open it.

FURTHER READINGS

JOHN BANVARD

The greatest keeper of the Banvard flame was John Francis Mc-Dermott, and his 1958 book, *The Lost Panoramas of the Mississippi*, though long out of print, is well worth finding. Not only is it thoroughly illustrated and researched, it also discusses the minor industry of imitators that sprung up around Banvard's innovations.

Any modern account of John Banvard is indebted to the pioneering scholarship of John Hanners. He wrote his 1979 Michigan State University dissertation on Banvard—"The Adventures of an Artist." Sections of it are reworked and wedged into his book *It Was Play or Starve* (Bowling Green State University Popular Press, 1993); a shorter, illustrated version turns up in his article "John Banvard and His Floating Theatres," *Traces of Indiana and Midwestern History*, Vol. 2, No. 2, (Spring 1990).

Two of the few scholarly efforts to precede those of McDermott and Hanners are Joseph Arrington's "John Banvard's Moving Panorama of the Mississippi, Missouri, and Ohio Rivers," *Filson Club History Quarterly*, July 1958; and Doane Robinson's "John Banvard," *South Dakota Historical Society*, Vol. 21 (1942). A broader and more recent account is also given in Ried Holien's "John Banvard's Brush with Success," *South Dakota Magazine*, September/October 1997.

The New York Public Library has two interesting sidelights on Banvard's life: "The Holy Land," an article on his Middle Eastern travels, in *Gleason's Pictorial Drawing Room Companion*, 1854, pp. 388–89); and an account of the building of the ill-fated Glenada castle, "Banvard, the Artist, and His Residence," in *Ballou's Pictorial Drawing Room Companion*, 1857, p. 312. But the best insight into Banvard's life comes from his own (and sometimes unreliable) accounts in the Banvard Family Papers (Minnesota Historical Society, St. Paul, Minn.). Other archives include the Banvard file at the Watertown Regional Library, Watertown South Dakota, and the Banvard Collection at the South Dakota Historical Society, in Pierre, South Dakota.

As for Banvard's own publications, the New York Public Library houses *Banvard's System of Short-Hand* (1880) and *The Origin of the Building of Solomon's Temple* (1886). Banvard's seminal accounts *Banvard's Panorama of the Mississippi River* (Boston, 1847) and *Banvard, or the Adventures of an Artist* (London, 1851) are rarities indeed, though some larger university libraries have them on microfilm. The New-York Historical Society has an original printed copy of the latter.

Banvard's masterpiece remains vanished, of course. But what of his competitors? Most of their work seems to have met a similar fate, with one notable exception. A 1200-foot moving panorama based on Bunyan's *Pilgrim's Progress* was executed in 1850 by some of New York's top painters (including Frederic Church) and traveled around the country. Amazingly, it turned up whole in 1995 at the York Institute Museum in Saco, Maine, where it had been utterly forgotten in a storage area for nearly a century. It has been restored and shown to the public; Holland Cotter's account of the exhibition, "A Pilgrim's Perils in an Ancestor of B-Movies," with some dramatic color illustrations, appeared in the Sunday, April 4, 1999, issue of the *New York Times*.

WILLIAM HENRY IRELAND

There is a wealth of material out there, thanks in large part to a series of facsimile reprints made in the late 1960s and early 1970s of most of the primary sources involved in the Shakespeare forgery scandal. The 1799 combined edition of *Vortigern* and *Henry the Second* (1799) is easy to find in major research libraries and used book searches, as is Ireland's fascinating *Confessions of William Henry Ireland* (1805). A variety of attacks and counterattacks from the time, including Edmond Malone's *An Inquiry Into the Authenticity of Certain Miscellaneous Papers . . .* (1796), Samuel Ireland's *An Investigation of Mr. Malone's Claim to the Character of Scolar, or Critic* (1798), and George Chalmers's *An Apology for the Believers in the Shakespeare-Papers* (1797), are all also widely available. Some of the original forgeries may also be found at the British Library.

The most readable recounting of the Ireland tale is John Mair's *The Fourth Forger* (1938), although Bernard Grebanier's more detailed *The Great Shakespeare Forgery* (1965) is also quite good. Jeffrey Kahan's monograph *Reforging Shakespeare* (1998) has a strong whiff of dissertation about it, and he grinds his ax down to a little nub; he's absolutely determined to prove that Ireland was a malicious criminal mastermind. Still, it's the best-researched of all the accounts of Ireland, and a useful corrective to the many lapses in credulity by earlier writers.

There is also a novel that used the Ireland scandal—*The Talk of the Town* (1885) by James Payn. It's rare, and the only copy I've come across is at the New York Public Library.

JOHN CLEVES SYMMES

For sheer novelty value, it's hard to beat the anonymously written (and incorrectly attributed to Symmes) 1820 novel *Symzonia: Voyage of Discovery*, by "Capt. Adam Seaborn." The Arno Press put out a facsimilie volume in 1974, though even that is hard to find now.

The two best explanations of Symmes's theories are *The Symmes Theory of Concentric Spheres* (1878) by Americus Symmes, which can be purchased in microfilm for one (1) arm and one (1) leg from the British Library; and James McBride's *Symmes's Theory of Concentric Spheres* (1826), available at the New York Public Library. Thomas Matthews's critical *Lecture on Symmes's Theory* (1824) and Jeremiah Reynolds's *Remarks on a Review of Symmes' Theory* (1827) are both in the Beinecke Library at Yale University. A microfilm of Symmes's original 1818 broadside can also be found at Columbia University.

One of the best posthumous accounts of Symmes is in the October 1882 issue of *Harper's New Monthly*, pp. 740–44; many later accounts simply rehash this article. Victoria Nelson's self-indulgent, though erudite, account of hollow earth theories through the ages can be found in the Fall 1997 issue of *Raritan*, pp. 136–66. There is an excellent chapter on Reynolds and Symmes in William Stanton's 1975 book *The Great United States Exploring Expedition of 1838–1842*, and Martin Gardner gives an entertaining account of later hollow earth quacks in his 1957 classic *Fads and Fallacies in the Name of Science*.

For examples of the motions made in Congress on behalf of Symmes, see *The Debates and Proceedings in the Congress of the United States* (later titled *Register of Debates in Congress*) for March 7, 1822 (Senate Proceedings), February 3, 1823 (House Proceedings), February 7, 1823 (Senate Proceedings), and February 10, 1823 (House Proceedings).

RENÉ BLONDLOT

The first place to go is Blondlot's own book, *The N-Rays: A Collection of Papers Communicated to the Academy of Sciences* (1905), available at the New York Public Library and the University of California at Berkeley. Watching his argument unfold, complete with diagrams and photos of N-ray phenomena, you start to understand how this man could have become so convinced of his own theory. Other contemporary descriptions can be found in Henri Bordier's *Les Rayons N et les Rayons n1* (1905) and Alphonse Berget's *Le Radium at Les Nouvelles Radiations (Rayons X et Rayons N)* (1904); UC Berkeley possesses copies. For an account from the medical side, see Dr. Margaret Cleaves's 1904 book *Light Energy*; I was able to find a copy at UC San Francisco. One example of how N-ray hoopla came to the general public is in Edward Romilly's "Human Radiations. N-Rays. Facts and Queries" (1904), a curious booklet in the collection of the British Library. Their copy still has the two little glass screens helpfully pasted inside the front cover for readers to perform their own experiments.

Much of N-ray controversy was fought in the pages of science journals, though, because it exploded and then imploded too quickly for many books to be published on the subject. See *Nature* magazine for 1903: December 24; for 1904: January 21, January 28, February 18, March 3, March 10, March 24, April 7, Sept. 29; for 1905: June 29. Also, see *The Lancet*, for 1904: February 6, February 20, February 27, March 5, March 12, March 19, March 26, April 9, April 16, April 23, November 12, December 10; for 1905: January 7, January 14.

For Robert Wood's own account of his visit to Blondlot's lab, see the lengthy quotation in William Seabrook's 1941 biography, *Doctor Wood*. Modern accounts of the scandal can be found in Irving Klotz's "The N-Ray Affair," *Scientific American*, May 1980; Irving Langmuir's "Pathological Science," *Physics Today*, October 1989; and Isaac Asimov's *Out of the Everywhere* (1990).

FRANÇOIS SUDRE

Unless you happen to be within walking distance of the National Library in Paris, it can be difficult to find information on Solresol in the offline world. François and Josephine Sudre's masterwork *Langue Musicale Universelle* (1866) and Aimé Paris's vitriolic *La Langue Musicale* (1846) and *Un Correction à M. Sudre* (1847) are all at the Library of Congress. *Rapports sur la Langue Musicale* is in the Music Room at Yale University; you'll often find that Sudre's few surviving works are misfiled in the music sections of libraries. Pages 31–38 of Louis Couturat and Leopold Leau's *Histoire de la Langue Universelle* (1907), available at the New York Public Library, contain what amounts to an obituary on Solresol. David Whitwell's very useful if occasionally repetitive history of Sudre, *La Téléphonie and the Universal Musical Language* (1995), is sold as a photocopy directly from Professor Whitwell himself. Call California State University (Northridge) and ask the music department for his extension.

The online world is rapidly growing as a source of Solresoliana; any resources listed here will surely be out of date before this even reaches the press. But for now the sites to look for are Stephen Rice's excellent page, which includes his translation of Boleslas Gajewski's *Grammaire du Solresol* (http://www.ptialaska.net/srice/solresol/

intro.htm); Jason Hutchens's page (http://www.amristar.com.au/
~hutch), and Greg Baker's page (http://www.ics.mq.edu.au/~gregb/
solresol/index.html).

Curiously, the notion of music conveying emotional content or
generalized messages achieved brief artistic vogues among composers.
In 1881, J. A. Goodrich published a slim volume titled *Music as a
Language*, which attempted without much success to show how specific emotions and ideas were conveyed by certain chord intervals and
counterpoints. Over a century later, Professor Joseph Swain attempted the same feat with his 1997 book *Musical Languages*, with
about the same lack of convincing results. No one seems to have
advanced much beyond the oboe section saying "Ha ha ha ha ha."

EPHRAIM BULL

Ephraim Bull's papers are at the Concord Free Public Library, and
the librarians there are tremendously helpful. Foremost among the
horticulture books of Bull's era are *The American Grape Growers Guide*
(1852), by William Chorlton, and Andrew Fuller's *The Grape Culturist*
(1864), both of which went through many editions. Also see J. Fisk
Allen's *Practical Treatise on the Culture and Treatment of the Grape Vine*
(1859) and Robert Buchanan's *Culture of the Grape, and Wine-Making*
(1852). Coming later are Viala and Ravaz's *American Vines (Resistant
Stock)* (1903) and George Hussman's *American Grape Growing and
Wine Making* (1915). These books are widely available at research
libraries and through antiquarian booksellers.

There are numerous accounts of old Concord, including Town-
send Scudder's *Concord: American Town* (1947), Allen French's *Old
Concord* (1919), and Josephine Swayne's *The Story of Concord* (1939),
and in Franklin Sanborn's memoirs *Sixty Years of Concord 1855–1915*,
edited and published by Kenneth Cameron in 1976. Brief mentions
of Bull may be found in editions of Hawthorne's letters, as well as in
two biographies by Julian Hawthorne: *Hawthorne and His Circle*
(1903) and *Hawthorne and His Wife* (1885).

Sir Henry Bessemer's life is chronicled in his *Autobiography* (1905), which can be had for a high price from antiquarian dealers; those with an engineer's cast of mind will find themselves in good company as they read Bessmer's narrative. The history of Dr. Welch can be sought out in William Chazanof's *Welch's Grape Juice: From Corporation to Co-operative* (1979). An odd sidelight of its history crops up in the company's own 1921 volume *Grape Juice as a Therapeutic Agent*, which is carried by a surprising number of antiquarian dealers, but is equally difficult to find in most libraries.

The most complete account of Bull is Edmund Schofield's in the Fall 1988 issue of *Arnoldia*; shorter accounts can also be found by Barbara Wallraff in the January/February 1980 issue of *Garden*, by Dorothy Manks in the October 1966 issue of *Horticulture*, and in the Fourth Quarter 1910 issue of *The American Breeders Magazine*. The *Meehan's Monthly* editorial is in the March 1894 issue. All are available through the University of California at Berkeley. Finally, U. P. Hendrick's *A History of Horticulture in America* (1950) does not discuss Bull much, but does give a well-researched context for understanding him and the rise of native hybridization and seed propragation in his era.

GEORGE PSALMANAZAR

Much of my chapter is drawn from Psalmanazar's own remarkable work, *Memoirs of* **** (1765). It is shocking that this book has been out of print for more than three hundred years now. Copies can be found, fortunately, at a number of major research libraries, such as the New York Public Library, the Library of Congress, and the University of California at Berkeley, and in the rare book room of the San Francisco Public Library. It is slightly easier to find his infamous fraud *An Historical and Geographical Description of Formosa* (1704). It went through a second edition in 1705 and multiple pirated and translated editions; in 1926 a small run (750 copies) of facsimile copies of the first edition were printed. Many major research libraries have either the original or the facsimile lurking in their rare book rooms— or at least they think they do. When I asked for one such Psalmanazar volume at the New York Public Library, it was found to be "missing." Psalmanazar books fetch thousands of dollars, and I suspect that someone knew the value of that book better than the library did.

The *Dictionary of National Biography* has a wonderful and exhaustive entry on Psalmanazar, longer than most of its entries for kings and prime ministers. More recently, Justin Stagl's *A History of Curiosity: The Theory of Travel 1550–1800* (1995) has an excellent chapter on Psalmanazar. The standard biography, though, remains Frederick J. Foley's *The Great Formosan Impostor* (1968). It is not an easy book to find, although the New York Public Library has a copy. It was published through the Jesuit Historical Institute—oh, Psalmanazar would be horrified—and is a well-researched and even-handed volume. And to date, no one has had any luck at guessing Psalmanazar's real identity, but I often wonder whether the name of his "Formosan philosopher" Chorche Mathcin is some kind of clue.

ALFRED ELY BEACH

Beach is his own best source. His marvelously illustrated 1868 volume *The Pneumatic Dispatch* can be found at the Science and Business branch of the New York Public Library, as can the *General Description of the Broadway Underground Railway* (1871) and *To the Friends of Rapid City Transit* (1871). For the opposition, see *Unanswerable Objections to the Broadway Underground Railroad* (1873). For a Beach railway postmortem written while it was still in living memory, see James Blaine Walker's *Fifty Years of Rapid Transit* (1917). And the late attempt at a London pneu railway appears in the July 12, 1877, issue of *Nature*.

Modern railway enthusiasts are a fine source of misinformation on Beach. I do recommend, though, Charles Hadfield's exhaustive history of British pneumatic railways, *Atmospheric Railways: A Victorian Venture in Silent Speed* (1967).

For a sense of Beach's wide-ranging interests in science and technology, just read any pre-1896 issue of *Scientific American*, or his wonderful (if short-lived) annual *Science Record* (1873). Anyone with a serious interest in his railway should also read through the 1867-to-

1872 volumes of his magazine. The outlines of the man himself can be sussed out from the obituary on the front page of the January 11, 1896, issue of *Scientific American*.

Finally, there is one very simple way to see what Beach's railway looked like, and blown up far larger than any plate in this book could manage. Go to a Subway shop—the fast-food chain, you know, where you can buy a six-inch Cold Cut Trio?—and lo! Pasted upon the walls are pictures of Beach's invention. Whoever was designing the chainwide decor for Subway simply clipped out a bunch of old public-domain illustrations of subways, including three that originally ran in *Scientific American* in the 1870s. Look for the pictures that depict an almost perfectly round (save for a slight groove in the bottom) brick-lined subway tunnel, and a rounded subway car interior. These are Beach's own handpicked illustrations for what was to be an ultra-million-dollar venture.

Graze pensively on your Baked Lay's Sour Cream and Onion chips. Ponder the vagaries of ambition.

MARTIN TUPPER

No matter how obscure he becomes, the sheer tonnage of his published output ensures that there will always be a Tupper—though you're more liable to find him as a prop book in a furniture store than on any library shelf. Still, almost any used-book web site or antiquarian dealer will have a few copies of *Proverbial Philosophy* or *Complete Works* around, often quite cheaply. Since it was published in a small run, long after his popularity had faded, it is harder to find his autobiography, *My Life as an Author* (1886), though the University of California at Berkeley has a copy. (Bizarrely, a Spanish translation—*Autobiografía*—turned up in Rio de Janeiro in 1969. The New York Public Library has one.) His numerous other efforts are also floating around used-book stalls, and all are at the the New York Public Library; the parodies that these efforts earned can be found in Volume 6 of Walter Hamilton's *Parodies of the Works of English and American Authors* (1889).

Tupper's obituary can be found in the November 30, 1889, issue of the London *Times*, p. 10, while there is a postmortem of Tupper's reputation in the February 26, 1938, issue of the *Times Literary Supplement*, p. 137. John Drinkwater damns him with faint derision in his contribution to the critical collection *The Eighteen-eighties* (1930). Just about the only other article on him is an interesting sidelight on his American tour and his relationship to Whitman: "To Destroy the Teacher: Whitman and Martin Farquhar Tupper's 1851 Trip to America," published in the Spring 1996 issue of the *Walt Whitman Quarterly Review*, pp. 199–209.

There is very little book-length scholarship on Tupper. Only one biography has been written: Derek Hudson's fine *Martin Tupper: His Rise and Fall* (1949), which is surprisingly easy to find used or at major libraries. The only critical study of his work is a curious obscurity by Ralf Buchmann, *Martin F. Tupper and the Victorian Middle Class Mind*, published in Bern in 1941. It was originally written as a thesis for the University of Zurich. It makes for amusing reading, because Buchmann really despises Tupper—though often Tupper is just a convenient stand-in for everything about Victorianism than Buchmann hates. Still, it's strange that in the midst of the greatest slaughter of this century, this grad student spent months jumping up and down on the cold corpus of an author that nobody even reads anymore.

ROBERT COATES

The only book-length account is John Robinson's 1891 biography *The Life of Robert Coates*. It's rather padded out, but essential nonetheless. I've never found it for sale anywhere, but both the New York Public Library and the University of California at Berkeley have copies.

Contemporary accounts can be found in *Reminiscences and Recollections of Captain Gronow* (1862) by Rees Gronow and in the March 1813 issue of *The European* magazine, pp. 178–83; this article also has the best-known engraved portrait of Coates. UC Berkeley has an original print copy of this magazine in an impressively weighty and beautifully tooled old binding. It was with great reluctance that I finally returned it.

For an account of the "party invitation" hoax played on Coates, see the 1862 volume of *The St. James' Magazine*, pp. 488–89. A brief overview of Coates's life is also to be found in the August 19, 1865, issue of London's *Once a Week* magazine, pp. 232–37.

AUGUSTUS J. PLEASONTON

As so often happens, this chapter came about by accident. I was loitering around the stacks of old books in the basement of the University of California at San Francisco library, this being my wont, simply plucking random books off the shelves and flipping them open. Victorian hydrotherapy books, 1868 treatises on dental sugery, and all kinds of turn-of-the-century strangeness: *The Milk Diet*, or *Good Health: By One Who Has It*, or *Viavi Hygiene* . . . and a beautiful little blue book caught my eye. That's when it all started.

Without question, the first book to seek out is this masterpiece of eccentricity by A. J. Pleasonton, *The Influence of the Blue Ray of the Sunlight and the Blue Colour of the Sky* (1876, 1877); there are copies at the Library of Congress, the New York Public Library, and major research libraries like those at UC Berkeley and UC San Francisco. It is worth possessing, really, although any antiquarian dealer lucky enough to have one will surely charge you upwards of $200 for a tight copy.

The other books around the blue glass movement are harder to find: John Carboy's *Blue Glass a Sure Cure for the Blues* (1877) is on microfilm at UC Berkeley, and the original copy is in the Rare Book Room of the Huntington Library in Los Angeles. The Library of Congress has Henry Beidler's *Blue Glass Sun-Baths as a Curative* (1877) and Thomas Gaffield's *The Action of Sunlight on Glass* (1881). Edward Mack's *Blue Glass March* is in the Rare Book Collection at the University of Pennsylvania library. Thomas Gaffield's *The Blue Glass Mania* (1877) is at the National Library of Medicine (National Institutes of Health) in Bethesda, Maryland. *Josh Billings' Trump*

Kards: Blue Glass Philosophy can be found at the Bancroft Library at UC Berkeley. Seth Pancoast's *Blue and Red Light: Or, Light and Its Rays as Medicine* (1877) and Edwin Babbitt's *The Principles of Light and Color* (1878) are also at UC San Francisco, and Babbit's book was even reissued in a 1967 abridgment with annotations by the twentieth century color enthusiast Faber Birren.

There were a number of periodical articles about the craze, including *Scientific American* in 1877: February 24, March 3, 10, 17, 24, April 7, June 23, and July 7; and *Medical and Surgical Reporter* in 1876: April 22, August 5; and in 1877: April 7, 14, and November 24. *The Manufacturer and Builder* had scathing commentary in August 1871, June 1876, March 1877, June 1877, and June 1879. *Harper's New Monthly* had an item on colored light experiments in April 1870, and the London *Times* carried a brief notice of blue glass treatments on February 20, 1877. Finally, the poem "The Scientific Housewife" is taken from the July 2, 1895, issue of *The Railway Surgeon*.

As for modern articles on Pleasonton or blue glass, save your time: there aren't any. The last word on Pleasonton came with the London *Times* obituary on August 1, 1894; just the year before, Cyrus Edson was already nostalgically speaking of blue glass in his March 1893 article "Fads of Medicial Men" in the *North American Review*. The final word written at all on blue glass seems to be in Henry Collins Brown's *Valentine's Manual of Old New York 1926* (1926). The Valentine's series is wonderfully written and prolific enough to be had cheaply from antiquarian dealers. Anyone professing an interest in the nineteenth century or in New York City should buy a shelfload.

Details about the colorful fraud Dinshah Ghadali can be found among the droll wit of *Nostrums and Quackery*, last published by the American Medical Association in 1936. The AMA put out a series of corrosive pamphlet attacks on charlatans early in the century, and these supplied my information on Chichester pills and "Doctor" Campbell: *"Female Weakness" Cures and Allied Frauds* (1915) and *Some Quasi-Medical Insitutions* (1916), both available at the University of Califonria at San Francisco. There are also many later light therapy texts there, including *Phototherapy* (1901) by Niels Finsen, *Light Energy* (1904) by Margaret Cleaves, *Light Therapeutics* by J. H. Kellogg

(1910), *Sunlight and Health* (1924) by C. W. Saleeby, and *The Seven Keys to Colour Healing* (1940) by Roland Hunt. Dr. Gerald Weissman's excellent *Democracy and DNA* (1995) provides useful contextual medical history, and Dr. Weissman very kindly helped me find research papers on modern UV therapies.

DELIA BACON

You're best off sticking with the original nineteenth-century sources. Bacon's *Philosophy of the Plays of Shakespere Unfolded* (1857) is reissued by an academic press every few decades or so, and so it's not too hard to find copies around. Used copies tend to be suspiciously pristine in condition.

Her earlier works make for much more pleasant reading. *Tales of the Puritans* (1831) and *The Bride of Fort Edward* (1839) can be found on microfilm in many libraries; the University of California at Berkeley also has original hardcover copies of both books. Catharine Beecher's "favor" to Delia, *Truth Stranger than Fiction* (1850), is much harder to find in print, but many libraries have it on microfilm.

The standard biography of Bacon is *Prodigal Puritan* (1959) by Vivian Hopkins; its style is a bit creaky, but it is well researched. Of the earlier commentaries on Bacon's life, the best two are probably Nathaniel Hawthorne's appreciation "Recollections of a Gifted Woman" in the January 1863 issue of *The Atlantic Monthly*, which was then reprinted in his collection *Our Old Home*, and Theodore Bacon's *Delia Bacon: A Biographical Sketch* (1888). The latter is difficult to find, but well worth it for the wealth of primary documents that it reprints. The San Francisco Public Library has a copy. And in a class all its own is Ignatius Donnelly's 998-page magnum loco opus— if you do not count his work on the lost city of Atlantis—*The Great Cryptogram* (1888).

And regarding the creepy *Hodie mihi, cras tibi* epitaph—you can see one in the graveyard of Greyfriars Church, in Edinburgh. Go on an especially cold and rainy day.

THOMAS DICK

The Complete Works of Thomas Dick (1856) contains crucial works like *Celestial Scenery, The Solar System*, and *The Sidereal Heavens*. There are numerous nineteenth century reprints of William Paley's primer *Natural Theology* (1802). The equally important *Bridgewater Treatise* (1836) by William Whewell might be harder to find, even though it went through at least ten editions. A different slant is provided by Sir David Brewster's *On the Plurality of Worlds* (1854), and a last gasp of natural astronomy turns up in J. W. Fring's *God in the Universe* (1914).

Richard Locke's hoax "Great Astronomical Discoveries Lately Made by Sir John Herschel at the Cape of Good Hope" (1835) has been reproduced on the web site "Moon Walk 1835," at http://users.visi.net/cwt/moonwalk.html. It's a crime that someone hasn't reprinted Locke's sci-fi classic. Modern accounts of the hoax can also be found in the book *To the Moon* (1968), by Hamilton Wright et al., and in the April 1969 issue of *American Heritage* magazine.

My chapter here only scratches one surface of natural theology and pluralistic worlds. For a much deeper account, I highly recommend Michael Crowe's *The Extraterrestrial Life Debate, 1750–1900* (1986); it is a work of impeccable scholarship. A new reprint of Crowe also mentions the recent completion of an Oxford University doctoral dissertation, "Observing God: Thomas Dick (1774–1857), Evangelism, and Popular Science in Victorian Britain and Antebellum America" by William Astore; I have not laid my hands on a copy of this dissertation yet, but any future writer on Dick probably should.

For other modern accounts of natural theology, see J. H. Brooke's article "Natural Theology and Plurality of Worlds Debate" in *Annals of Science* 1977, pp. 221–86, Richard Dawkin's *The Blind Watchmaker* (1987), and Robert Young's *Darwin's Metaphor* (1985). For an elegant piece of advocacy from the closest modern equivalent to a natural theologian, the astronomer Owen Gingerich, see his essay "Is There a Role for Natural Theology Today?" from *Science and Theology* (ed. Murray Roe et al., 1994), which is reprinted at http://www. leaderu.com/real/ri9501/natural.html. Further debate over the anthropic principle can be found in Martin Rees's *Just Six Numbers* (1999) and John Barrow and Frank Tipler's *The Anthropic Cosmological Principle* (1998).

After this chapter, my debut in *McSweeney's*, was written, I stumbled across an article that appeared in the February 16, 1850, issue of *Chamber's Edinburgh Journal*. Ruefully titled "Specimen of Successful Authorship," it makes for heartbreaking reading.

> Everyone has seen, or at least heard of, Dr. Dick's [works]. . . . Now what is the condition of this active and successful author? He is an old man—scarcely less than eighty years old: he entertains in his house a middle-aged wife and a family of orphan grandchildren. Being a retired schoolmaster, he enjoys a pension of £20 a year, besides about as much more from realized property. Now and then he writes a new book, or puts an old one through a new edition, and from that derives a few extra pounds. The sum of the whole is—POVERTY—poverty so great, that the postage of an American letter complimenting the author on his books often leaves him and his family with no resource for a dinner but the herbs in his garden.

Bear in mind that in Dick's era, it was the recipients of mail who were expected to pay the postage, and British authors rarely saw any money from the pirated editions of their work in the U.S. Dick did eventually receive an additional pension in his last few years, but still, imagine being aged and with scarcely three or four pounds income a month, and going hungry with your family while fan mail pours in with postage due. Looking up at his beloved stars may have been the old man's only solace.

ACKNOWLEDGMENTS

From the day that I first voiced aloud an extraordinarily vague notion—"What if I wrote a book about things that didn't work out?"—my wife, Jennifer, has been there for me. She has been this book's first advocate, its first reader and editor, and it simply could not have been written without her.

I am also deeply indebted to Dave Eggers for this book's existence. After the first couple of chapters got dozens of rejections like "I've never heard of these people that you're writing about"—as if that weren't the *point* of the book—in desperation I sent a chapter to Dave with the note "Everybody hates this, maybe you will too." And to Dave's great credit, at a time when everyone else couldn't even be bothered to go past the cover letter of an unknown writer, he read and understood *exactly* what I was doing. This book is in many ways a child of his *McSweeney's* magazine, and he has helped it every step of the way.

Becky Kurson read my work in *McSweeney's* and lavished praise and attention on it, becoming an extraordinary agent on my behalf. Tim Bent of St. Martin's Press took a chance on an oddball book and then gave it more attention than I could have hoped for from anyone. On the home front, both my son Morgan and I thank Marc Thomas for being such a great Uncle Zonker to my Doonesbury. And, lest I forget, thanks to my friends and my parents; over the years they all have humored a fellow who, rather than seeking out a steady job and paying rent on time, lived on ramen and bought old books instead.

Finally, my thanks to the very patient librarians at the New York Public Library, the Library of Congress, the British Library, the University of California, Dominican University, Golden Gate University, San Francisco State University, Johns Hopkins University, the San Francisco Public Library, the Concord Free Public Library, the Huntington Library, the Shakespeare Birthplace Trust, the Folger Shakespeare Library, and the National Library of Medicine. Libraries exist to preserve the thoughts and deeds that no one else has time for anymore, to collect items that might not be used for another ten, fifty, one hundred years—if ever. It is this last uncertainty that makes libraries the most heroic of human creations.

ABOUT THE AUTHOR

Paul Collins writes for *McSweeney's*, and his work has also appeared in *eCompany Now* and *Lingua Franca*. While writing this book, he lived in San Francisco, where he taught early American literature at Dominican University. He recently moved with his family to rural Wales, where he is now completing his next book.